THE GOLDEN DOOR

THE URBAN LIFE IN AMERICA SERIES
RICHARD C. WADE, GENERAL EDITOR

THE GOLDEN DOOR

Italian and Jewish Immigrant Mobility
in New York City 1880–1915

THOMAS KESSNER

New York
OXFORD UNIVERSITY PRESS
1977

"Epistle to a Godson," by W. H. Auden. From *Epistle to a Godson and Other Poems* by W. H. Auden, copyright © 1969 by W. H. Auden. Reprinted by permission of Random House, Inc.

"A Worker Reads History," by Bertholdt Brecht. From *Selected Poems,* translated by H. R. Hays. Reprinted by permission of Harcourt Brace Jovanovich, Inc.

"Lost America," by Pete Hamill. Reprinted by permission of New York Post. Copyright © 1972, New York Post Corporation.

"The Italians American Style," by Mario Puzo. Copyright © 1967 by The New York Times Company. Reprinted by permission.

To my wife, Rachel

Foreword

For the past two decades American scholars have been engaged in an intense examination of social mobility in American life. At the profoundest level, these studies examine the general notion that American society has been historically an open system which offered great opportunity for advancement to its poor and newcomers. Initial examinations emphasized the barriers to upward mobility and suggested that spectacular success stories were proportionately few and the real world of the underclasses was filled with grinding poverty, stunted ambition, and abandoned hope. Moreover, this work often utilized the most sophisticated quantitative methods, fortifying the conclusions with scientific sampling and statistical analysis.

More recent studies, however, are beginning to qualify that earlier judgment. Employing the same tools and drawing on comparable data, scholars are finding that the amount of upward mobility was measurably higher than anticipated, especially in young and rapidly growing cities. To be sure, the Horatio Alger saga has not been exhumed, but the facts more nearly sustain the older assumptions of significant opportunity and success in urban America. *The Golden Door,* dealing with the two largest immigrant groups in the nation's largest city, brilliantly argues the newer view.

Part of the explanation for the low mobility results of earlier research can be found in the size of the towns studied. Most were small and old, often they had comparatively stable economies. Indeed, these factors made them attractive to scholars. They provided a tidy and discrete topic with manageable numbers and usually ample data. It was possible to make generalizations based on large samples as well as to trace a significant number of individuals. Even those authors who found higher mobility often chose smaller cities for examination.

Thomas Kessner has had the audacity to attack New York City, the Mount Everest of urban history. The numbers involved are staggering. Between 1880 and 1919 over 23 million immigrants came to American ports; New York admitted 17 million of these. Most, of course, merely passed through and settled in the interior, but millions stayed. The two largest groups caught in the sieve were the Jews and Italians. *The Golden Door* analyzes how well they did during their first thirty-five years in New York City.

Though the results are comparable, the experience of the two groups was not. The commitment of the Italians who came to New York was limited. Many sought little more than to make some money rapidly and return to the homeland. They left family behind, took what unskilled jobs the city offered, accumulated modest sums, and jumped on the steamer for Italy. Jews, on the other hand, escaping persecution, broke their ties with Russia and brought the whole family to Gotham. No matter what happened to them here, there was no turning back.

Moreover, the Jews, historically if not by choice, were urban dwellers, hence they came to America with certain skills that kept most of them out of the manual laboring class. But their modest competence was no passport to riches; for the most part, they filled the poorest paying semi-skilled and white-collar jobs. The Italians arrived fresh from the countryside with little urban experience. They occupied the lowest blue-collar rung. Seeking to accumulate some money quickly, they seldom settled into steady jobs with the possibility of long-run improvement.

The deeper commitment to their new home led Jews to place more emphasis on education than the Italians did. Many of the latter arrived after school age, and since there was a great imbalance in the sexes, family formation was necessarily slow. Many married at home and shuttled from New York and Italy. But even when the number of youngsters grew, Italian children were found hard to lasso either by public or parochial schools. Utilizing special censuses, Mr. Kessner demonstrates the importance of this educational dimension in calculating the differing rates of occupational mobility.

Despite the difficulties and differences, the two groups substantially improved their position in the last decades of the nineteenth century. The author employs the phrase "New Immigrant" to include both Italians and Jews and concludes that though they "began the decade (1880) at the bottom of the Promised City's social order" they "rose out of the manual class at a rate of 37 per cent in the same decade." This upward movement is markedly higher than scholars have found in other American cities. In the next decade, the figures for Brooklyn are even more striking; 57 per cent moved into a higher category. Moreover, downward slippage was less (10 per cent) than one has been led to expect from other studies.

There are many qualifications to these figures. Jews did better than Italians; the material from which the figures are drawn are in many ways inadequate, the sheer numbers guarantee some inaccuracies. Yet Mr. Kessner's problems are not much different from those facing any scholar dealing with social mobility. And the care and caution he brings to the analysis fortify his arresting conclusions. Nor is he unaware of the growing literature that surrounds the topic. The final chapter is a judicious review of other scholarship and an explanation of why New York's experience is in many ways different from that of other cities.

The Golden Door also describes the patterns of residential change of the New Immigrants. Often improved occupational status was expressed by movement to a better neighborhood away from the old ghettoes. Indeed, the author views the original areas of concentration as not just places of wretched housing, inadequate jobs, poor schools, and endemic disorder, but as staging grounds for upward mobility. He does not minimize the dreadful condition of the ghetto, but he also sees certain benign qualities which provided the New Immigrants with some cultural continuity until they were ready to venture outside. Italians and Jews moved uptown in large numbers, some formed new concentrations, others opted for mixed neighborhoods. And Brooklyn, also a point of direct entry to many New Immigrants, produced similar patterns of residential mobility.

Mr. Kessner presents his case with all the modern quantitative paraphernalia, but he translates his statistical evidence into clear English. The most extensive tables form two appendices; others are placed unobtrusively into the text. In addition, he has mastered more conventional sources, often now disparagingly labeled "impressionistic." Hence *The Golden Door* blends the newest methodology with an older historical tradition to produce an eminently readable and original book. Moreover, it deals with the question of ethnicity which has recently dominated the writing on American society. Thus, like other volumes in the *Urban Life in America* series, it illuminates a contemporary problem by putting it into historical perspective.

New York   RICHARD C. WADE
August 1976   GENERAL EDITOR
                                        URBAN LIFE IN AMERICA SERIES

Introduction

A century ago Frederick Law Olmsted pointed to the bias of traditional histories which ignore the masses.

> Men of literary taste . . . are always apt to overlook the working-classes, and to confine the records they make of their own times, in a great degree, to the habits and fortunes of their own associates, or to those of people of superior rank to themselves, of whose sayings and doings their vanity, as well as their curiosity, leads them to most carefully inform themselves. The dumb masses have often been so lost in this shadow of egotism, that, in later days, it has been impossible to discern the very real influence their character and condition has had on the fortune and fate of nations.[1]

Convinced of the validity of Olmsted's complaint and motivated by their own interest in the common folk, "new urban historians" have turned to investigating the history of "anonymous Americans." This interest in American history "from the bottom up" has led to a number of inquiries into the process of social mobility in the United States. Studies have focused on the lives of the poor, the immigrant, and the laboring classes to explore the validity of America's image as a land of even-handed opportunity.[2]

xii   INTRODUCTION

Historians have analyzed the process of mobility in such di-
verse cities as Newburyport, Massachusetts, Atlanta, Omaha,
Boston, Birmingham, Alabama, and Poughkeepsie, New York.
The findings, although far from uniform, provide significant new
information. But the issue is far from decided, for as Stephan
Thernstrom, whose pioneering 1964 work *Poverty and Progress*
attracted many scholars to the subject, has written, "When we
possess rather detailed knowledge about the common laborer of
Newburyport but lack comparable observations about . . . New
York City it is risky to generalize. . . ." [3]

New York was not only the largest and most important American city, it was also the most cosmopolitan, welcoming the
bulk of Europe's emigrants to the New World and representing
to them the American promise of mobility. No city, not even
this great metropolis, is America in microcosm, but if we are to
have a fuller picture of mobility in general, and immigrant mobility in particular, New York's story is essential.

In the years between 1880 and World War I, European immigration fed the core of America's industrializing urban centers.
Many expressed the fear that these foreigners were the single
most dangerous element in the growing cities. They appeared so
unassimilable, especially the "New Immigrants" from eastern
and southern Europe. Even those who accepted the conventional
picture of swift American mobility feared that progress was too
much to expect from these unwashed hordes; here might be an
implacable proletariat.

The two major immigrant groups to settle New York City in
this period were the New Immigrant southern Italians and east
European Jews. Both were forced by circumstances to find a
better life away from home, but this innocent hope was made
more complex by the need to adapt to an alien environment in
the midst of immediate and pressing needs. Few of the newcomers could sit back to weigh their options. As quickly as they
settled, often within days and sometimes within hours of landing, they had to take their first jobs.

These immigrants provide a perfect population for testing mobility in New York. They started at the bottom; they were poor
and badly equipped. How they fared tells us much about the
process of growth and progress in New York and America.

It has been an historical commonplace that the Russian Jewish immigrant shot up the economic ladder quickly. In their impressionistic study of New York's ethnic groups, Nathan Glazer
and Daniel Patrick Moynihan claim that "most of the Irish had
taken three generations to work themselves out of poverty, the
Italians two. The Jews have moved somewhat faster." Moses
Rischin detailed the story of this success in his important study
The Promised City. Here he presented the conventional picture
of Russian Jews who by dint of ruthless underconsumption, de-
bilitating hard life and labor, and a vital drive for material success achieve the American dream.[4]

It is clear that Jews were mobile. But how mobile? Were they
as mobile as society generally believed? In 1933 *Fortune* felt the
need to publish a series of articles, later reprinted as a book, to
deny the myth of Jewish economic control. And what about the
Jews who remained poor? They wrote less and have presented a
lower profile to historians but were they the exceptions, or have
our perceptions been distored by hearing only from those who
were successful and articulate?[5]

In his recent study of the Italian-American experience, *Half
Bitter, Half Sweet,* Alexander De Conde accepts the idea that
"Italians moved ahead on a smaller scale and a generation later
than members of other significant ethnic groups, particularly the
Jews. . . . They took longer than the Jews to acquire large capital and make their way in America's competitive business world."
But Humbert Nelli's informed study of Chicago's Italian community disputes this, arguing that assimilation carried the southern Italian into the mainstream of American society and economy rather quickly, often within one generation. He does not
deny that many Italian immigrant neighborhoods retained their
flavor and character beyond the first generation. He argues, how-

ever, that this should not be interpreted as a lack of mobility, for a close study of these neighborhoods indicates that they seldom had the same Italians for more than a short time.[6]

Stephan Thernstrom's recent monograph on Boston found "Italian occupational achievement on the low side . . . ," while "the Jewish record was especially remarkable" for its progress; but his Jewish and Italian samples are too small to be definitive. Moreover, the best place to test the issue is New York City. As Marshall Sklare has written, "Even if reliable data were available from every other Jewish community in the country the lack of material about New York City would mean that a valid demographic portrait of American Jewry would still be unavailable." This holds true for the Italian experience as well.[7]

Among the major sources used in this study are federal and state censuses and city directories. These sources, like all others, do not escape shortcomings. Peter Knights has described the ante-bellum censuses as ranging from mediocre to pathetic. Post-bellum censuses are better but cannot avoid the distortions Knights complains of. Taken over a period of time, rather than simultaneously, the census represented the sum of populations of various block areas on different days and was not, therefore, the real city population at any given time. Moreover, as an inventory of population, the census betrayed important shortcomings, especially when dealing with ethnic slums. The language barrier was real and at times impermeable. Corner houses falling on the edge of the areas assigned to enumerators were sometimes missed. Immigrant fear of officials played a role, as did the fears of the census enumerator. Individuals boarding with families or living in hotels were often overlooked. And the possibility of exclusion was not the only inaccuracy. Dependent on individual testimony, the census was no more than an approximation of the truth.[8]

The city directories, which were published primarily as listings for local businessmen, are even less exhaustive. These vaunted Rosetta stones of our urban past have gaps that plague every study forced to rely on their information. Nonetheless, the directory which supplied the name, occupation, home, and business address of most heads of household is one of our few sources for information about otherwise inaccessible millions.[9]

If history were to measure validity in terms of a flawless reconstruction of the past, these shortcomings might be crucial. However, even the most perfervid historicist would not make this claim today. The approximate past must do. Toward this end the census and the directories are more objective and reliable than diaries, letters, newspapers, contemporary accounts, and folk songs. Used carefully and with imagination they provide as good an approximation of the past as we are likely to find.

The raw occupational data drawn from these sources, involving over 400 different job titles, had to be simplified in order to permit manageable analysis and meaningful description. These assorted occupations were aggregated into five different class levels, according to a system of classification that is described in Chapter Three. The use of this "five-step scale" will permit the results of this study to be compared with other recent investigations of occupational mobility.

In order to check these findings the data were subjected to a second analysis using a new scaling system devised by Professor Donald Treiman. This Standard International Occupational Prestige Scale, developed as a universal measure of occupational status, assigns numerical values to over 500 different job titles according to a variety of considerations. By and large, the Treiman scale analysis corroborated the findings that resulted from the conventional five-class methodology.[10] Considerations of style and space have persuaded me to avoid introducing Treiman scale computations in the text, but scholars interested in this information may refer to my doctoral dissertation.[11]

The analysis of these data involved the use of quantitative techniques. Quantification can be a dangerous tool because numbers imply degrees of exactness that the sources and the methodology often cannot support. Oscar Handlin, in an overall

critique of this new trend, has correctly observed that "every effort at quantification, in the end, operates within the parameters
set by the limitations of the observed data." And Norbert
Wiener's dictum that economics is a one- or two-digit science
should be kept in mind. It is true that in some of their less careful moments quantifying historians speak in significant figures to
four decimal places when their method and data can only support more general—and more honest—and still very useful conclusions such as "more," "many," "less," and "few." [12]

In most cases, however, exactness is not the point. Sharp, very
precise conclusions are justifiably suspect. The real value of the
quantitative approach is not its precision, but rather that it adds
another tool to the historian's craft. The flurry caused by Robert
Fogel and Stanley Engerman's controversial quantitative study,
Time on the Cross: The Economics of American Negro Slavery,
is sufficient retort to contentions like that of Arthur Schlesinger
that "all important historical questions are important precisely
because they are not susceptible to quantitative answers." The
issue is not whether quantification is acceptable. With the sources
that are presently available one of the few ways to study America's masses and their past is to sample and analyze the data
quantitatively. Only after this has been accomplished can the
historian go on to employ non-quantitative judgments about the
deeper meaning of his findings.[13]

The argument of this book should be easily discernible from
the organization of the chapters. The first chapter introduces the
setting, establishing the framework of time and place. The second
chapter analyzes characteristics of Italian and Jewish migration
that might have some bearing on occupation and mobility. Chapters Three and Four trace the changes in occupational profile
for both groups between 1880 and 1905. Chapters Two, Three,
and Four establish the ethnic context for the discussion of mobility in Chapter Five. The immigrant ghetto, neighborhood change,
and geographic mobility are discussed in Chapter Six. The final
chapter deals with comparative mobility and ethnicity.

Those so inclined will notice that this represents a somewhat different approach from recent quantitative investigations of mobility. In general the story does not center on how the data were gathered, what methodology governed their analysis, or the statistical evidence itself. I have tried to assemble the statistics within a narrative structure that addresses the broader issues of mobility and ethnicity in New York City.

I cannot claim that this book will bring the discussion of mobility in America to a definitive conclusion. Studies of mobility in the United States are still very much like the proverbial blind men touching different parts of the elephant—no single description is inaccurate but all are incomplete. However, I do hope that this study of New York will help move the description away from the flanks and closer to the vital organs.

Acknowledgments

I am pleased by the opportunity to express my gratitude to friends and colleagues who have shared their time and knowledge with me. Few groups share as fully or as selflessly as the scholarly community, and this book like many others is better for it.

It is a distinct pleasure to acknowledge my foremost debt to Professor Kenneth T. Jackson of Columbia University. He helped me define the topic, elaborate a methodology, and improve both style and content by challenging my assumptions and demanding a clarity of argument I was prepared to avoid; his kind and steady support encouraged me to deal with a number of fierce research obstacles.

Professor Walter Metzger's encouragement and close reading of an earlier version of this manuscript were both gratifying and helpful. His sharp sense of structure and organization drew my attention to a number of issues which led me to exploit my data more effectively. Professors Herbert Gans, Humbert Nelli, David Rothman, and John Hammond read the entire manuscript and provided trenchant criticisms and valuable suggestions. Sheldon Epstein and Robert Hecht also read parts of the manuscript and

I have benefitted from their observations. Professor Bernard Klein, chairman of the Department of History and Philosophy at Kingsborough Community College of the City University of New York, and my colleagues in the department deserve my gratitude for a variety of favors and suggestions. It is acknowledged gladly.

Donald Treiman, Peter Decker, Abram Jaffe, Aryeh Hertzig, Stephan Thernstrom, Clyde Griffen, Rosalyn Weinman Schram, and the late Stephen Bever, at various stages of my research offered technical guidance. Invariably these scholars took time from their own pressing research commitments to help me refine methodological procedures, and I am grateful to them.

Although I am not able to specify the long list of individuals whose numerous kindnesses made my research tasks more pleasant I do wish to acknowledge my appreciation to the staffs of the New York Municipal Reference Library, Manhattan and Brooklyn County Clerks, New York Public Library, Columbia University Libraries, and the Kingsborough Community College Library.

In working with the computer I was often dependent on the expertise of others. I am particularly indebted to the consultants at the Columbia University Computer Center and the City University of New York Computer Center. I wish also to note my appreciation to David Berger and Lou Lampert of the Kingsborough Community College Computer Center and Larry Fogel of the Federal Reserve Bank of New York who graciously provided me with programming aid at a crucial juncture.

The good fortune of a Summer Research Grant from the National Foundation for Jewish Culture permitted me to devote the summer of 1974 to research and writing. At Oxford University Press I had the benefit of working with Susan Rabiner and Leona Capeless who both provided editorial assistance with intelligence, good judgment, and the kind hand of friendship.

My wife, Rachel, brought to this project three gifts: patient support, intelligent criticism, and a willingness to suffer through the preparation of this book with good grace and careful typing. For these, and her other gifts for which I and our children are grateful, I have dedicated this book to her.

To my parents, who rejected despair and bitterness after Hitler, and framed my ambition for scholarship in an atmosphere that placed the highest priorities on civility and humanity, I owe a special debt.

Brooklyn, New York   T. K.
March 1976

Contents

Tables

THE GOLDEN DOOR

I

The Immigrant City

They came from Belfast and Palermo and a thousand other desperate sinkholes. They left behind their families, their language, the landscape of their childhood; they bid farewell to Hebrew scholars, olive trees, the Shannon's sweet waters and they marched into steerage, where a lot of them died of typhus and smallpox, where some ate rats to survive, and all were battered by the hard indifference of the Atlantic. It was, to all of them, worth it. They were going to New York.

Pete Hamill,
"The Lost America"

In 1876, the Civil War over and Reconstruction ending, the United States turned to celebrate its century of independence. Philadelphia was chosen to exhibit the nation's development by housing the Century of Progress Exposition. The adopted home of Benjamin Franklin and Betsy Ross, this one-time national capital still displayed America's most revered symbol, the Liberty Bell, with its fitting Biblical inscription: "Proclaim liberty throughout all the land unto the inhabitants thereof." Philadelphia by its own history of expansion and progress—it had grown from a small Quaker town two miles square to a bustling commercial metropolis of over 800,000 inhabitants in an area of 129 square miles—exemplified the young country's century of growth.[1]

At this Exposition a huge sculpted arm bearing a torch was exhibited for the first time. A gift from the French people, it had been designed by Frédéric Auguste Bartholdi as a modern symbol of the American quest. Shortly after the Exposition closed the arm carrying Liberty's flame was moved out of Philadelphia. It took its place high above a pedestal displaying a bronzed message to the disenchanted of all nations:

3

> Here at our sea washed sunset gates shall stand
> A mighty woman with a torch, whose flame
> Is the imprisoned lightning, and her name
> Mother of Exiles. From her beacon hand
> Glows world wide welcome; her mild eyes command
> The air bridged harbor that twin cities frame,
> "Keep ancient lands your storied pomp!" cries she
> With silent lips. "Give me your tired, your poor,
> Your huddled masses yearning to breathe free,
> The wretched refuse of your teeming shore.
> Send the homeless, tempest tost to me,
> I lift my hand beside the golden door!" [2]

To people in the United States and around the globe the new statue with its offer of welcome to the oppressed ("your sonnet gives to its subject a raison d'être," James Russell Lowell wrote to Emma Lazarus) quickly supplanted the more modest Liberty Bell as the nation's strongest symbol.* Americans readily accepted the image of world haven, and foreigners believed it. "Other lands," wrote the Polish immigrant man-of-letters, Henry Sienkiewicz, "grant only asylum, this land recognizes the immigrant as a son and grants him rights." Significantly this warm call to the world's needy was not located in Philadelphia, Boston, Chicago, or Washington; the Statue of Liberty guarded instead the world's pre-eminent entrepôt—New York harbor.[3]

To a modern reader Emma Lazarus's words ring somewhat tinny, overblown, and even condescending. But the immigrants who passed this statue close to a century ago saw themselves in precisely the mold the poetess cast—wretched, wasted, and uprooted bodies in search of new lives and broader horizons. Old World chains had shackled them to primitive economies and op-

---

* The poetess was in New York six weeks when a committee planning to set up the statue "Liberty Enlightening the World," represented by William Evarts, enlisted her in a fund-raising effort to secure a pedestal for the statue. She contributed a manuscript sonnet entitled, "The New Colossus," which was to be auctioned off. James Russell Lowell, a poet in his own right and American ambassador to England, wrote her: "I liked your sonnet . . . much better than I like the statue itself . . . an achievement more arduous than that of the sculptor." [H. E. Jacob, *The World of Emma Lazarus* (New York, 1949), 177–80.]

pressive governments. They now came to a Brave New World in
search of respite and opportunity. "If," in the words of an immigrant son, "they sickened at last of poverty, bigotry and kings,
there was always America." Between 1880 and 1919 over 23 million Europeans emigrated to America to seek out this promise of
freedom and opportunity.[4]

Over 17 million of these immigrants landed in New York.* "Of
all the great cities," observed the United States Industrial Commission's 1901 *Report on Immigration,* "New York [is] the most
intimately concerned with [immigration], since of the . . . immigrants who have come to these shores . . . no less than . . .
about 71 per cent have entered at that port." These immigrants
came to New York in search of change. In the process they
changed New York into a world city of myriad national strains.[5]

An Englishman passing through the city in the 1880s could not
contain his amazement with the un-Americanness of the cosmopolitan port. "An Irishman landing there cries, 'Be dad! It's for
all the wurrld like Corrke!' A German exclaims, 'Ganz wie Berlin,'
the Chicagoan asks 'what's the next train for the United States?' "
But another English visitor, Therese Yelverton, pinpointed it
more accurately. "Although in America it is not American, New
York is New York and nothing else." † New York represented the
Immigrant City *sui generis,* not a mere symbol of the New
World, but that for which the New World stood.[6]

Before 1880, western Europeans, including over five million
Irish and Germans, dominated the immigrant influx to the United
States. Warned to avoid the large cities, many of these Old Im-

---

* The total number of immigrants admitted at American ports between
1880 and 1919 was 23,492,630. Of this total, 17,097,640 entered through
the port of New York. Boston and Charleston admitted 1,395,724, and
Philadelphia was next with 938,647.

† To the urban poet Walt Whitman, New York was "a city of the world!
For all races are here; all lands of the earth make contributions here." ["City
of Ships," *Leaves of Grass,* John Kouwenhoven, ed. (New York, 1950), 233.]

migrants settled on farms, and in small towns or villages. "The pith and marrow of Ireland," *The Irish American* preached in 1849, "do not stop in cities to spread their money and fool away their time; they go directly into the interior." Those who did settle in New York were described by Archbishop John Hughes as "the poorest and most wretched population that can be found in the world—the scattered debris of the Irish nation." It was commonly believed that only those who could not afford the trip inland or lacked the drive remained in the port cities to form an urban sediment. New York City, reported the Industrial Commission, "acts like a sieve letting through the physically sound, the energetic and the ambitious; keeping back the infirm, the very poor and the lazy." [7]

If New York was a sieve, it held back far more than the Industrial Commission realized. Whatever their motivation or lack of it, many western European immigrants established large and politically powerful ethnic communities in a host of American cities, but particularly in New York. The street-wise Danish-born photographer-journalist Jacob Riis, writing in the 1880s, remarked that a map of Gotham's ethnic districts "would show more stripes than a zebra and more colors than any rainbow." Nonetheless, the predominant hues would be "green for the Irish prevailing in the West Side . . . and blue for the Germans on the East Side." [8]

By the time Riis recorded his observations the sources of American immigration had already begun to shift, and he found two new colors splashing across lower Manhattan.

> The red of the Italian forcing its way northward along the line of Mulberry Street . . . and after a lapse of miles, in the "Little Italy," of Harlem, east of Second Avenue. On the West Side the red [is] overrunning the old Africa of Thompson Street, pushing the black of the negro rapidly uptown . . . occupying his home, his church, his trade. . . .
>
> Hardly less aggressive than the Italian, the [gray of the] Russian and Polish Jew, having overrun the district between Riv-

ington and Division Streets, east of the Bowery, to the point
of suffocation, is filling the tenements of the old Seventh Ward
to the river front, and disputing with the Italian every foot of
available space in the back alleys of Mulberry Street.[9]

These "New Immigrants" from Italy and Russia began to come
in increasing numbers at the same time that western European
immigration tapered off. The extent of this well-documented shift
in immigration can be illustrated by comparing the "Old" and
"New" immigrations for two years, 1882 and 1907. In the earlier
year, 648,000 Europeans crossed the Atlantic to America; 87 per
cent came from the countries of northern and western Europe
while only 85,000, or 13 per cent, arrived from eastern and southern Europe. The German Empire—the largest single source of
immigrants—contributed 251,000 people, 39 per cent of all European immigrants.[10]

Henry James expatriated from the United States in this year,
1882. He returned twenty-five years later, confronting a United
States that struck him as different and alien. The Irish and Germans no longer dominated the cities, and the varied unfamiliar
tongues of southern and eastern Europe made discordant sounds.
He complained of a "sharp sense of dispossession." The source of
James's discomfort is not difficult to locate. In the year of his return 1.2 million people immigrated to America. Old Immigrants,
the broad backbone of Euorpean immigration in 1882, only accounted for 19 per cent of the new settlers, while 972,000, or
81 per cent, arrived from southern and eastern Europe. Italy
alone contributed 286,000 people, more than triple the total New
Immigration in 1882; Russia contributed 259,000 immigrants, a
fifteen-fold increase over the earlier figure.[11]

These New Immigrants poured into the cities. Five of every
six Russian Jews settled in urban communities, as did over three-
quarters of the Italians. They clustered in decaying and congested districts which accentuated their own highly visible debilities. Nativists like A. L. Wayland scurried for their pens to
question the wisdom of unrestricted immigration:

> We allow every nation to pour its pestilential sewage into our
> reservoir; at last we so far arouse ourselves to strain out the
> Mongolian gnat at the Golden Gate while we open wide our
> mouth at the narrows to swallow the Italian camel, the Polish
> Dromedary, the Hungarian elephant, and any pachyderms that
> present themselves.[12]

Nativists notwithstanding, cities, and especially the great metropolis at "the narrows," continued to attract newcomers. Urban
life and its trappings appealed to the New Immigrants. The eth-
nically veined cities throbbed with the sights, sounds, and fra-
ternal clubs of European cities and seemed to offer better opportunities in industry and commerce. Even with their lugubrious
slums, conditions were often better in the bigger cities. The Immigration Commission noted: "A comparison of the conditions in
a great city like New York or Chicago with those in some of the
smaller industrial centers such as mining and manufacturing
towns shows that average conditions as regards overcrowding are
very materially worse in some of the small industrial towns." [13]
For these and other reasons the New Immigrants chose to settle in the cities and rebuffed attempts at dispersing them. Concerned with this urban predilection, the Senate Industrial Commission studied its causes in the hope of preventing or redirecting
the immigrant concentrations. Its own studies, however, illustrated the drawbacks of rural settlement. The Commission told
of a group of Russian Jews from Odessa who emigrated to the
United States in early 1880 intending to bypass the cities for
farm life. This group landed in New York, purchased 760 acres
in Oregon for $7,800, and with some help from immigrant aid
societies raised the money for rail fare across the continent. They
settled the farm property, but a series of setbacks convinced
these immigrants that "farming was not a good business." Moreover, facilities for education, which they considered very important, were not available in the Oregon hinterland. "After three
years, 12 families left and before the fourth year was over all had
removed . . . back to New York." And how did they fare in the

overpopulated city that everybody wanted them to avoid? According to the 1901 Commission report, "One is now a chemist, one is a druggist, and one is an engineer, two are lawyers, two are dentists, one is a superintendant of a hospital, and one returned to Russia. . . ."[14]

New York's appeal rested on a firm economic foundation. Chief among its attractions was its great harbor, which, in addition to welcoming over 95 per cent of the New Immigrants, handled more than two-thirds of the nation's imports. So great was the volume of trade passing through the world's busiest port that the customs duties collected there bogged down the United States Treasury with unwanted surpluses. Not until 1910 did the great port's share of national imports dip below 50 per cent.[15]

In addition to the bustling wharves and docks, New York contained all of the nation's major securities markets and its most powerful investment banks. New York City banks served as the linchpin for national finance, with total deposits approximating those of all other cities' national banks combined. Bank loans—reflecting the ambition and confidence of Empire City investors—exceeded by over $900 the average loan made in second-place Boston.[16]

This ambition and confidence could be seen most clearly on the floor of the New York Stock Exchange. Early in 1880, investors pushed the level of sales up to 700,000 on peak days; by 1886, over 1,000,000 shares changed hands in a single day. Such financial growth also freed city commerce from the control of foreign capital. In 1869 the New York security market swelled with $1,465,000,000 invested by foreigners. By 1879 New Yorkers were pumping their own investment capital into other nations, as a $3,000,000 loan floated for the Province of Quebec indicated.[17]

An expanding economy placed New York at the forefront of industrial growth. Over the decade of the eighties, the census reported that total invested capital in the city rose from $181 million to $426 million. Between 1860 and 1890, to cite an important example, the number of textile firms in New York grew from 600 to 10,000, and employees in this business increased from 30,000 to 236,000—mostly immigrants.[18]

Growth in retail trade went hand in glove with this industrial development. Lower Manhattan from Broome and Grand Street to City Hall Park accounted for a major portion of the country's dry goods business. Huge retail establishments—Arnold Constable and Co., Lord and Taylor, Bowen McNamie and Co., R. H. Macy's, and the largest and most diversified, A. T. Stewart's—heralded the new department-type store along Sixth Avenue below Twenty-Third Street. Establishments such as these also supplied many immigrant New Yorkers with jobs. Stewart's alone employed close to 3,000 workers; immigrant shop girls, porters, day laborers, and tailors among them.[19]

This throbbing economy impressed visitors to the island metropolis. Theodore Dreiser marveled at its quality:

> What stinging quivering zest they display. How beauty is willing to sell its bloom, virtue its last rag, strength an almost usurious portion of what it controls, youth its very best years, its hope or dream of fame, fame and power their dignity and presence, age its weary hours, to secure but a minor part of all this, a taste of [New York's], vibrating presence and the future that it makes.[20]

To an Italian visitor, New York was "La mecca del dollaro." "Nothing," complained another visitor, "is given to beauty, everything centers on hard utility." Some chafed at the sight of a people who ordered their priorities to the clang of the cash register, but no one denied New York's unique economic success. This economic strength provided incoming immigrants with hope for an alternative to the misery of Old World poverty. A strong economy meant broad job opportunities, and this in turn meant that it might be possible to make enough money to keep families together—something their own homelands apparently could not offer. Thus, the immigrants sought out the Promised City in the belief that it could support them and offer their children an even greater comfort.[21]

Moreover, in New York there was hope for more than mere sufficiency. As banker-manufacturer John Britton said, "A man here may be a common day laborer, but if he has the right material in him there is no reason why he should not occupy the best place in the nation." Kings and nobles were left behind in Europe and with them the rigid and inflexible systems they headed. Italians fled a motherland where success was not achieved so much as inherited. And for Russia's Jews the concept of mobility—of achieved success by virtue of merit and ambition—had been severely hampered by persecution.[22]

In New York they knew that mobility was possible. They heard exciting tales of poor men who rose to the top. The aforementioned A. T. Stewart's department store stood as one monument to this sort of progress. Stewart arrived in the city, a young Irish immigrant from Belfast, in 1820. He held a variety of jobs including that of teacher in a private school until he journeyed back to Ireland for a £500 inheritance. After investing this money in Irish lace he set up a small 12- by 30-foot shop in lower Broadway. Stewart and his wife shared a one-room apartment above this store. In 1846 he moved into a marble-faced store at Broadway and Chambers. Then, in 1862, he built a new steel and stone structure that stretched over an entire square block between Ninth and Tenth Streets on Broadway and reached eight stories high—the largest retail store in the world.

In 1864 an English visitor wrote of this ex-school teacher: "Stewart is the great 'dry goods merchant' of New York. . . . He is I suppose, next to the President, the best known man in America. For 'dry goods' are a surer road to fame than politics and legislation." For the single year 1868, Stewart reported income of over three million dollars, the highest in the city. Sales in his stores for the three years before he died in 1876 totaled $203 million. The orphaned Irish teenager of 1820 had realized the American promise in spectacular fashion.[23]

The newcomers hungered for opportunity, and examples like Stewart's sustained the popular Horatio Alger myth of rapid mobility. Indeed, mobility was not only held out as a possibility, it was put forth as a moral imperative. As Russell Conwell * said over six thousand times during the eighties and nineties in his famous "Acres of Diamonds" speech:

> The opportunity to attain great wealth is . . . within the reach of almost every man and woman. . . . I have come to tell you . . . that the men and women sitting here, who found it difficult perhaps to buy a ticket to this lecture . . . have within their reach "Acres of Diamonds" . . . you ought to have money. . . . it is your Christian duty to do so. . . . Let us remember there is not a poor person in the United States who was not made poor by his own shortcomings. . . . It is all wrong to be poor anyhow.

Such banal social thought reinforced the prevailing concept of swift mobility for the deserving.[24]

A nation where it was wrong to be poor caught the imagination of Europe's masses. They left the Old World behind to those who feared to dream. To the question posed by W. H. Auden— "where are you going said Fearer to Farer?"—they would have responded, "To the Golden Land." And for a large number the Golden Land was New York.

But not A. T. Stewart's New York; not the "singing crystal street," Fifth Avenue, which sparkled with Stewart's magnificent marble palace and William Vanderbilt's $3 million French Renaissance mansion, and the homes of H. O. Havemeyer, Hollis Huntington, William Rockefeller, and Charles Yerkes; not the New York where on New Year's Day the city's wealthy added to the festive milieu by leaving their curtains partially drawn to display the elegant furnishings and princely appointments of their urban castles. The immigrants quickly learned to their disappointment that the Immigrant City was one of dizzying contrasts—"a lady in a ball gown with diamonds in her ears" while

---

* Conwell, 1843–1925, was a poor boy who became a lawyer after a struggle, but was not very successful. His wife's death in 1872 turned him to preaching and he became a blazingly successful Baptist minister nationally known for his sermons.

"her toes were out at the boots"—and *their* place was at the bottom. As dreams of patrician velvet made way for the reality of plebeian corduroy, Fifth Avenue faded into Mulberry Bend and "Bandit's Roost." [25]

The difference between the two, between their dreams and the reality they confronted, could be disheartening.

> All the time I hear about the grand city of New York [explained the Italian immigrant Alessandro DeLuca]. They say it is something to surprise everyone. I learn New York is twice, three, four, ten times bigger than Italian city. Maybe it is better than Milano. Maybe it is better than Naples . . . I think I am going to great city, to grand country, to better world, and my heart deveolp big admiration and a great noble sentiment for America and the Americans.
>
> I arrive in New York. You think I find here my idea?

And Anzia Yezeirska, the Jewish novelist, recalled peering out of her East Side window as a child. "I looked out into the alley below and saw palefaced children scrambling in the gutter. 'Where is America?' cried my heart." [26]

Dissatisfaction and disillusion were inevitable, as nearly all immigrants idealized America and no real nation could live up to their gilded expectations. But the city slums would have been disillusioning under the best of circumstances.

For most of the New Immigrants, Manhattan's slum section— "that very different and most radically foreign plexus known as the East Side"—became their new home. One of the wards in this district, the Sixth, was described in an 1879 *Report* by the Association for Improving the Conditions of the Poor. The investigator painted a sordid scene of rotten and decaying tenements packed to overflowing with poor tenants.[27]

One such abode was at 5 Jersey Street. "Here . . . on lines strung across were thousands of rags hung up to dry; on the ground piled against the board fences rags mixed with bones, bottles and papers; the middle of the yard covered with every imaginable variety of dirt." The underground cellars off the yard

were even worse. Windowless and dank, these quarters were shut
off from the outside air and often were stuffed with people:

> Opposite the door stood a stove, upon which meat was being
> cooked; to the right stood a bedstead roughly constructed out
> of boards, in the left hand corner a similar one. The small room
> contains another. These board bunks were covered with 3 or
> 4 blankets, and would each accommodate 4 men. There was no
> other furniture in the room which was so dark that we could
> only see by waiting till the eyes became accustomed to the
> light. There was scarcely standing room for the heaps of bags
> and rags, right opposite them stood a large pile of bones,
> mostly having meat on them, in various stages of decomposi-
> tion. . . . The smell could be likened only to that of an ex-
> humed body. There were nine men in the room at the time of
> our visit, but a larger number occupy the room.[28] *

"By 1879," reported Kate Claghorn, "[Jersey] street was swarm-
ing with Italians of the ragpicker class." [29]

New York's Italian colony had grown steadily after 1860. In
that year the census counted 1,464 foreign-born Italians, chiefly
from the northern regions of the kingdom. This early contingent
was often dismissed by the community at large as nothing more
than a "little handful of Italians . . . mainly a vagabond but
harmless class of organ grinders, rag pickers, bear leaders and
the like." Nonetheless, this colony included a number of professional musicians and artists, who fed the growing city's hunger
for continental culture. Most of these early Italian settlers took
their place, as had the older immigrants who preceded them, at
the bottom of the economic ladder. They filled unskilled jobs and
did day labor on the busy wharves. Others, the "fantastic van-

---

* Despite the surroundings, the investigator concluded: "Jersey Street at
first sight looks like a pestilence breeding, law breaking colony. . . . [how-
ever] no more peaceable, thrifty, orderly neighbors could be found than those
Italians."

guard of the brawny army to follow," worked at the fringe of the city economy, sifting refuse in search of rags, grinding hand organs, and vending fruits and statuary.[30]

They moved into the fetid and decaying "Five Points" section, concentrating in "the foul core of New York's slums," Mulberry Bend. Their barracks-type tenements commonly held from ten to fifty families each. "In the same room," wrote the noted churchman and philanthropist Charles Loring Brace, "I would find monkeys, children and men huddled together." The children served as an integral part of the household economy, shining shoes, sweeping walks, picking rags, or selling flowers to passersby.[31]

Conditions in Italy worsened during this period. The success of New World orchards in Florida and California ruined many orange and lemon growers in Calabria, Sicily, and Basilicata. This sudden jolt disrupted southern Italy's already precarious agricultural economy. Moreover, the high tariff walls established by the French government exacerbated Italy's troubles by wreaking havoc on the vintners of Apulia, Sicily, and Calabria, major centers of the Italian wine industry. Production of other foodstuffs slowed and the kingdom's beautiful landscape framed a stark portrait of unemployment and poverty unparalleled in all of Europe.

These unprecedented hardships set thousands to flight. Entire villages and rural towns carried their dialects and local loyalties to the streets of New York. Fed by Italy's chronic peasant poverty and viciously skewed land system (resembling in many ways the conditions of pre-famine Ireland), the Italian colony in New York grew apace. Between 1860 and 1880, 68,500 people left Italy for the United States, and in 1880 New York held 12,000 foreign-born Italians.[32]

As this community continued to grow under the pressure of deteriorating conditions in Italy, its newer arrivals were viewed by government researchers with greater approval:

> During these years the itinerant class—ragpickers, organ grinders and the like—which predominated in the earliest Italian

migration was being replaced by another class—the stable elements in the home country . . . whom only extreme poverty
induced to break the bonds . . . to their native land. Called
here by the industrial expansion after the Civil War this class
came as unskilled day laborers . . .[33]

According to a noted authority on Italian immigration, "The for-
mative years of Italian immigration may be said to have been
completed" with the 1880s.[34]

The spreading colony in lower Manhattan still could not compete with the Irish or Germans in numbers or in political and
economic power but the Fourteenth Ward already carried the
sobriquet "Little Italy." Italians competed for day labor and
made moves toward the industrial sector, generally challenging
the stereotype that "the Italians are an idle and thriftless
people." [35]

The ethnic grooves carved by the early settlers continued to
direct the currents of Italian life in the city. Like most foreigners
they preferred to live among their own. In setting up their "Little
Italy" they carefully retained their Old World subdivisions. The
local traditions and hatreds of numerous *paesi*, like the pungent
cheeses which the Italians brought with them, proved sufficiently
hardy to cross the sea and retain their original sharpness. The
pinched streets of lower Manhattan were divided into distinct
communities, and these provincial variations persisted twenty to
thirty years later. Mott Street between East Houston and Prince
held the Napoletani; the opposite side of the street was reserved
for Basilicati. Around the corner the Siciliani settled Prince Street,
while two blocks away the Calabresi lived on Mott between
Broome and Grand. Mulberry Street was strictly Neapolitan, and
Hester Street, running perpendicular to Mulberry, carried the
local color of Apulia.[36]

Once the Italian immigration set its course, it rapidly gathered
momentum. After a while it did not seem possible for more of
them to fit into New York's congested districts, and in 1901 the
Italian Commissariat of Emigration suggested that Italians settle

away from the metropolis. Alessandro Mastro Valerio, editor of *La Tribuana Italiana Transatlantica,* wrote, "The only means to rebuild the reputation of the Italo-American in general, is the plow." Settling in congested urban areas, while so much open land beckoned inland, was the Italian's original sin in the opinion of the Industrial Commission. They could only be redeemed "by going back to the agricultural life on the soil of their new country. The moral of the fable of Anteo, who was strong only so long as he was united to the soil, ought to be recalled to their vivid and poetic imaginations . . . it applies to their case." [37]

Such pleadings notwithstanding, Italians continued to swarm into the city and ignore the hinterlands. By 1900, 145,000 Italians lived in Gotham. The Italian playwright Guiseppe Giacosa complained that the "clothes, food and living quarters of the common Italians in New York and Chicago present a spectacle of such supine resignation to poverty, of an ascetic indifference to life's pleasures that . . . one expects to find among the Chinese." It may have offended Giacosa, but clearly such adversity did not diminish New York's popularity. No rural community, no agricultural settlement, could compete with the grand city and in 1920, 391,000 Italians were living there, almost as many as foreign-born Irish and Germans together.[38]

Like that of their Italian partners in the New Immigrant adventure, the trajectory of Russian immigration climbed rapidly. One lone Russian immigrant entered the United States in 1851. Forty years later, in 1890, 35,600 walked out of steerage onto American soil, and the wave crested in 1907 with 259,000 immigrants. The story of Russian emigration differs from the Italian, however, in one important respect: most of those fleeing Russia were escaping an urban "pale" to seek refuge from persecution as well as economic hardship.

The majority of these refugees were Jews fleeing yet another ruler in the tragic trek that had marked their diaspora experience. The turning point for Russian Jewry was the assassination of Tsar Alexander II in 1881. The succeeding regime fell under the control of a "kind of wooden ruling machine, to whom the living units of mankind are nothing, while the maintenance of . . . 'order' is everything": Konstantin Pobodonostev. "Order" meant the church and the autocracy, and this left no room for Jews and their particularism.[39]

In the best of times the Jews of Russia lived as "aliens as to rights and citizens as to obligations." Now they became enemies. Pogroms broke out "spontaneously." Michael Davitt, the Irish nationalist leader, described one such pogrom:

> From their hiding places in cellars and garrets the Jews were dragged forth and tortured to death. Many mortally wounded were denied the final stroke. . . . in not a few cases nails were driven into the skull and eyes gouged out. Babies were thrown from the higher stories to the street pavement. . . . Jews who attempted to beat off the attackers were quickly disarmed by the police. . . . The local bishop drove in a carriage and passed through the crowd, giving them his blessing as he passed.[40]

Economic pressure was applied through the infamous May Laws of 1882, which severely restricted the rights of Jews to settle in cities, curtailed their religious rights, and closed most professional, industrial, and agricultural pursuits to them. Poverty, always a threat, now became a reality, as 40 per cent of Russia's Jews were forced to depend on doles and charity. "They toil hard for a living so scanty that a rusty herring and a slice of onion is considered the tip of luxury and prosperity." A major resettlement program forced Jews from familiar territory and cruelly accomplished its purpose: "There . . . are scores of watchmakers in small towns where the towns-folk have no watches." Unmoved, Pobodonostsev happily declared that "one-third will die out, [and] one-third will leave the country. . . ." Minister of the Interior Count Ignatiev was equally candid, telling a delegation of Jews, "The western borders are open to you." Between 1881 and 1891, *before* the worst pogroms, 150,000 Jews left Russia. All but 15,000 went to America. (Even in Palestine, Russian Jews were met by cries of "Madman, irresponsible dreamer! Why have you come . . . move to America!") [41]

As with the Italians, the patterns established by the early Jewish immigrants from Russia in the sixties continued with minor changes over the next half-century. The early east European Jewish community clustered around the old German neighborhoods on the Lower East Side and many entered the German-dominated clothing industry. This industry proved especially attractive because it included a number of German Jewish entrepreneurs who were sympathetic to the religious needs of their co-religionists (e.g., no work from Friday sundown to Saturday night).

Other Russian Jews took to the streets for an income, stepping onto the lowest rung of the entrepreneurial ladder as vendors and peddlers.

> When the newly arrived Israelite asks what he shall do to make a living [quoted the *Asmonean* magazine] he is most commonly advised to go and peddle. . . . he goes on from day to day, changes the basket for the bundle, the bundle for the horse and wagon peddling, and finally . . . emerges a sleek, thrifty merchant. Have the history of one of these men and you have the history of them all.[42]

These peddlers swarmed over the Lower East Side selling bread, dry goods, Sabbath candles and hundreds of other items from rickety pushcarts or heavy barrels. Bustling thoroughfares like Hester Street overflowed with kerchiefed women and bearded men doing business of a sort: "Suspenders, collah buttons, 'lastic, matches, henkeches—please, lady, buy." Other eastern European Jews earned their living as jewelers, carpenters, painters, and retail shopkeepers.[43]

By 1880, the Jewish colony accounted for virtually all of the 13,571 Russian and Polish immigrants living in Manhattan.[44] They pressed into the Tenth Ward, "marking the beginning of that settlement which every year with a greater circumference is known as distinctively the Jewish quarter." Population density per acre in this ward increased from 273 in 1860 to 432 in 1880.

Already in 1883, the Association for Improving the Conditions of the Poor found this district overcrowded. On Essex and York Street an AICP investigator encountered 200 people squeezed into a single house that was subdivided into sixteen separate overcrowded apartments. By 1890 the ward bustled with 524 inhabitants per acre, the highest density in the city.* No wonder Rudyard Kipling compared New York to a "Zulu Kraal," and Arnold Bennett found that every window and door "seemed to sweat humanity." [45]

Jewish aid societies were concerned about these urban concentrations. In a sharply worded letter the Jewish Emigrant Relief Fund of New York wrote back to Europe that American cities did not hold the panacea for Russian pogroms. Too many of these refugees settle "in this city and crowd the filthy tenements in a certain section on the East Side. . . . The squalor, misery, and dirt of these tenements and their insufficient sanitary appointments must be seen to be understood." Like successful Italians, comfortable Jews feared the effects of slum concentrations on their ethnic image. They called for rural settlement. Such settlement would "make . . . the most effective step to stamp out prejudice against the Jew." They proved no more effective than their Italian counterparts. The romance of the farm did not blind the new settlers to the practical attractions of the Promised City; by 1920 Russians represented the single largest ethnic group in the city, numbering 480,000.[46]

As the city expanded, it elaborated into a downtown business district and outlying residential sections. Despite the unattractive

---

* New York ranked sixth in population density among world cities, but below Harlem it had a greater destiny than any other city. To Kipling the city was a "long, narrow pig Trough," and its streets "first cousins to a Zanzibar foreshore, or kin to the approaches of a Zulu Kraal." [Bayrd Still, *Mirror for Gotham* (New York, 1956), 208.]

surroundings, land values in centrally located downtown areas shot up. Lower Manhattan lots selling for $80 in the early forties climbed as high as $8,000 by 1880. The poorest immigrant working class, forced to live close to the factory district, squeezed into the substantial knickerbocker houses left behind by the departing upper class. Too expensive now for single families, these residences were subdivided into five and six separate apartments. The elegant façades remained, but sagging foundations trembled under loads they were not designed to support. At the same time landlords aggrandized every available space to expand their profitable properties. The garden was supplanted by a rear house; on top of both houses came more apartments, and the "court" style was established, producing dense slums "strung along both rivers like ball and chain, tied to the foot of every street." [47]

By 1880 a new style of tenement, representing the fond hopes of the model tenement reformers, emerged in the misshapen form of the dumb-bell. Retrospect is often unkind, ridiculing well-meant and honestly conceived efforts unfairly. Nonetheless, it is difficult to look at the dumb-bell design and believe that a commission of judges, including the president of New York's Board of Health, could find no better plan for decent downtown housing from among the 200 submitted to them in 1878. The scheme called for four families on each floor and provided each with a narrow twenty-eight-inch shaftway for light and fresh air. Even then, Dr. A. N. Bell, editor of the *Sanitarian,* saw in the winning design an "ingenious design for [a] dungeon." [48]

Disheartening as these conditions undoubtedly were, in their moments of reflection the newcomers accepted them; the bottom was the natural place to begin and they did not expect to remain there forever. They looked to New York's promise of opportunity and mobility—both occupational and residential. Better jobs and better homes in better neighborhoods beckoned. The two huge twin towers rising out of the East River to support the Brooklyn Bridge symbolized this "go ahead" spirit, opening an entire borough for the immigrant laboring class, while the spreading surface transit system opened another route out of the slums. By 1880, Manhattan's surface transit system carried over 150 million riders, an annual average of 125 rides for every New Yorker.[49]

The immigrants had faith in New York's promise. This much is evident in their writings. But then it must be kept in mind that mobility to poor and tortured Europeans was much like Dr. Samuel Johnson's story of the dancing dog: The amazing thing was not how well he did it, but that he did it at all.[50]

They came from towns and villages where caste and religion represented rigid class markers, and they settled in a flexible city where change was celebrated.

> You find there Jews born to plenty, whom the new conditions have delivered to the clutches of penury; Jews reared in the straits of need, who have here risen to prosperity; good people morally degraded in the struggle for success amid an unwonted environment; moral outcasts lifted from the mire purified and interbred with self respect; educated men and women with their intellectual polish tarnished in the inclement weather of diversity; ignorant sons of toil grown enlightened—in fine, people with all sorts of antecedents, tastes, habits and inclinations. . . .[51]

The Old World of monarchical Europe was a society in which individuals were locked into their fathers' and forefathers' stations in life, and their aspirations for the future were seen,

> As a named and settled landscape
> Their children
> Would make the same sense of
> As they did
> Laughing and weeping at the
> Same stories.[52]

In New York opportunity was not so oppressively imprisoned by the past. It was allowed to unfold in the spontaneous atmosphere of an expanding capitalist economy. New industries and the phenomenal expansion of New York's commerce produced many new jobs and new classes of wealth, and more important, a fluid society. In this situation, newcomers were afforded an opportunity to seek new roles. They did not have to fall into any one particular niche, for the expanding economy was constantly opening up new possibilities.

Clearly this society offered the opportunity for mobility. But how much? And for whom? An acute, if somewhat jaundiced, observer of New York immigrant life reported that, "The Italians and the poor Jew rise only by compulsion. The Chinaman does not rise at all. . . ." We turn to study this compulsion by learning how close it brought the Italians and their New Immigrant partners, the Russian Jews, to the success they sought.[53]

To do that, to compare these two groups fairly, demands the realization that Italians and eastern European Jews were not alike. Products of different cultures, and immigrants by virtue of different problems, they brought diverse backgrounds to the converted opera house at Castle Garden where steerage passengers were processed. The newcomers leaving the station, turning to the problems of securing a job and a place to live, were obviously affected and limited in their choice by their previous experience.

II

The Immigrant Context

The immigrant is not . . . a colonist or settler who creates a new society and lays down the terms of admission for others. He is rather the bearer of a foreign culture.

John Higham,
"Immigration"

Emigrating, the Italian working class brings away with it from the mother country all the little world in which they were accustomed to live; a world of traditions, of beliefs, of customs, of ideals of their own.

L'Italia

"The new immigration," observed the influential Dillingham Commission *Report on Immigration* in 1911, "has been largely a movement of laboring men who have come in large part, temporarily, from the less progressive and advanced countries of Europe in response to the call for industrial workers. . . ." These immigrants, the Commission concluded, represented an inferior type. They assimilated more slowly, "they" were more inclined to disease and crime, "they" were less literate, "they" were more rural and transient. In short, "they"—immigrants from Italy, Greece, Poland, Russia, Spain, Turkey, and Austria-Hungary— were less desirable.[1]

The Dillingham Commission had been appointed in 1907, with the expectation that its findings would provide a set of verified facts on the sensitive immigration issue.* President Theodore

---

* The Commission was composed of three Senators, three Representatives, and three Presidential appointees and chaired by Senator William P. Dillingham of Vermont, who favored immigration restriction. The key member was

Roosevelt put great faith in the Commission's work, hoping to use its reports "to put before Congress a plan which would amount to a definite solution to this immigration business." [2] Like many other purportedly "objective" and "scientific" studies, this one, which took more than three years to complete and involved the work of over three hundred people, confidently endorsed the conventional view of America's recent immigrants.* Its widely accepted statistics-studded forty-one-volume *Reports* buttressed a Manichean interpretation of American immigration. The Old Immigrants had been noble and necessary, but as Woodrow Wilson wrote in his popular *History of the American People:* "The immigrant newcomers of recent years are men of the lowest class

presidential appointee economist Jeremiah Jencks, also a restrictionist, who was warned by T.R., "Don't put in too many professors." [Oscar Handlin, *Race and Nationality in American Life* (New York, 1950), 78–80.]

    * The Immigration Commission, *Reports*, XXIII, recorded testimony on the issue of immigration and its restriction. One of the more interesting submissions was Thomas Bailey Aldrich's nativist poem "The Unguarded Gates":

> Wide open and unguarded stand our gates,
> And through them press a wild, a motley throng—
> Men from the Volga and the Tartar steppes,
> Featureless figures of the Hoang-Ho,
> Malayan, Scythian, Teuton, Kelt, and Slav,
> Flying the Old World's poverty and scorn;
> These bringing with them unknown gods and rites,
> Those tiger passions, here to stretch their claws.
> In street and alley what strange tongues are these,
> Accents of menace alien to our air,
> Voices that once the tower of Babel knew!
> O, Liberty, white goddess, is it well
> To leave the gate unguarded? On thy breast
> Fold sorrow's children, soothe the hurts of fate,
> Lift the downtrodden, but with the hand of steel
> Stay those who to thy sacred portals come
> To waste the fight of freedom. Have a care
> Lest from they brow the clustered stars be torn
> And trampled in the dust. For so of old
> The thronging Goth and Vandal trampled Rome,
> And where the temples of the Caesars stood
> The lean wolf unmolested made her lair.

from the South of Italy, and men of the meaner sort out of Hungary and Poland, men out of the ranks where there was neither skill nor energy, nor any initiative of quick intelligence." [3]

The Commission aligned the many nationalities in two groups and forced the statistics into this schema. Then chief researcher Jeremiah Jencks and his staff argued that the data supported this division. Despite the tables, charts, and other quantitative paraphernalia, they dogmatically misread the data. By their own findings the Commissioners showed the widely divergent character of the southern and eastern European immigrants. The various nationalities, grouped together as the New Immigrants, often differed more radically from each other than from the preferred western Europeans. [4]

For the purposes of the present study it is important to note the distinctions between New Immigrant Italians and Jews before going on to compare rates of social mobility. It is probably unwise to apply the approach of one noted historian—"I have assumed that . . . innately Negroes are, after all, only white men with black skins, nothing more, nothing less"—to the study of Italians and Jews. [5] Products of different cultures, they each brought to the New World a unique European past which played an important part in setting the course of their American experience. Thus we turn to these background differences before treating the consequent issue of social mobility.

One of the most significant differences between Old and New immigrants involved the issue of transiency. Commonly labeled "the birds of passage" syndrome, it referred to "the male laborer who comes to the United States with the intention of earning and saving money while employed here, and who, satisfied with his competence . . . returns home. . . ." Steamship rates were relatively cheap (a steerage ticket between Naples and New York cost $15 in 1880) and there were those males who crossed the ocean to seek not a new home but only temporary employment.[6]

Once here they took the menial jobs which others shied away from. Day labor, for example, accounted for 65 per cent of their employment. Accustomed to a low standard of living, they subsisted on the barest necessities, squirreling away as much as they could and sending these savings back home. "The southern and eastern European wage earner," W. Jett Lauck explained, "is usually single or, if married, has left his wife and children abroad. He has no permanent interest in the community in which he lives or in the industry in which he is employed. His main purpose is to live as cheaply as he can and save as much as he can. . . ." If the job market slackened, or the "bird" piled up sufficient savings, he returned to his European home.[7]

Such transiency narrowed the newcomer's sights to short-range goals. He generally neglected to learn the language or to make other long-term commitments to his new surroundings. Instead, with little specific training, he entered the lowest levels of the job market. Business and petty enterprise, which required investment and promised only gradual progress, were largely ignored. Similarly, the transient spurned clerical work because such higher-status jobs often did not offer better wages than day labor and only paid off in the long run as stepping stones to white-collar careers. The "bird of passage" kept his eye firmly trained on maximizing immediate rewards and eventually returning to Europe.[8]

Clearly, transiency bore on occupational mobility and progress; how characteristic was it of the New Immigrants, and more specifically of the Italians and Jews? The Immigration Commission responded to this issue directly, opening a chapter on "Permanent and Temporary Immigration" with the flat assertion that "In the matter of stability, or permanence of residence in the United States, there is a very wide difference between European immigrants of the old and new classes." [9]

As early as 1874, one of the first students of Italian emigration, Leone Carpi, noted that "thousands of Italians go in search of

work abroad, then come back within a year or two bringing with
them a small amount of savings, along with," Carpi could not let
the opportunity pass, "some bad habits." In his masterful 1919
study of Italian emigration, the distinguished Harvard economist
Robert Foerster agreed: * "The emigrants expect, in leaving Italy,
not to develop ties abroad, but only to lay by dollars." And Giovanni Florenzano, author of *Della emigrazione Italiana in America,* added, "our immigrants carry their mother country in their
hearts and maintain a political tie with it . . . , they return as
soon as they have put together a small nest egg. In this respect
they are different from the English, Irish and Germans who go
to America to become citizens." [10]

The impressionistic literature, of which the above is merely a
sampling, abounds with references to the pervasiveness of Italian
repatriation. Although the United States Commissioner General
of Immigration did not publish figures on this return movement
until 1908, Italian records are available and they bear out the
impressions.

Between 1892 and 1896 the average figure for Italian repatriation from the United States stood at 20,000. Expressed another
way, for every 100 Italians emigrating to the United States in
that period, 43 were going in the opposite direction back home
to Italy. By 1907–1911 the rate of average annual return had
spiraled to 150,000 individuals, averaging 73 repatriates for every
100 Italian immigrants.

These statistics are based on the compilations of the *Statistica
della emigrazione.* The American statistics for the post–1908
years cannot really be said to match the Italian figures closely.
There are variations, sometimes quite large,† between the two

---

* Foerster indicated the centrality of repatriation in the Italian immigration experience by opening his book with the following keynote quote from
E. Morpugo: "He abandons the niggardly soil as the swallow forsakes the
inclement skies, he returns to this familiar and cherished hut as the bird re-
pairs its old nest."

† For the three years 1908–1910 Italian figures total 419,142, while American figures compiled by the Commissioner-General of Immigration add up
to 308,977.

sets of data but, in the words of Robert Foerster, "nothing suggests the two series are irreconcilable." [11]

Whether the American or Italian figures are accepted, it is clear that this reflux played an important and impressive role in the history of Italian-American immigration, and helped make tenure in the New World "strangely temporary" for many Italians. Diomede Carito summed it up by recalling the words of an Italian in America who told him, "Doctor, we brought to America only our brains and our arms. Our hearts stayed there in the little house in the beautiful fields of our Italy." [12]

Just where on the occupational ladder were those Italians who chose to return to Italy within a short period after their arrival? The answer bears upon the validity of future conclusions on Italian-American mobility. If returnees were higher-status Italians, their repatriation would have the effect of depressing the overall record of Italian-American mobility, by draining off the successes. If, on the other hand, the reflux represented primarily low level job-holders, the effect would, of course, be quite different.

Records on Italian repatriates indicate that a minimal number of Italian-born professionals—one in 250—left the United States. Over 80 per cent of the return flow consisted of farm and common laborers. Moreover, 96 per cent of those leaving the United States for Italy traveled third class. Apparently the return movement did not draw its people from the successful classes.[13]

Statistics on the eastern European Jewish immigrants show no comparable repatriation. Their flight was not spurred by economic exigencies alone, but also by the determined persecutions of an antagonistic officialdom. Their departure was therefore stamped with finality, and they carried with them few nostalgic recollections of a beloved mother country. When the wandering Jew filled his migrant's pack and locked his synagogue, he slammed the door on a situation that the American ambassador to St. Petersburg, John W. Foster, compared to the barbarities of the Dark Ages.[14]

The Dillingham Commission was forced to recognize the Jew-

ish immigrants as exceptions to its New Immigrant stereotype:
"Conspicuous among the newer immigrants as exceptions to this
rule are the Hebrews, who . . . indicate a degree of permanency
not reached by any other race or people. . . ." From 1908 to
1912, 295,000 Russian Jews entered the United States and fewer
than 21,000 re-emigrated to some other country. While the average repatriation for all New Immigrants (with Jews excepted)
stood at 42 per cent, the percentage for Russian Jews hovered
around 7 per cent. This strikingly low figure indicated a resettlement of remarkable permanence. For better or worse they set
down roots, while others, more ambivalent about the conditions
which drove them from Europe, were more transient.[15]

Repatriation statistics provide only a partial picture of transiency. The previous discussion, concerned with the backflow of
American immigration, neglects those immigrants who lived and
worked as transients, but did not leave this country. Demographic
data on the sex and age makeup of the two immigrant groups
provide a sharper picture of differences between the immigrants
while also broadening the analysis of transiency.

The New Immigration as a whole was made up mostly of males
in their wage-earning years. Over the twelve-year span, 1899–
1910, males accounted for nearly 75 per cent of southern and
eastern European newcomers, and 83 per cent of the entire influx
was between the ages of 14 and 44. The very low number of
women and children pointed conclusively to a non-family migration and implied a primarily economic motive behind the immigration.[16]

Italian immigrants fit this general pattern quite closely. Indeed
their sex ratio was even more skewed than that of most other
New Immigrant nationalities. Of the 64,000 Italian immigrants
who entered the United States in the years 1882–1883, for instance, males accounted for 56,000, or 88 per cent. In the years
of peak migration between 1880 and 1910 an overwhelming majority of the immigrants from Italy were male, approximating
80 per cent for most years.[17]

The vast majority of these newcomers, over 83 per cent, fell in the 14–44 age group. Children and the aged consistently accounted for insignificant proportions of the Italian wave. Between 1899 and 1910 less than 6 per cent of all incoming Italians were over 44 years old, and the fraction represented by those under age 14—11 per cent—was not much larger. Even allowing for the prevailing custom of staggered immigration, where the head of the family or an older son migrated first, this one-sided distribution is remarkable.[18]

The meaning of these figures is apparent: The Italian immigration was, by and large, a nonfamily movement of males in their productive years. These single men * came to make some money and go home. "When winter comes and out of door work grows slack or when the labor market is depressed," Edwin Steiner observed, "these unattached forces return to Italy, and bask in the sunshine until conditions for labor on this side of the sea grow brighter." [19]

Others who did not particularly care about returning to Italy nonetheless did not settle down. Without family ties to restrict them, they moved freely across the city and country, often joining the "birds of passage" in seeking the most attractive short-range opportunities, ignoring business and enterprise.

Official immigration statistics on Jews as a distinct ethnic group were first gathered after 1899. In that year the Commissioner General of Immigration discarded the practice of categorizing immigrants by national origin in favor of "racial" categories and used the heading "Hebrews" for the first time. Fortunately, the United Hebrew Charities, concerned with the effect of the large Russian Jewish influx on its own philanthropic priorities, collected detailed information on Jewish immigrants landing at New York between 1886 and 1898. These figures reveal a fairly even ratio between the sexes—58 per cent male and 42 per cent female. Official statistics for the next twelve years reaffirm this

---

* Although largely a male phenomenon, transiency was also observed among the Italian women. Some of them came to "earn a dowry so that they might return to Italy with brighter prospects of finding a husband." [Louise C. Odencrantz, *Italian Women in Industry* (New York, 1919), 26.]

ratio with a very slight increase in the proportion of females. Over this entire period the contrast with Italians remained sharp. For the years between 1899 and 1910, when females constituted 43 per cent of the Jewish group, the figure for Italians was 22 per cent, almost half.[20]

The balance between the sexes indicates that the Jewish immigration was a family movement, and age data confirm this impression. These data, available in the U.H.C. surveys for 1886–1898 and the Immigration Commission *Reports* for the subsequent period to 1910, suggest that the Jews were more likely than most other immigrants to bring children with them. The U.H.C., which defined children as under age sixteen, found that more than one-third of all incoming Jews fell into that category, and the Commissioner of Immigration's statistics for the later period counted 25 per cent under age fourteen.[21]

Clearly Jews migrated in family units. They may not have all come together, but the large number of women and children indicates that the decision to relocate was firm, and that it involved permanent resettlement. Plans and goals would therefore be expressed in long-range terms. Whatever their future would be, they knew that for them it would be shaped in the New World.

Studying the make-up of the two groups and the comparative levels of repatriation provides insight into some differences in attitude and aspiration. Even more important with regard to their economic future was the fund of occupational experience that they brought with them. The jobs filled by Europeans in the countries they left behind, it is true, did not invariably determine their New World occupations, but their Old World experience did cast their abilities in very specific molds, setting parameters for progress. Peasant laborers did not, after all, harbor dreams of professorships.

Jews and Italians, it is clear from Table 1, differed in occupational experience, which helps explain why these two immigrant groups which arrived in the United States during the same period and often settled in adjoining sectors of the same city established different economic patterns.

TABLE 1 OCCUPATIONAL EXPERIENCE OF ITALIAN, JEWISH, AND ALL IMMIGRANTS ARRIVING IN THE UNITED STATES, 1899–1910

Professional	Italian	Jewish	All Immigrants
Actors	605	232	8,108
Clergy	874	350	8,917
Engineer	543	484	17,779
Musician	2,803	1,624	9,907
Sculptor & Artist	1,611	357	6,216
Teacher	599	2,192	14,558
Physician	617	290	5,085
Miscellaneous	1,705	1,926	29,167
Total Professionals	9,336	7,455	99,737
Professionals as Per Cent of Total with Work Experience	.5	1.3	1.4
Skilled			
Barber & Hairdresser	19,156	4,054	32,097
Carpenter & Joiner	3,928	36,138	141,326
Clerk & Accountant	22,318	17,066	94,544
Dressmaker	3,928	16,303	38,369
Mariner	18,788	402	79,016
Mason	37,984	2,507	73,899
Miner	23,283	252	82,856
Painter & Glazier	2,430	16,387	25,758
Seamstress	14,751	23,179	56,048
Shoemaker	44,823	23,519	101,283
Tailor	30,316	145,272	212,059
Miscellaneous	54,201	110,744	476,327
Total Skilled	275,906	395,823	1,423,582
Skilled as Per Cent of Total with Work Experience	15.6	67.0	20.2
Miscellaneous			
Farmer	19,410	1,008	114,144
Farm Labor	563,200	11,160	1,652,040

TABLE 1 OCCUPATIONAL EXPERIENCE OF ITALIAN, JEWISH, AND ALL
IMMIGRANTS ARRIVING IN THE UNITED STATES, 1899–1910 (*Continued*)

Professional	Italian	Jewish	All Immigrants
Labor	767,811	69,444	2,531,299
Merchant/Dealer	15,203	31,491	139,392
Servant	106,851	65,532	998,206
Miscellaneous	10,564	8,354	90,610
Total Miscellaneous	1,483,039	186,989	5,525,691
Miscellaneous as Per Cent of Total with Work Experience	83.9	31.7	78.4
Total with Work Experience	1,768,281	590,267	7,049,010
No Occupation Stated	516,320	484,175	2,506,717
Total Immigration	2,284,601	1,074,442	9,555,727

Source: Computed from United States Immigration Commission, III, 130–178.

Table 1 shows that very few Italian professionals emigrated to
the United States. Their high-status positions were place-specific
and did not travel well. Italian lawyers, ignorant of American law
and custom, after landing in the cities were often not better off
than common laborers. And unless physicians established a clientele within their own immigrant community they too were forced
to take up pick and shovel alongside illiterate compatriots. "All
of them," the Italian Information Office said of the immigrant
professionals, "meet bitter disillusionment and are often forced
to take up humble and arduous occupations." "Hardly have they
landed," G. P. Riva, Italian Consul-General at New York la-
mented,

> when they discover that America is not for them. Wanting
> knowledge of the language and every other resource, they come
> to the consulate and ask for succor in repatriation. How many
> think themselves lucky if they can find employment as waiters
> on board a vessel bound for Italy.[22]

This pattern generally applied to all immigrants. The United
States Industrial Commission on Capital and Labor concluded:

"There is abundant opportunity for the unskilled day laborer, or for the tradesman, but the average educated European finds himself at a serious disadvantage in competition with Americans for the better grade of commercial or professional positions." So particularly dire was the shortage of professional Italians that when the prominent journalist Adolfo Rossi attempted to launch an ethnic newspaper in 1882 he had great difficulty in finding an Italian sufficiently educated to "write his own tongue accurately." [23]

Musicians, sculptors, and artists, representing close to half of all Italian professionals coming to the United States, were conspicuous exceptions to this rule. Growing prosperity afforded Americans more time and money for entertainment—New York's Metropolitan Opera opened in 1883—and musicians detected a growing market for their skills. Moreover, differences which hampered Italians in other areas provided them with a valuable patina of continental culture in the arts. "A too facile assimilation to established ways," Robert Foerster shrewdly noted, "may even make profit less easy." [24]

Skilled hand labor served an important role in technologically backward Italy, but it did not command large wages. Daily wages for masons as late as 1907 averaged between 50 and 60 cents a day, while master printers earned only a dollar a day. In the larger cities, skilled mechanics commanded between $1.00 and $1.50 per day, while smaller city craftsmen averaged 50 to 60 cents less. In 1911, when the famed black American educator Booker T. Washington toured Italy, he observed that urban regions in the south were terribly backward, displaying a larger class "living in dirt, degradation, and ignorance at the bottom of society," than any other cities he knew. Thus, artisans had sufficient motive to leave Italy. Nonetheless, the number of skilled Italian immigrants to the United States was not large; only two in thirteen were skilled craftsmen. [25]

Those Italians who came with skills often found decent jobs at their old callings. Many masons, for instance, who learned their trade by hacking stone out of the Alps and Apennines in lumber-short Italy, put this experience to use in helping build and decorate New York's large apartment houses. Nonetheless, in 1907, when one in every four American immigrants came from Italy, they provided only one in 150 arriving plumbers, one in 74 locksmiths, and one in 38 of all machinists.[26]

By far the largest segment of incoming Italians—84 per cent—fell into the nebulously titled "miscellaneous" category. This category of eleven different vocations included such unrelated occupations as banker and servant. Such incongruous grouping presents a potential problem in interpreting Italian immigration. However, after removing all but the unskilled categories we find that very few Italians have been subtracted. The four categories bankers, agents, manufacturers, and merchants/dealers represented only .9 per cent of the total Italian immigration, and only one per cent of all Italians in the miscellaneous category. Thus, the remaining group of unskilled workers dominated the Italian influx, comprising 83 per cent. The focus can be narrowed yet further. Of the 1,768,281 Italians with any work experience, 1,331,011 were either farm or common laborers.

In sum, this was a peasant migration primarily from the agricultural regions of the south, heavily dominated by unskilled laborers. Dr. Allan J. McLaughlin, who was in charge of the United States Public Health and Marine Hospital at Naples, characterized "the *contadino,* the man from the country" for Senator Dillingham as

> a healthy animal, ignorant, but with splendid adaptability, quick to learn, bright, considering that he is a descendant of a race ill treated for centuries. . . . They are very rugged and strong. . . . They are capable of doing a day's work and possess a great deal of endurance. The United States gets the cream of those who have enterprise enough to exercize an initiative. In fact, one of the complaints of the present day of Italian officials is that the very best young blood of the Italian plebes is going out of the country.[27]

Other observers concurred in this description. They were especially impressed with the industriousness of the contadini. The

Rev. N. Walling Clark told the Immigration Commission that "they are ready to work and work hard, from early morning to late at night." Indeed, he was convinced that "there is no emigrant . . . from Europe who is a better worker, a man who has more power of enduring work, and he is a willing worker who has the desire to work." No Horatio Alger hero offered more.[28]

The Jews of eastern Europe had a very different occupational history. Medieval restrictions had prevented them from pursuing agriculture, funneling them instead into commerce and petty enterprise which produced their historical role as middlemen to Europe. Although by the nineteenth century these restrictions had loosened up somewhat, the May Laws of 1882 reinstituted their full range in Tsarist Russia. These laws prohibited Jews from buying and selling farm lands or entering a long list of preferred professions and constricted them even more narrowly than before to small-town life. This explains why in an overwhelmingly agricultural economy only 3 per cent of Russia's 5,000,000 Jews held farm-related jobs.[29]

Table 1, which summarizes occupational data on Jews and Italians, shows a disproportionately large number of Jews without occupations. While this category accounted for between one-fifth and one-fourth of all Italians, it held almost half of all incoming Jews. This curious difference can be explained by the number of women and children in the Jewish immigration. Women and children generally reported no previous occupation and therefore swelled the "without occupations" category.

The pronounced variation in the skilled and miscellaneous categories was far more significant. Fully two-thirds of all gainfully employed Jews worked at skilled crafts, an uncharacteristic statistic for New Immigrants, or indeed any immigrants. Only 16 per cent of all previously employed Italians and 20 per cent of all occupied immigrants belonged to this category. Within the skilled occupations, Jewish experience was heaviest in the clothing trades (one of the few industries traditionally open to European Jews), in which one of every three arriving Jewish workers earned his living. The remaining immigrant craftsmen knew town

trades—butchering, carpentry, shoemaking—which they had practiced in the segregated Jewish townlets of the Russian Pale of
Settlement.[30]

Nonetheless, these skilled immigrants represented the least
skilled of Russia's Jews. "*Ver geht kein America?*" went a common
saying, "*Die shnayders, shusters, und ferdganovim* [Who leaves
for America? The tailors, shoemakers and horse thieves]." Professional Jews were scarce. Of the 6,000 Jewish clergymen reported
in the Russian census of 1897, fewer than 350 left for America in
the subsequent twelve-year period. Other professional categories
were equally sparse, with the notable exception of teachers and
musicians. Most of the teachers who came had not actually
served in the Russian schools—such positions were all but closed
to Jews—but rather as *m'lamdim* or elementary level religious
teachers supported by the local communities. Jewish musicians
apparently shared with their Italian counterparts the feeling that
prosperous America could support entertainers better than their
own strapped local communities.[31]

The comparatively small miscellaneous category further sets
this immigration off from the typical European pattern. The
figures for Jewish farmers and laborers were unusually low. Interestingly, although Jews would quickly become merchants and
peddlars, only 5 per cent of those emigrating to the United
States were merchants or dealers. Moreover, it is noteworthy that
despite the high number of women in the Russian-Jewish immigration, they accounted for only a small proportion of all immigrant servants.

Thus the New Immigrant Jews brought over to their new
world the city skills that they had cultivated in their restricted
communities. Among those filing out of steerage were over
145,000 tailors, 23,000 shoemakers, and 17,000 clerks and accountants. Grodno, however, was not New York, and it was far from
clear that their Pale experience would help them in Gotham.*

* One problem they would encounter was anti-Semitism. Although they
did not suffer persecution in the United States, the New Immigrants, both

In contrast, most of the Italians had a peasant background. Despite this, they refused to go into farming. Joseph Lopreato writes that for the *contadino*

> farming was a punishment, not only for his ill-nourished stomach but for his soul as well. It sickened his self. It humiliated his sense of being. It reduced him nearly to the status of the donkey and the goat, animals that he constantly brutalized as an outlet for his anger . . . but farming in America? That was absurd.[32]

Whatever the reason, these country-raised Italians did not seek out America's farms.* Consequently, they had to adapt on two levels, to a new country and to an urban environment. Unless they expanded their skills their peasant experience equipped them only for the periphery of the city economy as menial laborers.

More than one-fourth of the adult immigrants admitted to the United States between 1899 and 1910, according to the Dillingham Commission, "could neither read nor write." Yet American society placed great emphasis on literacy (the nation would be

Italians and Jews, did encounter discrimination. Henry Adams, steeped in the prejudices of his patrician class, showed how intense these feelings were: "The Russian Jews and the other Jews will completely control the finances and Government of this country in ten years or they will all be dead. . . . The hatred with which they are regarded . . . ought to be a warning to them. The people of this country . . . won't be starved and driven to the wall by Jews who are guilty of all crimes, tricks and wiles," said the man who could not understand why America had not put his gifts to better use. [John Higham, *Strangers in the Land* (New York, 1968), 93.]

* That Italian peasant farmers should show so little attention to American farms is explained by Constantine Panunzio thus: "The *contadini* were not farmers . . . but simply farm laborers . . . seldom owning their own land, . . . They are not . . . acquainted with the implements of modern American farming." Their tools were a mattock, axe and wooden plow. "When they come to America, the work which comes nearest to that which they did in Italy is not farming or even farm labor, but excavation work." [*The Soul of an Immigrant* (New York, 1928), 77–78.]

thrown into virtual trauma during World War I as a result of
Army intelligence tests that indicated a drastically lower level of
literacy than expected). Immigrant shortcomings in this area
thus caused concern.[33]

Indeed, literacy, or the lack of it, played an important role in
immigrant fortunes. Mario Puzo, the Italian-American author,
recalls that illiteracy often caused immigrants to narrow their
aspirations to the thinnest line of existence.

> My mother wanted me to be a railroad clerk. And that was her
> highest ambition; she would have settled for less. At the age
> of sixteen . . . when I let everybody know that I was going
> to be a great writer. . . . she quite simply assumed that I had
> gone off my nut. She was illiterate and her peasant life in Italy
> made her believe that only the son of the nobility could pos-
> sibly be a writer. . . .[34]

The *padrone* (immigrant contractor) was another example of the
role literacy could play in immigrant success. Because he could
read and write while others could not, he managed the fortunes
of fellow countrymen to his great profit.

Literacy (at least for the purposes of immigrant records) was
determined at the point of entry with two questions put to all
immigrants: "Can you read?" "Can you write?" Of all immigrants
over the age of fourteen, between 1899 and 1910, 27 per cent
answered both questions, "No." Not surprisingly, the Italian immigration with its concentration of peasants and farm laborers
had a very high rate of illiteracy. The average figure for all
Italians—despite the fact that north Italians separately had a low
proportion of 12 per cent—was 47 per cent.[35]

The Jewish immigrants, who lived in a setting that provided
greater access to education, were far from universally literate.
More than one in four, 26 per cent, could not read or write, reflecting the restrictions of Russian law and their own custom
which kept them out of the native school system. The large
proportion of females, who were generally less schooled than

the men, is an additional cause for the high figure. In any event, with respect to illiteracy Jews fit the New Immigrant pattern; literacy figures for the Old Immigrants had been far more respectable.*

The millions who poured out of steerage and onto Castle Garden and Ellis Island brought some resources tied in their bundles, hidden in their stockings, or pressed between the pages of a book. This, they hoped, would launch their success, or at least pay for their necessities until the bountiful America supplied a job. Some were even moderately wealthy, and if there was enough money to open a small neighborhood business in the immigrant quarter, this might in time, and with hard work, produce a man of means.

Immigrant financial records are imprecise. The immigrant law of 1893, however, provided that ship manifests state whether each incoming alien possessed at least $30, and if not the ship captain was obliged to record the amount brought along. In 1903 the stipulation was changed from $30 to $50. Since "The financial resources of an immigrant frequently . . . [had] an important bearing on his admissibility," this was probably sufficient incentive for the immigrants to report their money.[36]

On the basis of Port Inspector Reports it appears that few of the New Immigrants came with considerable liquid wealth. North Italians came over in the best circumstances, averaging over $30 for each immigrant who reported money. Southern

* Although the question merely asked if they could read, it was probably interpreted by most of the immigrants as whether they could read their native tongue. Most Jews could at least *read* Hebrew. "The most ignorant 'man of the earth' among our people can read the holy tongue [Hebrew], though he may not understand the meaning of the words." [Abraham Cahan, *The Rise of David Levinsky* (New York, 1917), 88.]

Italians, however, were considerably poorer, with slightly over
$17. The average sum for all Italians between 1899 and 1910 was
$19.45. The mean for Jews was $29.09.[37]

Although with respect to transient or permanent immigration,
work experience, and literacy the Italians and Jews were very
different, the two groups were alike in bringing little capital with
them. Both would start by looking for jobs, as few Jews or Italians
brought enough money to establish their own businesses.

Thus, a close comparison of the two groups indicates a good
deal of disparity. But if these differences are clear, their implications are not unambiguous. Repatriation, for example, may not
have impressed Senator Dillingham or Jeremiah Jencks as desirable—but their criticism was leveled at the impact of this split
loyalty on assimilation. The effect of the "birds of passage" syndrome *on mobility* is open to many interpretations. Rootlessness
allows for a "follow the main chance" attitude, which often gave
the Italian laborer wide latitude to seek out the best-paying jobs.
And what if he was truly successful here? Nothing prevented
him from deciding to settle and bring over the rest of his family,
which is what many did.

Moreover, it is clear that those going back were often the
least successful. W. B. Bailey pointed out in a 1912 article titled
"Birds of Passage," that "the result of such migration [is often to]
limit the fall in wages and to free the community from the necessity of supporting a number of unemployed. . . . Our country
owes a debt of gratitude to Europe in that every group of returning immigrants contain some whose vitality has been impaired by
severe labor. . . . [and] industrial accidents. . . ." This meant
that group mobility was enhanced because the least successful
were washed back home.[38]

That the Jews were more urban, came over as a family unit,
and settled more firmly, does not in itself predict the course or
rate of their mobility. "There are," Stephan Thernstrom has concluded, ". . . a good many discrepancies between the ranking of
immigrant groups in terms of various handicaps and their ranking

in terms of occupational performance after their arrival." It is easily proven that the Italians were largely of rural peasant background and as a result passed on a set of values for education, work, thrift, and ambition that differed from the ideas and attitudes of the Jews of Russia. How this affected their experience in the United States is the subject of the succeeding chapters.[39]

III

Immigrant Occupational Distribution

A large proportion of the great New York clothing industry . . . is in Russian Jewish hands, as well as a fair proportion of the trading in these goods, both wholesale and retail. . . . The needle industries . . . have remained the great field of Russian Jewish business activity in New York.

> Isaac Rubinow
> "Economic and Industrial
> Condition of the Russian
> Jew in the United States"

Historians determined to illumine America's past from "the bottom up" have been placing the "common people" under increased scrutiny. Taking up Berthold Brecht's challenge—

> Who built the seven towers of Thebes?
> The books are filled with the names of kings.
> Was it kings who hauled the craggy blocks of stone? . . .
> Where did the masons go? . . .
>
> Every ten years a great man,
> Who paid the piper?
>
> So many particulars
> So many questions.—

they have been trying to fill in the particulars and answer questions about the masons. But the study of inarticulate and inaccessible masses is more easily aspired to than achieved, and in their ardor for the task some scholars have been forced to draw water from such rocky sources as folk tales and songs.[1]

The student of New York's anonymous Americans is, however, more fortunate. He has at his disposal an assortment of firsthand census reports with millions of biographical sketches of people from all walks of life. These records provide glimpses of the men "who hauled the craggy blocks," immigrant workers like Louis Malisprini, Abraham Falk, Augusto Muzzio, and Tobias Krakower. The study of these men, and others like them, brings into focus "the tangle and mat of . . . growth between the tall trees of success, the shabby chambers crowded with aspirants and climbers, . . ." which fascinated such naturalist writers as Theodore Dreiser.[2]

In 1880, 46-year-old Louis Malisprini, a native of Genoa was a recent newcomer to New York. With his wife and five children, Malisprini lived in a tenement on Sullivan Street in lower Manhattan's Italian section. His teen-age sons attended the city schools while his two younger daughters remained at home with their 30-year-old mother.[3]

Like many other recently arrived immigrants, Malisprini found that his Old World experience was poor preparation for life in an industrial metropolis. He had little choice but to work at unskilled labor.

> The same individuals, [wrote Robert Foerster] had they lived two thousand years ago, would not have been harnessed to tasks materially different from those they toil at today. Not only have they lacked all specialized training, but they have even reached adult years without an elementary inculcation of reading and writing. . . . They have worked out of doors, betaking themselves wherever a strong back and compelling arms were needed. . . . To the rest of the world it has fallen to utilize them as they are.[4]

It is not surprising then, to learn that Malisprini and his spouse were both illiterate.

Tobias Krakower, a Russian Jew, left his homeland before the onset of full-scale persecutions. Like most Jews who settled in New York, he lived on the Lower East Side, helping create a milieu that was not quite Russian—the dread of official persecution was absent, and Jews were permitted to join all others in reaching for the golden ring—but nonetheless more Russian than

American. The touchstones of his east European *shtetl* surrounded him: the synagogue, a burial society, the kosher butcher,
a Yiddish language newspaper. Even his occupation, tailor, came
directly from the Russian Pale. Although the 23-year-old Krakower was himself literate, his wife, born in Russian Poland, could
neither read nor write.

Like most other immigrants, 56-year-old Augusto Muzzio did
not have sufficient capital to invest in a shop with its fixed
costs and overhead. He did, however, want to try his hand at
New York's growing retail business and sometime before 1880
turned to peddling fruit. A sympathetic writer sketched the type
of life Muzzio might have led vending his fruits on the city
streets:

> I remember watching an old pushcart vendor one sweltering
> afternoon in summer . . . and I was never more impressed
> with the qualities which make for success in this world . . .
> patience, and good nature and sturdy charitable endurance.
> . . . He was a dark, gray headed, grizzle cheeked "guinea" or
> "dago" as he was scornfully dubbed by the Irish policeman
> who made his life a burden. . . . Some few peaches had fallen
> awry, and these he busily straightened. One pile . . . he re-
> plenished from baskets of hitherto undisturbed peaches, care-
> fully dusting the fuzz of each one with a small brush to
> heighten their beauty, and add to the attractiveness of the
> pile. . . .[5]

Muzzio's son Augustine, 31, lived with the family, contributing
to its support by working as a laborer. His 18-year-old sister
worked in one of the candy factories that had sprung up in the
downtown area. Two younger girls attended school.

Abraham Falk was 40 years old in 1880. Russian Poland—that
sector of Poland which fell to Russia after partition in the late
eighteenth century—had been his home, but deteriorating conditions caused him to leave before 1862. He crossed the ocean and
settled in Manhattan. After more than eighteen years in New
York, Falk was still illiterate, and together with his 18-year-old
daughter and 16-year-old son toiled at making cigars, a common

occupation among Bohemian and Jewish immigrants in the Promised City's tenements. Falk's four other children promised at least one improvement in status over their father. They learned to read and write in the public school.

Having glanced at these individuals (who fit so well George Eliot's description of "men who lived faithfully a hidden life and rest in unvisited tombs") we might conclude that their anonymity was well deserved and it need not be disturbed. They lived—let it be said plainly—prosaic, common lives, undistinguished by achievements of note. Forgettable men, forgettable lives. Except that in the aggregate these anonymous aliens who settled in New York were a crucial element in its development. They contributed to its unique economic success and helped make its heterogeneous culture. And by their experience they tested America's commitment to the promise of fair and rapid progress for all.[6]

The previous chapter elaborated some of the differences between New Immigrant Jews and Italians before they entered New York. This chapter considers the immediate effects of those differences by analyzing immigrant occupational distribution in 1880 and 1905.

Admittedly such still-life occupational profiles do not permit an analysis of economic mobility beyond indicating the progress of each group *qua* group.* They do, however, show what jobs were open to Italians and Jews, how quickly the newcomers were able to achieve upper-level occupations, and, perhaps of equal significance, what role they played in New York's evolving economy. Moreover, by providing a picture of New Immigrant

---

* It is important to underscore this caveat because it is easy to misread the ensuing discussion as a description of occupational mobility. Comparing, for example, the occupational distribution of New York's Italians in 1880 with 1905 will tell us very little about the success or lack of success of the first group twenty-five years later. The 1905 population represents certainly some of the 1880 wave and their children, but, much more, later arrivals. The population in 1905 is then, for all intents and purposes, a different Italian population. For a fuller discussion of this point, see pages 105–6.

development these data permit us to draw important comparisons between Italians and Jews.

In 1880 the city of Manhattan—only after 1898 was Manhattan consolidated with the other boroughs into Greater New York— boasted a unique work force of over half a million souls in a total population that exceeded 1.2 million. In what was still primarily an agricultural nation, with only 33 per cent of the population involved in industry or commerce, the Empire City, with more than 70 per cent of its work force in these sectors, was clearly unique.[7]

Other characteristics contributed to the metropolis's uniqueness. More than half of the city's working population was foreign-born, providing New York with the largest immigrant labor force in the world. The influence of these workers was not restricted to any one sector of the economy, as they competed with the American-born for jobs in all fields. Indeed, available census statistics indicate that the distribution in broad occupational categories did not vary markedly between aliens and natives.[8]

New York's two major immigrant colonies did, however, differ from each other quite sharply. The Old Immigrant Irish and Germans, who provided three-fourths of the immigrant labor pool, were drawn to different parts of the city economy (see Table 2). The Irish concentrated on the service jobs. One of every two Irishmen was reported occupied in this category, which included domestic servants (24,000) and common laborers (20,000). The Germans, on the other hand, took to industrial occupations, with more than half in manufacture-related businesses, especially the clothing trades, which they dominated, together with native-born American women.[9]

The radical shift in American immigration which came to national attention in the late eighties and nineties was felt earlier and more powerfully in the big cities. In 1880, before the New Immigration won its own sobriquet, Italian and Jewish communities began their rapid spread over lower Manhattan and into adjoining Brooklyn. These concentrated knots of newcomers drew the attention of natives and visitors alike because the foreign cultures stood out so distinctly. Perhaps less obviously, these foreigners displayed equally distinct patterns of occupational distribution.

Unfortunately, the United States Census for 1880 did not publish data on Italians or eastern Europeans. These groups were lumped together with a host of other nationalities in an "other countries" column. The manuscript federal census schedules for this year are, however, available and it is possible to reconstruct the occupations of the two New Immigrant communities by surveying these schedules.[10]

The general categories employed by the census divided the economy into five different sectors. These categories did not reflect differing levels of skill or status. Nonetheless, for the purpose of comparison with the published data, the shortcomings of the classification scheme will be ignored for the moment.

TABLE 2 OCCUPATIONAL DISTRIBUTION FOR ITALIANS, IRISH, RUSSIAN JEWS, AND GERMANS, BY PER CENT, NEW YORK CITY, 1880

	Italian	Irish	Jewish	German
Agriculture	0	.4	0	.7
Professional & Personal Service	47.4	51.4	3.8	21.0
Trade and Transportation	16.2	20.0	32.8	25.4
Mfg., Mechanical & Mining	36.3	28.1	63.5	52.8
Total in Sample	1,035	114,581	980	92,657

Source: Irish and German data are from United States Department of Interior, *Statistics of the Population of the United States at the Tenth Census* (Washington, 1883), 892. Sample data on Italians and Jews are drawn from the manuscript schedule of the Tenth Census of the Population, 1880, for New York and Kings Counties.

A comparison of the Old and New Immigrants in Table 2 points to some interesting and, in light of the Dillingham Commission's conclusions, unexpected similarities. The spectrum of occupations for the Italians closely resembled that of the longer-settled Irish. Both groups (who shared peasant origins) concentrated very heavily on service jobs, especially domestic service and common labor. "Trade and transportation," which included a divergent cluster of entrepreneurs, peddlers, clerks, and railroad laborers, accounted for roughly 20 per cent of the remaining Italians and Irish, and for both these ethnic colonies another one-third of the total took positions in the industrial sector.

Eastern European Jews differed significantly from both the Irish and Italians. Because of the low number of laborers and service workers among the Jews, they did not really match any of the groups in the table. But aside from this admittedly significant difference, the Jews did bear a resemblance to the Old Immigrant Germans (who, of course, had a number of Jews among them). Like them, but in even larger numbers, Jews gravitated to peddling, shopkeeping, and skilled industrial labor. Of every 10 Jews, 9.6 were occupied in one of these areas. Thus, broadly speaking, Italians trod the path blazed by the Irish, and Jews compared most closely to the Germans.

Unfortunately, that is all the insight that can be gleaned from the data presented in Table 2. The census categories, descriptive rather than analytical, reveal nothing about the relative status of the various ethnic groups. Day laborers and domestic servants were placed in the "professional and service" category; so were physicians and surgeons. A high percentage of immigrants in the service class could, therefore, mean a large number of janitors or day laborers, or the same statistic might reflect a collection of high-status lawyers, doctors, and government officials. This loose system of classification leaves too much to be desired.[11]

A hierarchical scale of occupations based on Alba M. Edwards's concept of the "social-economic grouping" and used in more recent studies provides a more sharply honed tool of analysis. The highest classification, "high white collar," includes professionals and major proprietors, managers, and officials. "Low white collar" embraces clerks, salesmen, semiprofessionals and petty proprietors, managers, and officials. The succeeding three classifications include the three levels of blue collar labor: skilled, semiskilled, and unskilled (including menial service labor).[12]

One additional refinement of the census approach carries the analysis yet further. The data presented thus far gather the foreign-born immigrants together with their American-born off-spring, heads of families together with their sons and boarders. The ensuing discussion studies only heads of households; a later chapter is concerned with the occupational history of the remaining household members.

ITALIAN OCCUPATIONAL DISTRIBUTION, 1880–1905

Table 3 summarizes the survey data for Italian household heads, according to the five-level occupational hierarchy. As might be expected, the high white-collar class in 1880 was very slight. One finds no lawyers, doctors, or engineers among the sampled households. Only two in every 100 Italians achieved a position atop the hierarchy, and they accomplished this by way of business success.

One-fourth of New York's Italians held low white-collar occupations, with peddlers * and shopkeepers forming the most im-

---

* The placing of peddlers in the low white-collar range is admittedly arbitrary and arguable. Clearly, few peddlers wore white collars and their earnings were often low. In the last analysis, however, I agree with the Edwards/Thernstrom classification that places peddlers in a white-collar class. They were entrepreneurs—albeit of the pettiest sort—and they were involved in risk-taking and investment. This opened for them an avenue of business progress closed to the average worker.

TABLE 3 OCCUPATIONAL DISTRIBUTION FOR ITALIAN HOUSEHOLD
HEADS, BY NUMBER AND PER CENT, NEW YORK CITY, 1880 AND 1905

Class	1880 Number	Per Cent	1905 Number	Per Cent	Difference *
I High White Collar	9	2.0	23	2.3	+ .3
II Low White Collar	112	24.9	181	17.8	− 7.1
III Skilled	59	13.1	221	21.8	+ 8.7
IV Semiskilled	31	6.9	165	16.3	+ 9.4
V Unskilled	239	53.1	425	41.9	−11.2
Total	450		1,015		

* Between 1880 and 1905, expressed as the difference between percentages.
Source: Sample data from Federal Census Schedules for New York and
Kings Counties for 1880 and from New York State Census Schedules for
New York and Kings Counties, 1905.

portent elements of this stratum. Musicians, who emigrated to
the United States in relatively large numbers, created the only
significant nonbusiness group in this class. The few clerks, salesmen, and semiprofessionals played inconsequential roles in the
Italian occupational spectrum.[13]

The bulk of this immigrant community earned its livelihood at
lower-status occupations. Three in every four Italians worked at
manual labor. Thirteen per cent of these blue-collar workers
took skilled jobs in assorted industries, working as confectioners,
shoemakers, masons, and tailors. Significantly, however, Italian
craftsmen did not dominate a single skilled craft. Instead, this
relatively small group was scattered among the various industries,
preventing the kind of control exerted by other ethnic groups
when they saturated a craft within an industry.[14]

The small semiskilled and service sector (7 per cent of the
manual-class) demonstrated a similar lack of focus. Except for
barbering, where Italians quickly won recognition, this division,
which included most factory and personal service jobs, provided
little hope for the capture of any single service or industry.

Lacking industrial skills, over 53 per cent of this immigrant

Italian community were obliged to assume unskilled jobs. Colorful organ grinders and the elegantly named *chiffonniers*—"with sacks on their shoulders rummaging the garbage cans, gleaning paper, rags, bones, broken glass"—were part of this group, but common laborers constituted the largest segment. Of every ten Italian households, common laborers headed four, working on the busy wharves, on construction sites, and on assorted public works, "employed at the most repulsive tasks, scorned by the workmen of other nationalities—carrying offal to the ships and dumping it in the sea, cleaning the sewers et similia. . . ." The pay was low, the work hard, and the tenure short.[15]

Overall, the Italian colony in 1880 showed the structure of a recent immigrant group, which had less to do with their American experience than with their Old World backgrounds. Rural, backward southern Italy had supplied them with little in the way of industrial skills, consequently their range of occupational choice was narrow. Most did manual work, and the occupational *cul de sac*, unskilled common labor, trapped a large number. Even the nominally white-collar contingent were mainly peddlers and vendors, skirting the edge of the white-collar classification.

Writing in 1881, Charlotte Adams sketched the metropolitan Italian community. She depicted the organ grinders, "wandering minstrels . . . who pass their summers playing on steamboats and at watering places"; and the unskilled workmen she found "everywhere." The recent newcomers were forced into these undesirable roles by their inexperience. They had brought "no intellectual capital but the primitive methods of farming handed down by their ancestors. . . . The idyllic life of an Italian hillside or of a dreaming medieval town is but poor preparation for the hand to hand struggle for bread of an overcrowded city." [16]

Over the next two decades this community was transformed from an ethnic enclave concentrated in the immigrant quarter to a collection of sprawling "Little Italies," populated by 145,000 foreign-born Italians and their offspring. And in the following five years, as the immigrant wave climbed to its crest, one million more came to the United States, adding tens of thousands to Gotham's Italian population.

This seemingly inexhaustible influx drove many involved with what Theodore Roosevelt called "the immigrant business" to join nativists in complaining that these recent immigrants were less needed, less wanted, and less capable than their predecessors. Europe, they cried, was scraping the bottom of the barrel and heaving this sediment across the ocean into America's congested cities. Writing in the *Annals of the American Academy,* John Mitchell charged that "In the early history of this republic every healthy immigrant arriving on our shores was an asset to us; but during the past 10 or 15 years . . . immigration has increased so rapidly and has reached such stupendous proportions that many of these immigrants . . . are in reality liabilities." Or as Mary K. Reely summarized in her brief for restriction, "The era of expansion when crude labor was needed in the building of railroads, etc., has passed." [17]

Despite such grim forebodings about the overabundance of immigrant labor in the midst of constricted opportunities, the status profile for New York Italians in 1905 shows improvement on a number of levels. Judging by a comparison of class data in Table 3, Italians suffered a declining white-collar class, but more than compensated with progress up the blue-collar ladder. Indeed a close look at the detailed job data (not given in Table 3) reveals that Italians stamped their mark on an array of jobs and industries, exerting a measure of control that they did not have in 1880.[18]

In the course of one generation the upper white-collar class increased slightly, and it included a few professionals in addition to the entrepreneurs. In spite of this increase at the top, the white-collar class as a whole would seem to have suffered decline. At first glance this white-collar dip appears quite significant, but closer inspection points to a different conclusion. The entire decline of the low white-collar class can be traced to the dwindling number of peddlers. Were peddlers excluded from consideration in 1880 and 1905, the low white-collar class would actually show a 1 per cent rise from 12.7 to 13.8 per cent.

By 1905, street trading, which in the previous decades provided poor men like Augusto Muzzio with the opportunity to try their hand at business, had become big business. A 1906 Report of the Mayor's Pushcart Commission described the process by which investors took control of peddling and converted it from a poor man's avenue of enterprise to their own purposes:

> The method employed has been a simple one—some well-to-do Italian sends various of his Italian neighbors to the office of The Bureau of Licenses and has them take out licenses in their own name, although they do not intend to peddle, nor do they supply the funds to pay the license fees required, but these are supplied by the "padrone" who then hires peddlers by the day or the week to sell goods for him and supplies each of these peddlers with a license for the time being.

One such peddling tycoon bought fistfuls of the necessary licenses and ran 170 different pushcarts; others controlled 66, 64, 62, 53, 50, and 45 such vending stands. Moreover, the city restricted peddling licenses to such New Yorkers as were either citizens or could produce "first papers." Consequently, while 12 per cent of New York's Italians in 1880 earned at least technical white-collar status as street traders, one generation later only 2 per cent peddled.[19]

At the same time the incidence of more substantial entrepreneurs climbed. Shopkeepers and artisans who dotted the neighborhoods with their groceries, saloons, and barbershops paced off a healthy 5 per cent increase from 1880 to 1905.

Regardless of these upper-class permutations, blue-collar work continued to dominate the occupational horizon. Within this broad class, however, one notes a 9 per cent boost in skilled workers. Italian craftsmen moved into a variety of choice manual occupations such as carpentry, shoemaking, and baking, occupations which in 1880 had been more "Jewish" than "Italian." But the most significant takeover took place in Gotham's largest industry, the clothing trades.

In the 1890s employers, seeking to avoid union demands, turned to the largely unorganized Italians who offered to work for less and brought them into the industry. "The Italian and his wife," the Industrial Commission explained, "will come to the shop together . . . There are numbers of cases where the Italian and his wife together work for the same price which the Jew receives for his labor alone, and in this way the Italian is able to crowd the Jew out of the trade." In an 1889 investigation a New York factory inspector found nary an Italian clothing factory in all Manhattan; two years later there were hundreds. At first, they were employed at semiskilled tasks as operators and pressers, but they eventually took skilled jobs as well, displacing Jewish tailors, designers, and cutters who either moved up or out of the industry.

Ten years after they originally stepped into the needle trades, Italians claimed 12 per cent of the industry's jobs. By 1904, the largely Jewish clothing workers' union reported the proceedings of a strike in English, Yiddish, and, signaling the prominence of a new ethnic group, in Italian. After studying the trends, the Industrial Commission expressed little doubt that "the future clothing workers in the country are not likely to be Jews, but the Italians." [20]

At the semiskilled level, the capture of another heretofore non-Italian branch of New York's economy resulted in a 10 per cent spurt over the generation. As late as 1880, 95 per cent of Manhattan's longshoremen were Irish. As in the clothing trades, a strike provided the crucial opening wedge for Italians. After a crippling Knights of Labor strike in 1887, employers resolved to break the Irish monopoly on the waterfront by introducing lower-paid recent immigrants. By 1896 displacement of the Irish began in earnest. In his authoritative study of *The Longshoremen* Charles Barnes described the takeover:

> The employment of Italians proved so advantageous that as soon as the wedge was in, the opening for them was certain to become wider and wider. The tremendous annual increase of

unskilled labor by immigration, the eagerness of the Italians for the work, their willingness to submit to deductions from their wages, leaving a neat little commission to be divided between foreman, saloon keepers, and native bosses—all these considerations insured the permanence of the Italian longshore work.[21]

Once a sufficient number became longshoremen *—earning an average of two or three dollars a week more than common laborers—an ethnic momentum was set in motion. "They stood together. Each Italian who found employment brought relatives. . . . If one secured a job as a foreman, he gave preference to his countrymen." Eventually they moved up into powerful positions as contracting stevedores. Seven or eight such stevedores were responsible for hiring almost all longshoremen who handled foreign commerce. The swift takeover accomplished, in the words of Robert Foerster, "one of the most striking examples of racial displacement in American industry." [22]

Only one other semiskilled occupation employed a significant number of Italians, and this, too, dealt with transportation. The various moving and delivering businesses that carted New Yorkers and their goods employed many Italians as hackmen, draymen, and teamsters.

Italian barbers were especially numerous in the service sector, supplying more than half of New York's haircutters, scissoring their way into a trade that had been controlled by Germans and Negroes. Italians also provided a large number of waiters and bartenders. One of every twenty Italians among New York householders worked as either a barber, waiter, or bartender.[23]

As the skilled and semiskilled fractions increased, the unskilled division decreased by 11 per cent. Nevertheless, unskilled labor persisted as the single largest occupational resource for New York

* Many questioned the efficiency of the Italians, writes Barnes: "It is evident that they have less physical strength than the Irish. On some piers it is said that 'one "white man" is as good as two or three Italians.' The Scandinavian-American Line, Hoboken, once worked a gang of Irish in one coal boat and a gang of Italians in another at the same time, and found by actual count that the Irish brought up two bucketfulls to the Italian's one." [Charles Barnes, *The Longshoremen* (New York, 1915), 9.]

Italians, providing 42 per cent of all household heads with jobs.
Here, too, Italians followed an already familiar pattern of ethnic
succession. Italian workers displaced the Irish in unskilled street
and construction work. New York's Inspector of Public Works
testified before Congress in 1890 that Italians constituted 90 per
cent of those involved in Gotham's public works. Over 4,000 Italians joined the crew that began excavation on the Lexington Avenue subway in 1900. In that year one of every four common
laborers in New York was Italian.[24]

When Constantine Panunzio arrived in the United States in
1902 he quickly learned that only "peek and shuvil" work was
available for Italians. One reason was that, "the 'padrone' perhaps makes a greater per capita percentage in connection with
securing and managing workers for construction purposes than in
any other line and therefore he becomes a walking delegate . . .
spreading the word that only 'peek and shuvil' is available." [25]

Whatever the reason, unskilled construction work was "the
great Italian beachhead" into the American economy. As urban
construction programs grew, Italian involvement grew apace.
When the Bronx aqueduct was built in 1904, 5,000 Italian workers were employed at the excavation, and in the same year they
played a large role in building Manhattan's Grand Central Ter-
minal. The comment made by the Maine Bureau of Labor—"It
would be difficult at the present time to build a railroad of any
considerable length without Italian labor"—applied to New York
with equal aptness. Indeed, many of the Italian laborers involved
in building Maine's railways were drawn from the Five Points
section of Manhattan. The padrone's lure probably sounded attractive, but the actual wages that they received were $1.25 a
day, "which is 25 cents less than wages paid to other nationalities." [26]

Other unskilled workers provided menial services. In 1894,
when Commissioner of Labor, Carrol D. Wright surveyed the
slum areas in New York, he found 474 foreign-born bootblacks,
of whom 472 were Italian. In 1900, 2,648 bootblacks were listed
for New York State; 2,561 were Italian.[27]

Thus the Italian occupational hierarchy remained basically blue-collar over the years 1880–1905. Important changes, nonetheless, did upgrade the manual categories, with more workers involved in skilled and semiskilled work than ever before. Ousting the Irish and other ethnics from the semiskilled and unskilled sectors and piercing the Jewish shell around the clothing industry, the Italians established their own influence. The overall picture indicates a greater span of active involvement in the economic mainstream by 1905. Immigrant restrictionists notwithstanding, the flood-tide of incoming southern Italians did not drag the occupational distribution downward below its 1880 position.[28]

Their toehold on the economy was, to be sure, at a low level, but as the foremost scholar of Italian immigration concluded: "While demonstrating less power in accomplishment than some of their hard-fibered predecessors they have been willing to fag in isolated places for many hours in the day." Their peasant background equipped them for this kind of hard work and solid, if somewhat stolid, accomplishment. It taught them to hitch their ambitions to the thinnest line of existence: a job and their daily bread, an ambition they clearly surpassed in New York.[29]

JEWISH OCCUPATIONAL DISTRIBUTION, 1880–1905

Between 1880 and 1905 the Jewish settlement on the Lower East Side with its various organizations, stores, and community politics took on the character of a small city. To those who reported its development, this community seemed to be fired by a hunger for material success and its accompanying security. Together with their urban European experience, this passion for economic prosperity produced a unique occupational development.

In 1880, 44 per cent among New York Jews held white-collar positions. Five per cent were in the high white-collar class as professionals and major entrepreneurs. The lower white-collar segment resembled their Italian counterparts in pursuing generally entrepreneurial occupations. And, as with the Italians, the size of this class is somewhat deceptive because of the large number of peddlers, just past the white-collar threshold.[30]

Having come to the United States with considerable entrepreneurial experience but little ready cash, peddling was a logical avenue of commerce for Russian Jews. Moreover, the successful example of the German Jews offered a riveting lesson:

> There was a man, a greenhorn—believe me he couldn't talk a word of English. [His brother-in-law got him a menial job.] He puts by a dollar or two. Then it comes a chance to rent a little store—a hole in the wall. So what does he sell in that store? Clothes? Shoes? Groceries? Maybe newspapers, cigarettes? not him. You wanta hear? A few fine combs. *Fine combs!* . . . Who could tell that from fine combs you can make a living. So you know what that man is today? A millionaire? Richer than Jacob Schiff!

True, or more probably not, many Jews believed that the Promised City's wonderful alchemy could indeed turn fine combs into gold. So they peddled, filling places like Ludlow and Hester Streets with carts, baskets, and the shouts of hawking.[31]

TABLE 4 OCCUPATIONAL DISTRIBUTION FOR RUSSIAN JEWISH HOUSEHOLD HEADS, BY NUMBER AND PER CENT, NEW YORK CITY, 1880 AND 1905

Class	1880		1905		
	Number	Per Cent	Number	Per Cent	Difference *
I High White Collar	27	5.2	145	15.1	+ 9.9
II Low White Collar	204	38.9	297	30.8	− 8.1
III Skilled	262	50.0	335	34.8	−15.2
IV Semiskilled	28	5.3	170	17.7	+12.4
V Unskilled	3	.6	16	1.7	+ 1.1
Total	524		963		

* Between 1880 and 1905, expressed as the difference between percentages.
Source: Sample data from Federal Census Schedules for New York and Kings Counties for 1880 and from New York State Census Schedules for New York and Kings Counties, 1905.

The unsightly wagons and baskets filled to overflowing with foods and other merchandise offended the sensibilities of some New Yorkers. Writing in the *New York Times,* one reporter described the community of peddlers who worked the streets of the Lower East Side: "This neighborhood peopled almost entirely by the people who claim to have been driven from Poland and Russia, is the eyesore of New York . . . the filthiest place in the Western continent." Peddling was repugnant and the people who practiced it even worse. But New York got used to these eastern Europeans with their stalls and assorted merchandise, and a few years later the *New York Tribune* reported more calmly that "the neighborhood . . . presents a quaint scene . . . black with purchasers and bright with the glare of . . . torches from the pushcarts." The major point, however, was the importance of this trade for the Jews. "Tailors or mechanics who are out of work hire a pushcart until they find a position. Recently landed immigrants are advised by their friends to take a pushcart until they can establish themselves in some business." The road may have been unlovely, but they kept their sights trained ahead.[32]

The rest of the lower white-collar class were mostly an assortment of shopkeepers. Grocers, bakers, and butchers attracted their customers with kosher and traditional foods, while the Jewish clothiers appealed to a wider clientele. Only 2 per cent of the entire sample were semiprofessionals or clerks.

Fifty-six percent of the Jewish working population did manual labor. Here, however, one finds a sharp distinction from the data for Italians. While 53 per cent of the Italian manual laborers were unskilled, only .6 per cent of the Jews fit this category. The bulk of the blue-collar workers occupied skilled positions. Glaziers, jewelers, shoemakers, and carpenters dotted the occupational landscape, but tailors dominated it. Of the large skilled class (50 per cent of all Jewish workers) three-quarters made the garments produced by New York's major industry, the clothing trades.

Jews brought needlework experience with them. In Russia clothing manufacture had employed one-third of the Jewish labor force. Thus, when these experienced Jews landed in the garment center of the world they easily slid into the needle trades. For "what kind of work could the Jew follow?" asked the authority on New York's clothing business:

> He was physically unfit for the heavier forms of manual labor, and his natural inclination toward business could not be gratified, owing to the fact that commerce requires capital. . . . The clothing industry was, previous to 1882, practically the only one in which Jews were engaged as employers of labor. It was but natural that the new arrivals should seek employment in it. . . . Furthermore, it did not interfere with their peculiar religious customs. . . .[33]

New York manufacturers sought out these raw immigrants. As one candidly admitted, "I want no experienced girls, they know the pay to get . . . but these greenhorns . . . cannot speak English and they don't know where to go and they just come from the old country and I let them work hard, like the devil, for less wages."[34]

The Jewish immigrants introduced the task system into the garment trades. Other innovations helped supplant the journeyman tailor and decentralize the production of garments. The Jew accomplished this by "his willingness to change the mode of production by using the sewing machine and division of labor against which the native tailor has shown a decided aversion. . . . [The] Jewish contractor was not merely a middle man; he was necessarily a tailor," who organized the labor and broke it down into less skillful tasks.[35]

This tailor often served as a subcontractor or "sweater" who distributed the goods to a flock of garment workers, invariably immigrants, under his wing. Squeezed by the industry's dogged competition, the "sweater" pushed wages down. The newly arrived Jews accepted the low wages. "His price," observed a less than admiring Jacob Riis, "is not what he can get, but the lowest he can live for, and underbid his neighbor." The bulk of this work was performed in the tenement where "there is no such thing as a dinner hour; men and women eat while they work, and the 'day' is lengthened at both ends far into the night." [36]

Simultaneously, as the Russian "sweater" drove out the German contractor, immigrant tailors and operators replaced the native garment workers. Many of these workers were women who were originally hired for their willingness to accept lower wages than men. Now the Jews edged them out, working for even less, and by 1900 they controlled New York's giant clothing industry. This provided them with investment and business opportunities as well as many skilled jobs for tailors and related craftsmen.

New Immigrant Jews in 1880 held a wider array of higher status jobs than the Italians. They had a larger white-collar class, but, more significantly, they invaded the $80 million clothing industry. Within the decade they controlled thousands of jobs in this industry. Sustained growth carried this industry forward to a point where in 1905 it was a $306 million business, employing one-quarter of all industrial workers in the city. The total industrial output of only three American cities exceeded the value of New York's clothing products in that year.[37]

Jesse Pope who studied the Jews of the clothing trade claimed that the Russian Jews came to the United States "unused to orderly industry, untrained in the crafts and violently attached to a religion and customs out of all adjustment to those of their new home . . . [and] were the most helpless and inefficient immigrants that have ever entered this country." If his analysis is correct then the clothing industry was their salvation, because it provided an outlet for their narrow abilities, allowing them to enter the economy at a higher level than other immigrants in 1880.[38]

Among the Jews the two lower blue-collar divisions, which accounted for 61 per cent of all Italian jobs in 1880, were insignificant. Together these two segments added up to 6 per cent. The semiskilled category included mostly garment workers, butchers, and barbers, while the unskilled grouping was less than 1 per cent.

After 1880 the Russian persecutions wound tighter, and over the next twenty-five years hundreds of thousands of Jews left for the United States. Most of them settled in New York. Beginning as an ethnic slice wedged between the Chinese, Irish, Bohemian, Italian, German, Negro, and Arab colonies, the Jewish *shtetl* in lower Manhattan grew to dominate the area.

A broad sample of New York's eastern European Jewish population in 1905 reflects the changes in occupational profile that attended this growth. The upper white-collar division showed a remarkable increase of 10 per cent (see Table 4), largely as a result of the number of major entrepreneurs. Although the professional segment did grow and included engineers, doctors, lawyers, and clergymen, four of every five household heads in the top stratum were businessmen. Clothing manufacture and real estate development were the most popular among these enterprises, and often both of these were related. Carefully taking advantage of available mortgage credit, even "sweaters" turned handsome profits on small investments as Jacob Riis reported:

> At the least calculation, probably, this sweater's family hoards up thirty dollars a month, and in a few years will own a tenement somewhere and profit by the example set by their landlord in rent collecting. It is the way the savings of Jewtown are universally invested, and with the natural talent of its people for commercial speculation the investment is enormously profitable.[39]

The expanded upper white-collar class was matched by an almost corresponding drop in the low white-collar fraction, primarily because of the same forces which adversely affected the Italian low white-collar grouping. Between 1880 and 1905, the incidence of peddling decreased by 75 per cent. Even newly arriving Jews apparently ignored street vending for other pursuits. This alone explains the 8 per cent decline in the low white-collar grouping. Otherwise, shopkeepers, in greater variety than before, maintained their proportion and, significantly, clerical positions increased in relative importance. Thus the number of insurance salesmen, real estate agents, and sales clerks grew, marking an important penetration of white-collar employment, despite the estimate of Heywood Broun and George Britt that as late as 1930, Jews were excluded from 90 per cent of the general office jobs available in the city.[40]

The blue-collar sector showed a clear downgrading from 1880. The proportion of skilled labor dwindled by 15 per cent while the number of semiskilled jobs picked up by 12 per cent, largely as a result of changes in the clothing industry which cut the percentage of Jewish tailors in half.

Italians, following the example set by the Jews, cut prices, accepted even lower wages and took jobs away from the Jews. Additionally, increased mechanization in the industry downgraded many tasks from skilled to semiskilled. The job that in 1880 required a skilled tailor was accomplished by a semiskilled machine operator in 1905. The statistics sum up the change: In 1880, only 3 per cent of the Jews did semiskilled garment work, one generation later 13 per cent held such jobs.

Other skilled crafts remained relatively unchanged, with housepainting, carpentry, cigarmaking, and shoemaking, in descending order of importance. Unskilled labor made a modest increase but nonetheless remained insignificant, with less than two of every 100 Jews in such jobs.

Over the twenty-five years from 1880 to 1905, as the number of Russian immigrants crested, the occupational spectrum for New York's Jewish community underwent some rearrangement. Peddling and tailoring, which sustained the early settlers, receded from their original centrality, and in this age of American enterprise Jews joined the mainstream in seeking success through business. And indeed among the first generation immigrants it was not medicine, law or even their vaunted thirst for education that carried them forward. It was business.[41]

One generation, spanning the presidencies of Rutherford B. Hayes and Theodore Roosevelt, marks the boundaries of this chapter's inquiry. In this period, when the United States welcomed more newcomers than ever before or after, the issue of immigration underwent deep and critical probing and emerged a far less respected ideal. Various groups intensified their efforts to close America's celebrated open doors, and Senator Henry Cabot Lodge fearfully advised that "the gates of the great Republic should no longer be left unguarded." One of the most popular arguments in the nativist arsenal accused the New Immigration of weakening the country by introducing millions of unlettered and unskilled foreigners who threatened to disturb the American economy's equilibrium. At the very least, a look at the occupation development of New York's Italians and Jews refutes this distorted thesis.[42]

Over these years the great metropolis, so far as can be measured by statistics, continued to progress undaunted by the New Immigrants. In 1880, over 16,000 industries in Manhattan and Brooklyn, representing $243 million in invested capital, manufactured $650 million worth of goods. At the forefront of industrial development, these two cities provided 275,000 workers with their livelihoods at an average salary of $434 a year. By 1900 the number of industries in the two boroughs had increased by one-fifth, to 20,000. Invested capital rose even more rapidly, tripling to $934 million. The working population increased by a factor of 1.6, and the average annual wage climbed by $99 to $533. The product of this economy was valued at $1.4 billion.[43]

Stephan Thernstrom has described a "level of minimum mobility." In effect, that mobility is often structural rather than personal. Thus, for example, the changeover in an economy from agriculture to industry in itself increases upper-level opportunities, creating a pulling effect, drawing lower-level workers into the newly opened upper ranks. In this sort of situation an upgrading of occupations will take place, but it is passive rather than active, attributable to the environment rather than the individuals or groups involved.[44]

This is an interesting caveat. Clearly New York's growing economy expanded the range of opportunities for all of its inhabitants. Thus in 1880, the city required 2,638 physicians, 3,008 lawyers, and 45,312 clerks, salesmen, and accountants. Twenty years later the number of white-collar positions increased significantly. The 1900 Census reported 6,577 physicians, 7,811 lawyers, and 113,177 clerks, salesmen, and accountants. Demand for white-collar professionals and workers clearly increased, and inevitably this opened more opportunities for New Yorkers who were sufficiently equipped to compete for these jobs. However, at the same time lower-level occupations increased as well. To take just one example the number of laborers shot up from 35,424 to 98,531 over the same two decades.[45]

If only upper levels had expanded and the need for unskilled labor had remained relatively constant or declined, immigrants would have been forced to equip themselves with the necessary skills and compete for skilled occupations and white-collar positions. In this case the structural argument could be made. But with the demand for labor expanding at *all levels,* unskilled immigrants were not forced to choose between acquiring new skills or no work. If they were willing to struggle and work hard, unskilled labor was available. In this situation ethnic predilections —previous experience, attitudes toward education, ambition for status and security—played far more important roles than the structural "pull effect" of the New York economy.

The lesser significance of structural as opposed to personal mobility is apparent from looking at the changes in occupation distribution for all New Yorkers. Between 1880 and 1900 the percentage of gainfully employed who were "laborers" dropped from 9.1 to 8.9 per cent; between 1880 and 1905, the percentage of Italians who were laborers dropped 11 points from 53 to 42 per cent. Obviously this change had less to do with the insignificant drop in demand for laborers than with intrinsic development within the Italian community.

In this respect New York resembled Boston, where Thernstrom found that although the white-collar class grew, the increase was

gradual. Only over long periods of time was this change meaningful. The changes in New York's occupational structure were
neither sufficiently rapid nor dramatic to account alone for the
kinds of progress exhibited by Italians and Jews between 1880
and 1905. And to the degree that the two groups differed in their
patterns of progress (since structural changes altered the host
environment for both immigrant communities) the separate patterns reflect ethnic distinctions.[46]

As a result of *their* European experience and their permanent
settlement Jews landed higher on the status ladder than Italians.
As Nathan Reich has written,

> Most of the Jewish immigrants had resided in towns and cities,
> and the bulk of them were artisans, petty merchants, semi-
> professionals, or young people without any special training, but
> easily adaptable to any number of urban, industrial or com-
> mercial occupations. It was quite natural for the Warsaw tailor
> to become the dressmaker of lower Broadway, or for the Pinsk
> peddler to blossom forth as the storekeeper of New York, or
> for the talmudic scholar of Vilna to make his debut before the
> American bar.[47]

In 1880 they formed a white-collar class that was 17 per cent
larger than the corresponding Italian stratum. By 1905 this difference had spread to 26 per cent.

Manual labor continued to provide more than half of all jobs
in both communities. As a consequence of the mechanization and
standardization of skilled tasks (as well as their own adaptation)
statistics for both Italians and Jews exhibited a rearrangement in
the blue-collar area. Italian workers in the skilled and semiskilled
strata, 20 per cent in 1880, shot up to 38 per cent a generation
later, while the unskilled sector dropped 11 per cent. Clearly the
Italian group which in 1880 had no choice but to accept unskilled jobs took advantage of increased opportunities for semiskilled work in 1905.

Jews did not have an unskilled category to speak of, and the
hefty increase in the semiskilled area in 1905 therefore did not

help lift people from the bottom, but rather drew upon those who in the earlier period might have taken skilled jobs. The effect was to bring both groups toward the middle of the blue-collar spectrum; a move up for the Italians, down for the Jews. This middling trend helped close the gap between the two groups of New Immigrants. A difference of 37 per cent at the skilled level favored the Jews in 1880. By 1905, it had been sharply cut to 13 per cent. Differences at the unskilled level, still enormous, dropped from 53 per cent to 42 per cent.[48]

Jews who had settled in 1880 found it easy to enter the clothing industry, and one very important consequence of their rapid, united move into the clothing industry was an early involvement in the labor movement. Jewish garment workers frequently united to express their shared needs. The earliest expression of these demands was a request for time off to conduct afternoon and evening religious services, and to be dismissed earlier on Friday afternoon.

Unlike the Italians who were originally fragmented in various trades, the Jews were concentrated, providing ground for a common consciousness. Early socialists and radicals like Abraham Cahan and Jacob Barondess were able to frame proletarian appeals in ethnic rhetoric and build a labor ideology among these workers. Although some Jews had joined the Knights of Labor, the tailors' National Progressive Union, or other variations, it was not until Morris Hillquit proposed an ethnic union that the Jewish labor movement really took shape in the United Hebrew Trades, founded in 1888. In 1897 the founding of the *Jewish Daily Forward* provided the labor movement with a press organ that was widely read among the immigrant Jews.

The Italians were only beginning to move into the needle trades and longshore work in large numbers, while the Jews continued to build their labor-union movement. Rudolf Glanz writes, "To the Jew unionizing was already a life work when the Italian only first began to look at the activities of the union." In its survey of immigrant union affiliation, the Dillingham Commission found Jews outnumbering Italians two to one. This earlier and larger union involvement among Jews often resulted in better pay and easier progress.[49]

From their initial jobs Jews aspired to become "sweaters" and then manufacturers and investors in real estate, producing a larger white-collar class by 1905. Speculation was something many of them learned in Europe, and it flourished in their New York neighborhoods. Abraham Cahan described it well:

> Small tradesmen of the slums, and even working men, were investing their savings in houses and lots. Jewish carpenters, housepainters, bricklayers or installment peddlers became builders of tenements or frame dwellings, real estate speculators. Deals were being closed and poor men were making thousands of dollars. . . .[50]

Italians, unable to transcend their lack of urban and industrial skills, at first took unskilled jobs—60 per cent fell *below* the skilled stratum in 1880. This pattern continued to hold Italians back (although the percentage did gradually decrease). They stuck to their peasant habits: "In all classes, the Italian of the first generation is somewhat slower than some other races to take on the habits and customs of the people he has come among." And transiency continued to erode whatever fund of experience had been built up. Moreover, transiency made the padrone indispensable. "Notwithstanding the abuses of the padrone, Italians cannot be induced to accept employment through other means." This apprenticeship at the bottom which kept Italians tied to the lower blue-collar levels and retarded their move into higher-status occupations was something the Jews were able to avoid.[51]

IV

The Immigrant Household and Its Occupations

The great [Italian] beachhead into the American middle class was initially established by strong backs and the laborer's shovel. Shovels to stuffed shirt Italians, are what watermelons are to stuffed shirt Negroes. . . . Yet one of the legends that most warms the heart is the story of the American Italian who presented his shovel, as a family heirloom, to his eldest son.

Mario Puzo
"The Italians, American
Style"

The economic well-being of the immigrant family was not built on the wages of one breadwinner alone. Household heads generally provided the major share of the family budget, but with seasonal employment a not uncommon scourge in the downtown communities, immigrant wives, offspring, and boarders made necessary contributions to the welfare and earnings of New Immigrant households. This chapter analyzes the role of these elements through the occupational lens.[1]

Married women in southern and eastern Europe had frequently helped their husbands on the farm or in family-owned businesses. But it was not common for women to leave the home for factory work. In New York, however, as in most of America's cities, farms were rare, and few immigrant husbands could open shops upon their arrival in America. Moreover, by the late nineteenth century, America's industrializing cities were rapidly moving ahead on the once controversial position of Alexander Hamilton's that "In general, women and children are rendered more useful by manufacturing establishments than they otherwise would be."[2] Children, single women, and even married women were being encouraged to participate in the developing factory-organized industrialization of America's cities—in fact, to relate their roles in society to this emerging industrialization. Immigrant wives were naturally ill-equipped for a system that was so bewilderingly different from what they had known and prepared themselves for in Europe.

At first, immigrant wives resisted the trend to factory labor. In 1880, only 7 per cent of the Italian households reported wives who held full-time jobs in addition to their other duties. This small sample of working women is too small to support solid conclusions about the sorts of occupations held by Italian women, but it does point to their scarcity, and to the degree that these figures can be taken as representative, they show an interesting resemblance to the occupational profile for Italian males. Thus, blue-collar jobs provided 90 per cent of this small group with work, close to half in unskilled occupations.

Actually, the number of Italian women who earned salaries is far larger than the 7-per-cent figure implies. "Italians," one recently settled *signora* told Mary Van Kleeck, "are different from American women, they don't like to work in factories and the men don't want them to do it. They must take the work home especially if they are married." Homework, which permitted these women to earn wages outside the factory system, occupied many Italian women who settled in New York after 1880. However, because the census failed to take data on such jobs no quantitative analysis is possible.[3]

It is, nonetheless, clear from contemporary accounts that this form of labor was very common in the immigrant neighborhoods. Aside from the fact that it satisfied the husband's demand that his wife stay home, it suited her busy schedule. She could work at home—after picking up the day's bundle at the shop—care for her apartment and family, and plan her work around her household chores.[4]

The clothing industry was one of the important sources for this homework. Despite the introduction of the task system and machinery, the "finishing" of garments continued to be done by hand. And this work was done primarily at home, by newly arrived Italian women. "Of the home finishers, in New York at least," wrote Robert Foerster, "the Italian women have been about seven in eight of all workers, earning $50–$125 a year." To an exploiting manufacturer they were, "as cheap as children and a little better." By 1902 Mabel Hurt Willet reported that Italian women monopolized the felling and finishing of garments, hand-sewing tasks that were amenable to homework.[5]

Italian wives also dominated the artificial flower industry.* This production of ornaments for the millinery trade required careful hand crafting and therefore resisted mechanization well into the twentieth century. The primitive status of the production process provided the basis for a flourishing homework system. A 1910 Russell Sage Foundation study found that more than half of the approximately 5,000 workers in this field did not report to a shop but earned their wages in their own apartments. Every spare moment was utilized to cut, paste, and fashion the millinery embellishments, and because necessity robbed such women of a bargaining position they earned abysmally low wages for their troubles.[6]

One such Italian family, typical of many, consisted of a grandmother living with a couple and their four children, aged 4, 3, 2, and one month. The mother and grandmother could not leave the house to work, and it was, of course, illegal for the young children to do so. Nonetheless, all except the father and the two youngest babies made artificial flowers. The three-year-old worked on petals,† her older sister, still too young for school, separated stems and dipped them into paste, while the two women placed

---

* "Formerly Americans and Germans worked at the trade," sulked one employer, "then the Italians and Jews came in and killed it . . . we cannot compete with them in cheapness of product." [Mary Van Kleeck, *Artificial Flower Makers* (New York, 1913), 30.]

† As late as 1910, when a 15-year-old required a special employment certificate to work in a shop, 10 per cent of those doing flower work alongside their mothers were under eight years old, and more than one-third were under 14. [Mary Van Kleeck, *Artificial Flower Makers*, 27, 100.]

the petals on the stems. One hour's work for the four workers produced a gross of flowers, and these 144 pieces earned them 10 cents. A twelve-hour day earned this team $1.20; a good week $7.00.[7]

Gradually, however, homework declined and the women entered the factories. In 1892 the New York State Board of Health passed reform legislation restricting tenement labor. One year later, 371 tenements were cleared and over 17,000 homeworkers were forced out.[8]

Theodore Dreiser portrayed the impact of the new legislation on an immigrant family:

> "So," says the inspector, stepping authoritatively forward, "finishing pants, eh? All three of you? Got a license?"
>
> "Vot?". . . . "What is it he wants?" says the father to child.
>
> "It is a paper," returns the daughter in Hungarian. . . .
>
> "Listen you," and he turns the little girl's face up to him, "you tell your father that he can't do any more of this work until he gets a license. . . ."
>
> ". . . Only one can work here. Two of you must go into the shop."
>
> ". . . No vork?" . . . "I do no more vork?"
>
> "No," insists the inspector, "not with three in one room."
>
> The Hungarian puts out his right leg, and it becomes apparent that an injury has befallen him. . . . Helping to sew is all that he can do.
>
> "Well," says the inspector when he hears of this, "that too bad. . . ."[9]

Between 1900 and 1915 the number of licensed homeworkers in Manhattan declined from 21,000 to 5,700, as mechanization and centralization contributed to the downtrend. Faced with the need to supplement the low wages garnered by their unskilled husbands and the constricting possibilities for jobs outside the factory, Italian women began to give up their prejudice against the shop. This was especially true of those who married in the United States. "Between the various races [and] . . . the Italians . . . there is a broad difference," a 1910 report on women wage-earners contended, "the girls marry earlier than among the other races, but on the other hand, many more remain at work in the shop than of the other races." [10]

The Dillingham Commission discovered that southern Italian women, more than all others, were likely to be gainfully employed. And in her study of *Italian Women in Industry*, Louise C. Odencrantz reported that Italians accounted for over 75 per cent of the women employed in the men's clothing industry in 1910, while they occupied more than 35 per cent of the jobs in the following industries: ladies' clothing, candy-making, paper-box manufacturing, laundry work and the tobacco trades.[11]

Between 1880 and 1905, Italian wives who sought work outside the home improved their opportunities to escape the unskilled category. By learning new skills and entering new trades they enhanced their qualifications. Skilled labor replaced rag picking and other marginal occupations as the largest job category. Women were especially drawn to the needle trades because sewing appealed to them as a clean and "feminine" type of work. A heavy advertising campaign by clothing manufacturers designed specifically for Italian-language papers helped burnish this appeal as employers sought to attract the low-paid Italian women to the factories.

Nonetheless, the attitude that women belonged in the home dominated both American and immigrant households. In 1905, under 6 per cent of all Italian families sampled in New York reported working wives. Most of the women who had to work still preferred homework when they could get it. As a 1908 survey of homeworkers showed, most of this type of work—as much as 98 per cent—continued to be done by Italians.[12]

The sample data suggest that it was even rarer for Jewish women to leave the home for work. Strong social attitudes reinforced the prophet's aphorism that "a princess's honor resides

indoors." Contemporary handbooks warned, in the words of the
National Federation of Settlements' study of *Young Working
Girls:*

> In many places girls work side by side with, or in the near
> vicinity of, men. They sometimes become careless in their con-
> duct, slack in manners and conversation, immodest in dress, and
> familiar to a degree that lays them open to danger. In many
> factories too, girls of low or even bad morals work. . . .[13]

These threats may have been losing their sting by the 1900s,
but *shtetl*-reared wives found them convincing. "Hebrew women,"
said a Bureau of Labor Statistics study, "almost invariably stop
work when they marry." Only 2 per cent of all Jewish wives took
jobs outside the home in 1880, and this number dropped to 1 per
cent in 1905. Even with this small group of working women, however, ethnic determinism played a part. The jobs these women
took did not resemble the occupational pattern of Italian women,
but rather that of Jewish men.[14]

Like their Italian sisters, however, Jewish women did do homework, and therefore this is but a partial depiction of their employment. The famous picture of an immigrant family sitting
around a clothing-laden kitchen table with mother and children
working, did indeed originate in the Jewish Tenth Ward. With
some asperity Jacob Riis called it Jewtown, and described it
thus:

> Take the Second Avenue Elevated Railroad at Chatham Square
> and ride up half a mile through the sweater district. Every
> open window . . . gives you a glimpse . . . [of] men and
> women bending over their machines, or ironing clothes at the
> window, half naked. Proprieties do not count on the East Side;
> nothing counts that cannot be converted into hard cash.[15]

Jewish homeworkers were widely used in the clothing industry
in its early period, especially in the "sweating" phase. But mechanization, tenement legislation, and competition from Italian
women sharply cut down on these jobs. When the work switched
from home to factory, Jewish women refused to take jobs in the

factories. Some joined their husbands in their neighborhood stores, but otherwise they allowed their economic function to recede.[16]

Thus, by 1908, despite the prevailing tendency "for the employees to be recruited from the same race as the foreman," the Bureau of Labor noted an exception in the clothing industry, where Jewish foremen hired Italian women. "No matter how great the poverty, the Hebrew men seldom allow the women of their family to do the [clothing] work at home, even though they may have been shopworkers before marriage." A canvass made in the same year assembled information on 488 home finishers in New York City. Not one of them was a Russian Jew.[17]

For married women in both Italian and Jewish communities the single most significant characteristic of shopworking wives was their scarcity. Be that as it may, immigrant wives did often work at home. For this we have the statements of various investigators, but unfortunately no census data. Apparently this practice of homework played an important role in the Jewish community before 1900, but declined sharply thereafter. For Italian women, however, it continued as an important source of needed income. At the same time some of the Italian women gave up their objections to factory jobs and left the home to punch clocks in the busy factories that ringed their neighborhoods.

IMMIGRANT OFFSPRING OCCUPATIONAL DISTRIBUTION, 1880–1905

Children of immigrant parents confronted American society with a training and an aspect that was patched together from two different worlds. Products of New World streets and schools, they were molded in an Old World pattern of upbringing. Different from their parents, they nonetheless were held at arm's length by native Americans as children of the uprooted. To New York's

economy they brought more attractive credentials than the first
generation; they spoke the language and handled American customs with greater ease and assuredness. But for all this they
could not escape their status as foreigners.[18]

The census sources impose certain limits on any attempt to
study the second generation. Only those immigrant sons and
daughters still living with their parents fall within the purview of
this survey. Consequently its conclusions are based on early
career patterns. Nonetheless, in view of the established correlation between career beginnings and subsequent development,
the findings are important. Moreover, they show the persistence
of an ethnic differential into the second generation.[19]

The occupational distribution for Italian offspring is given in
Table 5 below. Most of the Italian families in the 1880 sample
were recently settled, as the period of heavy Italian immigration
was just beginning. Perhaps this lack of American experience explains why none of the offspring held an upper white-collar position. It might also explain why the largest single category in the
lower white-collar class was composed of musicians, who brought
their skills with them from Italy. Burdened by their illiteracy,
the freshness of their arrival, and a degree of anti-Italian prejudice,* only 3 per cent of the total were employed as clerks and
sales workers. Peddling and retailing, which permitted them to
avoid the vagaries of an alien hiring process, were far more
popular, accounting for over one-third of all offspring in white
collars.[20]

Like their parents, the largest segment of these Italian-
Americans concentrated on manual labor. But, significantly, they
held more attractive blue-collar jobs than their fathers. Household heads were not afforded the opportunity of learning a skill.
As soon as they landed necessity forced them to plunge directly
into unskilled labor. The younger generation, however, acquired
new skills. Nineteen per cent of the offspring worked as confec-

---

* An interesting case of this prejudice surfaces in the census where an
enumerator in Brooklyn's Sixth Ward, tired of grappling with alien names
simply filled in "Dago" for a few Italian families.

tioners, cigarmakers, tailors, and at a variety of other skilled positions.

TABLE 5 OCCUPATIONAL DISTRIBUTION FOR ITALIAN AND RUSSIAN JEWISH OFFSPRING, BY PER CENT, NEW YORK CITY, 1880 AND 1905

| | Italian | | Jewish | |
	1880	1905	1880	1905
I	0	.9	.6	4.8
II	15.4	11.8	22.0	32.9
III	18.6	36.2	49.4	30.4
IV	17.6	27.3	27.0	30.4
V	48.4	23.9	.9	1.5
Total	188	586	318	724
Total Households Sampled	456	1,029	536	1,008

Source: Sample Data from Federal Census of 1880 and New York State Census of 1905.

Among the 18 per cent in semiskilled jobs, industrial labor predominated, especially in the artificial flower business, which attracted many of the girls. As young Julia explained, "Everybody else I know worked in it. It is the Italian's trade, and then I thought that when I get married I can still keep up at home." Among the males, barbering proved popular, rapidly becoming an acknowledged Italian art.[21]

Notwithstanding the large skilled and semiskilled strata, over 48 per cent of the group had to settle for positions at the very bottom of the ladder. Assorted jobs as rag pickers, common laborers, and shoe shiners placed close to half the Italian offspring at the fringe of New York's economy, no more tellingly involved in its ample growth and rewards than most of their parents. The peasant shovel was passed on from one generation to the next; no longer working the soft earth of Italy's farms it was now used to excavate sewers and aqueducts. Like it or not Italian youth wore the heavy yoke of their parents' past.

Twenty-five years later New York's bulging Italian community was more diversified. It included American-born and educated offspring with the children of recent newcomers, and the occupa-

tional spectrum for these sons and daughters, summarized in
Table 5, reflects a noticeable change from 1880.

Over this generation the upper white-collar class increased to
slightly below one per cent. No major businessman appeared in
the sample, in part because of the survey's bias toward youth,
but there were a few professionals, including a physician, two
pharmacists, an engineer, and a teacher. This element was quite
small in the overall group, but represented double the proportion
of professionals found among Italian household heads in the same
year.

Professional careers did not seem to appeal to most Italians. A
1904 study of New York Italians by *Charities* magazine counted
115 physicians, 63 pharmacists, 4 dentists, 21 lawyers, 15 public
school teachers, and a sprinkling of various other professionals in
a population that in 1900 exceeded 219,000. Peasant life in the
mezzogiorno had trained Italians to trim their aspirations to the
prevailing winds. They did not think in terms of careers or professional life. Work was something one did in order to earn
money. Life was not so much fulfilled by work as it was filled
with its drudgery. This attitude was often passed on to children,
even in New York's freer atmosphere.[22]

The same year as the *Charities* survey Lillian Brandt canvassed 143 Italian children aged 9 to 14 from the four Italian
schools run by the Children's Aid Society. Each child wrote a
letter outlining his vocational goals. Giulio's letter with its ambition for progress, but at the same time hemmed in by blue-collar
borders, was typical:

> Dear and most gracious Signora A. . . . ,
> My father has been two years in America, and he follows the
> trade of carpenter, and . . . he would like to make of me an
> honest industrious boy, with, at the same time, a trade better
> than his, and he sends me to school so that when I am grown
> I may be an educated man and useful to others.
>
> Later I wish to make machines for factories, and thus have
> better wages than others.[23]

Of all the children questioned, four indicated a desire to become physicians, two proposed law for their future vocation, and thirteen girls looked forward to teaching (pointedly, sewing was the subject most often cited). For the rest of the children, as apparently for most Italians, professional status gave off no special luster, which explains the low number of Italian professionals.

The lower white-collar class in 1905 was somewhat slimmer than in 1880. No longer, however, did peddlers and musicians dominate. The twin curtains of foreignness and discrimination which kept Italians out of clerical and sales positions in 1880 had parted somewhat. Young men and women worked in offices as clerks, typists, bookkeepers, and office helpers, and others took sales positions in New York's growing retail industry. Italian offspring differed markedly in this respect from their parents; only 1 per cent of all household heads did sales or clerical work compared with 8 per cent of their offspring. The remaining white-collar offspring were shopkeepers, and a few semiprofessionals.

Changes within the white-collar class notwithstanding, blue-collar occupations continued to provide most of the jobs. Indeed, the proportion of manual laborers grew somewhat. However, because this expansion of the blue-collar class was accompanied by its upgrading, due to enlarged skilled and semiskilled strata, the status of Italian offspring was actually enhanced.[24]

Needle trades accounted for a large share of this increase by providing opportunities for skilled Italians. The building trades, cigar-making, and candy-making played significant secondary roles in boosting the skilled sector from 19 to 36 per cent. As these industries mechanized they also produced a large number of semiskilled level opportunities and this category shot up by 10 per cent over the years. Male offspring also turned to barbering, driving drays, dock work, and menial service occupations. Indeed the variety of Italian occupations at the skilled and semi-skilled levels demonstrates a breadth of involvement in Gotham's progress that had not been evident in 1880.

This movement away from peripheral occupations was something that even the Dillingham Commission could not avoid no-
ticing. Concerned with the issue of assimilation and the question
of whether second-generation New Immigrants were showing
any progress away from the occupational mold of their elders,
the Commission launched a study of immigrant occupations.
Their study, based on the raw census data collected for 1900, was
not restricted to immigrant offspring living with their parents (as
is the 1905 sample presented in Table 5). Their findings for New
York State indicate important generational differences.

Unlike the clothing industry, which was important to both generations and provided many with occupational opportunities, in
other areas the Commission found clear generational variations.
In clerking or professional positions the younger generation
was clearly more involved, while the senior Italians showed more
merchants and peddlers. The major difference, however, appeared in the laborer category. Thirty-two per cent of the immigrant generation were laborers, while the figure for their offspring was 8 per cent. In broad swathe this kind of generational
variation is confirmed by the data for New York City in 1905.[25]

The Immigration Commission divided the generations by place
of birth—foreign-born immigrants, regardless of the age at
which they entered the country, were pegged "first generation,"
while American-born offspring came under a "second generation"
heading—implying that nativity had occupational significance.
The Commission did not, however, test this notion that American-
born Italians differed significantly from their Italian-born brothers
and sisters.

A breakdown of the 1905 sample by place of birth in Table 6
shows to the contrary that nativity proved to be of relatively
little occupational consequence. The Italian upbringing and background framed vocational aspirations and skills for the offspring,
regardless of nativity. The ethnic pattern proved the dominant
force. Place of birth had such slight effect that none of the status
levels varied by more than 5.3 percentage points between those

Italian offspring born in Italy and those born in the United States.

In a period when strictly defined sex roles led to powerful occupational predispositions, gender proved to be a variable of wider consequence than nativity, as Table 6 demonstrates. Moreover, with the enhancement of Italian occupational status by 1905, differences in job patterns between the sexes grew even more marked.

In 1880, the recentness of their arrival hampering occupational progress, sons and daughters had little choice but to accept unskilled blue-collar jobs. Differences between the two, because of this heavy concentration in the unskilled sector, proved slight. Those differences that did exist showed a greater inclination

TABLE 6 OCCUPATIONAL DISTRIBUTION BY
NATIVITY FOR ITALIAN OFFSPRING,
BY PER CENT, NEW YORK CITY, 1905

	American-born	Italian-born
I	0	1.2
II	15.6	10.3
III	34.1	37.0
IV	28.1	27.0
V	22.2	24.6
Total	167	419

OCCUPATIONAL DISTRIBUTION FOR ITALIAN OFFSPRING
BY SEX, BY PER CENT, NEW YORK CITY, 1880 AND 1905

	1880		1905	
	Sons	Dtrs.	Sons	Dtrs.
I	0	0	1.3	0
II	17.3	12.8	13.4	8.8
III	17.3	20.5	31.4	45.1
IV	14.5	21.8	22.8	35.8
V	50.9	44.9	31.2	10.3
Total	110	78	382	204

Source: Sample Data from Federal Census of 1880 and New York State Census of 1905.

among males toward the poles—more white-collar and more unskilled—while females flocked more readily to middling occupations.

A generation later the tendency for males and females to con-
centrate on different occupational categories intensified, as more
and more offspring freed themselves from unskilled labor. Italian
sons with 15 per cent in white collars outnumbered daughters at
the higher-level occupations. They also had a much larger fraction at the lowest rung, with 31 per cent in unskilled positions.
Females crowded into skilled and semiskilled jobs. Eighty per
cent were in one of these two blue-collar divisions, 25 per cent
more than the male proportion in such occupations.

In large part these differences resulted from the distinct roles
assigned to sons and daughters by the Italian family. Pressure was
applied to both sons and daughters to cut schooling short. But in
those families that did have white-collar ambitions for their children, girls were expected to sacrifice their prospects in favor of
their brothers. Mary Van Kleeck, secretary of the Committee on
Women's Work explained: "It is by no means unusual to find
girls . . . leaving school to go to work in order to give their
brothers a chance to have a better education. One Italian girl,
now earning $10 a week in busy season as a rose maker, left
school . . . six years ago, at the age of thirteen. . . ." She
worked sometimes until four and five in the morning to help
send an older brother to medical school, while another continued
his high-school education toward the same goal.[26]

For girls especially, school was considered superfluous. They
were expected to stay home and learn from their mothers. "The
Italian girl," wrote Lillian Brandt, "more than the average girl
expects to be occupied, and at an earlier age than the average
girl. . . ." "Why," went the typical question, "should she go to
high school when she's goin' to be married anyway?" Other girls
did not even get that far. One Italian mother explained to an
investigator that she didn't relish the prospect of her daughter's

education, "Why should she learn to write, she'd only write to her fellas." Yet another mother insisted on withdrawing her daughter from school just as she entered the graduating class. "That," said the unhappy daughter, "is how Italians are." [27]

These girls, however, did learn how to sew, make artificial flowers, and a variety of other skills that Italian mothers passed on. In 1880 this made little practical difference because the clothing trades and other industries were not yet open to Italians and the girls had to join the rest of the family in unskilled jobs. But when higher-level occupations did open up to Italians in the 1890's the young women qualified for skilled and semiskilled jobs. In 1905 fewer than 11 per cent occupied the bottom rung. [28]

Generally Italian sons also left school early. But they were less rigorously controlled than daughters. With more room to assert independence some continued their schooling in defiance of parental pressures. And in such cases where parents did value education the son came first. Hence they qualified for white-collar jobs as clerks, sales personnel and office workers in larger numbers than their sisters. Moreover, since the son was expected to follow his father's model, he became the partner if there was a family business or was aided in acquiring his own shop. This helps explain the white-collar differential. [29]

In the blue-collar area most skilled jobs for Italians were in the various garment industries, but sons did not have much training in needle skills, and most of these jobs went to the women. If males did secure skilled positions it was as shoemakers, masons, painters, stonecutters, machinists, and other "male" crafts that they learned from their fathers. Lacking their sisters' skills they filled fewer semiskilled occupations. Consequently 21 per cent more of the sons did common labor.

Had Italian household heads been very successful, this pattern of generational succession would have passed on stores and factories to the male offspring, and sons would have fared far better than their sisters in terms of occupational status. As it was, large numbers of Italian fathers still held unskilled jobs in 1905, and their sons reflected this by their own heavy concentrations in that sector.

Like their Italian counterparts, Jewish offspring in 1880 were primarily in blue-collar jobs. As Table 5 (page 79) illustrates, at this early point in east European settlement very few individuals qualified for upper white-collar positions. Lower white-collar opportunities were apparently more accessible and 22 per cent of the total occupied such jobs. In this same year Jewish household heads represented a considerably larger white-collar class (see Table 4). Generational variations went beyond these numbers. The older generation achieved white-collar status by shopkeeping and peddling. Enterprise was their only entree. Their offspring, however, had more diverse possibilities and filtered into sales positions. A few were even hired as secretaries and bookkeepers, although such jobs were rare. As with the Italians, immigrant status still hung heavily on their tongues and in their manners.[30]

Three of every four Jewish offspring did manual labor. Within this broad classification they occupied higher status levels than their Italian counterparts. While 48 per cent of the Italians did unskilled work, 49 per cent of the Jews (almost exactly the same percentage as their parents) could boast of skilled occupations. And almost none of them worked as unskilled laborers.

Tailoring, of course, held the key to their good fortune, providing 83 per cent of their skilled jobs. Their sympathetic network of relatives, friends, and co-religionists helped train and then place them. Although the younger generation seldom expected to stay in these jobs—"The statement has been repeated until it is trite," noted Jesse Pope, "that the Jew considers the [clothing] industry as a stepping stone to something higher,"—they were fortunate in beginning careers upon such a high "stepping stone," higher than most recent immigrants could expect.[31]

Cigar-making, originally controlled by Bohemians and Germans, also attracted large numbers of these "green" immigrants. When they found apprenticeship in the highly skilled union shops closed to them, they turned to the "scab shops" run by fellow Jews. These shops cut prices to compete and therefore paid lower wages, but they introduced the immigrant and his working children to a new trade. After a few years the now skilled craftsmen found it easier to move into the higher paying union shops.[32]

The industries that in 1880 hired the second generation— clothing, cigar-making, and, to a lesser extent, carpentry and jewelry—were industries where the first generation had exerted a measure of control. None of these represented second-generation conquests. Lacking previous white-collar experience and unable as yet to exploit New World educational opportunities, the Jewish offspring traced an unexciting pattern of succession behind their parents. The distribution of their occupations is what one might expect from recent immigrants with little money and low literacy, but sufficient urban experience and connections to escape the unskilled mud-sill of the urban economy.

Between 1880 and 1905, as Jewish household heads expanded their white-collar class, their offspring exhibited similar improvement. Upper white-collar positions, a mere .6 per cent of the second generation in 1880, multiplied to 5 per cent in 1905. But while fathers cast their success in entrepreneurial forms (businessmen accounted for three in four of the upper white-collar stratum), the younger generation moved into the professions. More than half of the highest class among the offspring were professionals, including doctors, dentists, engineers, pharmacists, attorneys, and teachers.[33]

Commerce had served the Jewish outsider well in Europe, but he reserved his greatest esteem for the professions. Talcott Par-

sons, Thorstein Veblen, Will Herberg, Lloyd Warner, and Louis
Wirth have all written of "the . . . propensity of Jews to enter
the learned professions," and "the fascination which professional
careers have had for the Jews." People with a healthy respect for
education, the Russian Jews thirsted for professional status. Abraham Cahan recalled a conversation with one of these immigrants:
"I was once consulted by an *illiterate Jewish peddler of thirty-
two* who was at a loss to choose between medical college and a
dry goods store. 'I have saved two thousand dollars, . . . some
friends advise me to go into the dry goods business, but I wish
to be an educated man and live like one.' " [34]

Medicine, especially, awed the Russian Jew:

> In the shtetl, the doctor was a remote presence, almost a myth,
> he rode in a carriage. His household shopping was done by
> domestics. His wife travelled abroad for her clothes and her
> cures. He was consulted by the Christian nobility, the Jewish
> rich, as well as the Hasidic wonder rebbes. . . .[35]

Moreover, the professions helped insecure Jewish offspring cir-
cumvent discriminatory hiring practices. "The Jew," Nathan
Glazer has written, "prefers a situation where his own merit receives objective confirmation and he is not dependent on the
good will or personal reaction of a person who may happen not
to like Jews." They also betrayed "a certain contempt for manual
labor . . . ," according to Isaac Rubinow, "a sad but inevitable
result of an enforced commercial life," in Europe. This attitude
which lavished respect on the man who kept his hands clean
helped make the Jewish factory worker a " 'man of one generation, neither the son nor the father of workers'; his father had
been a petty merchant or artisan, his son was to become a businessman or professional." [36]

The low white-collar division also expanded over the twenty-
five years after 1880. This growth from 22 to 33 per cent was
rendered even more meaningful by important shifts within the
low white-collar range. Law and drug clerks, absent from the
1880 profile, outnumbered peddlers in 1905. Such positions as

professional clerk and skilled office worker grew from 1 per cent in the earlier sample to 10 per cent a generation later, despite the exclusionary policies toward Jews of such companies as Western Union, New York Telephone, and most banks. Moreover, sales and stock clerking became the most popular of all low white-collar occupations, in part reflecting the prominent role Jews were now playing in New York retailing.[37]

Another area of significant growth, remarkable in view of the sample's youth, was in business. As peddling declined from 10 to 1 per cent, more substantial enterprise grew from 2 to 7 per cent. For those who found the professional route closed—and quotas in professional schools helped put up road-blocks—or unappealing, business fulfilled many of the same needs for independence. As Nathan Glazer has noted somewhat cynically:

> In Abraham Cahan's *The Rise of David Levinsky,* we read how the young immigrant going into business could, despite his accent, produce clothing as good as that produced by longer established Americans, and more cheaply. Only a rare businessman would not buy Levinsky's goods because of his accent. But if David Levinsky had been trying to rise to the vice-presidency of a huge corporation, he would certainly have found the going harder.[38]

While the white-collar class grew to 38 per cent, blue-collar work continued as the principal source of employment. And in this sector Jewish offspring, like their parents, reflected the downgrading of manual labor by mechanization. The number of semiskilled workers precisely matched the skilled class. Together they accounted for 61 per cent of the total. The unskilled sector remained insignificant over the years.

For the Italian offspring no differences of note emerged between the American-born and those born overseas. This was not the case for the Jewish offspring, as Table 7 below indicates. Those born in the United States, benefiting from an American education, clearly put this advantage to effective use. Well over half the American-born pursued white-collar careers, landing office and sales positions much more easily than their foreign-born brethren.

Gender, a significant variable among the Italians, proved equally important among the east Europeans. Table 7 persuasively demonstrates how closely sons resembled the household heads, while daughters followed a different pattern. In 1880 the white-collar figures for fathers, sons, and daughters were 44, 39, and 4 per cent. A generation later the similarity between fathers and sons was even closer, with the three white-collar sums reading 46, 45, and 27 per cent respectively.

TABLE 7 OCCUPATIONAL DISTRIBUTION BY
NATIVITY FOR RUSSIAN JEWISH OFFSPRING,
BY PER CENT, NEW YORK CITY, 1905

	American Born	Foreign Born
I	4.5	4.9
II	52.6	28.4
III	17.3	33.3
IV	22.6	32.1
V	3.0	1.2
Total	133	591

OCCUPATIONAL DISTRIBUTION FOR RUSSIAN JEWISH OFFSPRING BY SEX
AND COMPARED WITH HOUSEHOLD HEADS, BY PER CENT,
NEW YORK CITY, 1880 AND 1905

		1880			1905	
	Head	Sons	Dtrs.	Head	Sons	Dtrs.
I	5.2	1.1	0	15.1	6.3	2.7
II	38.9	37.4	3.5	30.1	39.1	23.8
III	50.0	42.5	57.6	34.8	33.0	26.5
IV	5.3	18.4	37.5	17.7	19.8	45.9
V	.6	.6	1.4	1.7	1.9	1.0
Total	524	174	144	963	430	294

Source: Sample Data from Federal Census of 1880 and New York State Census of 1905.

Compared with their brothers, few Jewish girls were trained to develop careers. The Jewish family, like the Italian, expected girls to devote their future to a husband and a family. Mary Van Kleeck, who reported that Italian girls were expected to sacrifice their opportunities in favor of their brothers, discovered similar circumstances among the Jews:

> The oldest daughter in a Russian family left normal school [teacher training school] after the second year in order that her elder brother might attend college. Her father was a tailor. Two younger children were in school. She explained that she wanted to go back to normal college, but for her brother a college education was "a matter of a life position," while for her it was not.[39]

Nonetheless by 1905 the white-collar element among the young women had increased from 1880 by a factor of 7.6, as they moved into typing, bookkeeping, and, on a higher level, into teaching.

Although these women held lower-level jobs than their brothers, when they are compared with Italian daughters different contrasts emerge (see Table 8). In 1880 Italians had a larger white-collar class, but blue-collar differences favored the Jews overwhelmingly. By 1905 many Jewish women (when not called upon to sacrifice in favor of their brothers) exploited New York's educational opportunities to acquire white-collar positions. Woods and Kennedy's contemporary study of *Young Working Girls* explained that they were unique because "they seem to understand the increased power which preparation gives. As one result Hebrew girls are everywhere crowding the high and commercial schools, and taking their place beside the children of families with a start of one or more generations." [40]

In the blue-collar fields Italian women successfully turned the tables on their Jewish sisters. In 1880, 58 per cent of the latter group did skilled work. This contrasted with 21 per cent for the Italians. But in 1905 the figures for the two groups read 27 and 45, with Italian women representing the larger figure. As the above figures indicate, Jewish daughters either could not or simply would not match Italians in skilled blue-collar labor. Italian girls had better training and greater regard for handiwork and they were far more tractable as employees.

TABLE 8 OCCUPATIONAL DISTRIBUTION FOR
ITALIAN AND RUSSIAN JEWISH OFFSPRING COMPARED
BY SEX, BY PER CENT, NEW YORK CITY, 1880 AND 1905

	Daughters			
	1880		1905	
	Italian	Jewish	Italian	Jewish
I	0.0	0.0	0.0	2.7
II	12.8	3.5	8.8	23.8
III	20.5	57.6	45.1	26.5
IV	21.8	37.5	35.7	45.9
V	44.9	1.4	10.3	1.0
Total	88	144	204	294

	Sons			
	1880		1905	
	Italian	Jewish	Italian	Jewish
I	0	1.1	1.3	6.3
II	17.2	37.4	13.4	39.1
III	17.2	42.5	31.4	33.0
IV	14.5	18.4	22.8	19.8
V	50.9	.6	31.2	1.9
Total	110	174	382	430

Source: Sample Data from Federal Census of 1880
and New York State Census for 1905.

When the Italian girl exhibits an interest in her trade it is an
interest in craftsmanship or in her own wages rather than in
general trade conditions. The Jewish girl, on the contrary, often
displays an eager zest for discussion of labor problems . . .
[she] will probably plunge at once into a discussion of her
trade its advantages and disadvantages, wages, hours of work,
and instances of shabby treatment in the shops, or of unsanitary conditions in the workrooms.[41]

When their paths crossed the results were not always happy.
Some of the Jewish women, often seeking issues of wider impor-

tance, had little regard for their fellow New Immigrants. "If they were more civilized," said one Jewish girl about her Italian co-workers "they wouldn't take such low pay. But they go without hats and gloves and umbrellas." [42]

Italian and Jewish males also differed from each other, especially at the two extremes of the occupational scale. Jewish sons consistently outpointed Italians in the white-collar category, increasing the differential from 20 to 26 per cent over a generation. Remarkable progress for Italian offspring closed the gap in skilled jobs from 25 per cent in 1880 to 2 per cent in 1905, and the semi-skilled stratum did not, at either point, show great variance. The upgrading of Italian achievements also cut a 50 point difference in the unskilled area to 29 per cent. Nonetheless, unskilled labor continued as the benchmark characteristic of the Italian occupational spectrum; Jewish unskilled, 2 per cent, Italians, 31 per cent.

What accounted for the different patterns? Certainly the fact that their parents differed in their cultural values was significant. And although another investigator of immigrant mobility "turn[s] to group values as [an] . . . explanation of differences in occupational achievement . . . [with] reluctance, because explanations of this type tend to be tautological and difficult to verify independently," this explanation does seem to be the most sensible. Such specific explanations as differential fertility do not help here, because it was the Jews who had the larger families.* Moreover, the important differences between the two groups appear

---

* Of the 16,191 individuals sampled, Italians averaged 2.62 offspring per family and Jews 3.21. Admittedly this data is unavoidably fragmentary. Many families had offspring in Europe and therefore seem smaller than they really were. Between 1880 and 1905 the average number of offspring in both Italian and Jewish families went up, not necessarily as a result of increased fertility but rather as an indication of the influx of sons and daughters of families already here. Thus the average number of offspring in Italian families sampled climbed from 1.90 in 1880, to 2.20 in 1892 and 2.97 in 1905. The average number of offspring for each Jewish family in these years was 3.12; 3.12; 3.30, respectively. In any event this data cannot be summoned in favor of the thesis which argues that larger family size correlates with lower economic status for both fathers and children.

from common-sense observations to be of sufficient significance to explain the occupational variation.[43]

Three touchstones help guide the discussion of cultural difference: attitudes toward family and community, attitudes toward economic goals and ambitions, and attitudes toward education.

In Italy very tight relationships within *la famiglia* undercut the development of broader ethnic relationships. "Outside of the family," writes Leonard Covello in his astute study of Italian life, "reigned indifference and often, even hostility . . . , *la famiglia* was the only social concept, and . . . any other term such as *paese* . . . or *villagio* . . . , had no other than a purely spatial connotation. It would be hard to find in southern Italy a synonym for the English word 'community,' [or] the Russian 'mir'. . . ." [44]

Nor, of course, would there be a synonym for *kehillah*. The *shtetl-kehillah* was a closely interrelated society. The authoritative study by Zborowski and Herzog explains:

> The structure and process can best be described by borrowing from physics the concept of a "field of forces." The relationships between the parts—their contrast, interdependence, and interaction—create a field of reciprocally functioning forces resulting in a dynamic equilibrium. . . . [The shtetl had a] closely knit community, where each is responsible for all and all are responsible for each, privacy is neither known nor desired.[45]

Where the *shtetl* outlook was that "life is with people," the prevailing attitude in the *paese* was one of "amoral familism." The consequences of these differences produced a Jewish community in New York that was more tightly knit, with strongly perceived ethnic obligations. Jews hired Jews, gave charity to Jews, and yes, often exploited Jews. But most important for the issue at hand, as Jews moved into business their co-religionists were pulled along into jobs.[46]

The two New Immigrant communities also differed in their aspirations, especially with regard to their offspring. The *shtetl* Jew often measured his own success by the achievements of his children. Tremendous pressures were placed on the children to fulfill the ambitions of their parents. "Because parenthood is so important, *nakhes fun kinder* [pleasure from children] is the epitome of joy. . . . through the child's success the parent is validated. . . ." These pressures, generally expressed as economic goals in New York, produced great tension between the generations, but as Nathan Hurvitz has argued these tensions themselves often had positive economic effects.[47]

There was little such pressure in the *paese*, where few harbored aspirations for themselves or for their children. The role of children in the farm communities was far more prosaic. They were viewed primarily "as an economic asset . . . poor married couple[s] relied heavily on children as a source of free manual help." Poor fathers with large families were envied for their ability to lie back and permit the children to work, and a common saying had it that "a father with many children is like a king with many vassals." Great pressure was brought upon the children to give up their childhood early to do something productive.[48]

Settlement in America had little effect upon these values. As Herbert Gans has written, "It would seem that not only are Italians much the same everywhere, but that there is a clearly identifiable Italian social structure that has changed remarkably little . . . from Italy to America." As it was in Italy so it would be in the New World. Children were expected to hold jobs and contribute to family income. They entered the job market before they could train for high-status careers. Consequently Italian offspring generally settled into manual labor.[49]

Probably one of the most significant distinctions between the two groups involved their attitude toward education. The Italian parent had little regard for schooling. "As the child approaches maturity . . . the parental demands upon the allegiance of the child in his economic role are made in no unmistakable terms. . . . The progress of schooling receives, at best, only secondary consideration." These parents feared the school as a competitor for control over their children. "The schools [make] of our children persons of leisure—little gentlemen. They [lose] the dignity of good children to think first of the parents, to help them. . . ." They resented the school as an inculcator of foreign values and for interfering in the economic exploitation of their children. This antischool persuasion became, in the words of the astute Italo-American educator Leonard Covello, "a cultural tradition." Upon reaching 14, when school attendance ceased being compulsory, and often even before, Italian children were withdrawn from class and sent to work. Others were pressed into work while still at school, captives of poor households and strong family control.[50]

The vaunted equalizer did not serve all equally, as Colin Greer complains in *The Great School Legend*. According to some estimates, 10 per cent of the Italian children in New York avoided school entirely. Other Italian children of peasant backgrounds did not stay in school long. After they left school these youngsters were forced to rely on their parents for training. This process assured that progress would be built slowly only after years of experience and exposure to urban industrial opportunities.[51]

Some Italian children, of course, did go on to high school, college and even beyond, but usually this was done without parental blessings. Because adult values did not reinforce school authority but rather competed with it, many Italian children who were considered quite bright in the classroom followed their own inclinations and dropped out of school. The future for such a child was not hard to predict. In the words of the Industrial Commission, he was "likely to become a laborer like his father."[52]

Jews accorded the academic ideal greater respect. Two studies of New York school children point up the direct effects of this ethnic difference. In 1908 a survey of fifteen Manhattan schools showed a disappointingly high number of immigrant offspring who were left back one or more grades. German students had the lowest rate of retardation at 16 per cent. Among the New Immigrants, 23 per cent of the Russian children were at least one grade behind; for Italians the figure was even higher at 36 per cent. Three years later another study, this one interested in determining the percentage of students who entered high school and continued on to graduate, again found a significant ethnic difference. Zero per cent of the Italians who were sampled graduated. Among all immigrants Russian children recorded the highest figure, as 16 per cent pursued their education to a diploma.[53]

Jewish immigrants placed great emphasis on education. Not only was it intrinsically valuable, but it was also a key to economic and social success. Jacob Riis understood well the attitude of the downtown Jews. "The poorest Hebrew knows—the poorer he is the better he knows it—that knowledge is power, and power is the means for getting on in this world that has spurned him so long, is what his soul yearns for. He lets no opportunity slip to obtain it." [54]

This devotion to school as a device for mobility impressed all who wrote on the topic. Thus the Industrial Commission wrote admiringly, "The poorest among them will make all possible sacrifices to keep his children in school; and one of the most striking phenomena in New York City today is the way in which Jews have taken possession of the public schools, in the highest as well as lowest grades." [55]

The following letter to the Yiddish language *Daily Forward's* popular "Bintel Brief" column is typical of this attitude.

> I am a widow . . . [with] five children. . . . I have a store and barely get along. . . . I am obliged to employ a salesman . . . if I were to withdraw my [15 year old] son from high school I could dispense with the salesman, but my motherly love and duty . . . do not permit me. . . . So what shall I do when the struggle for existance is so acute? I must have his assistance to keep my business going and take care of the other children; but at the same time I cannot definitely decide to take him out of school; for he has inclinations to study and goes to school dancing. I lay great hopes on my child.[56]

Such hopes were fashioned by a nonpeasant experience in Europe and by a cultural ideal that respected academic learning.

This helped equip Jewish children with the emotional and intellectual support that permitted them to benefit from New York's schools and colleges. Moreover, Jewish heads of household, as we have seen, settled more permanently and held more skilled jobs than did their Italian counterparts. Armed with stability and the greater economic security which flowed from the "better" jobs they held, Jews could afford to keep their children in school longer, something they wanted to do anyway.

For many Jewish children education did not stop at the compulsory age of 14, nor even with high school. In an age when college was often considered the fenced-off preserve of the privileged well-to-do, New York's City College offered the sons of working-class Jews the opportunity for higher education. "The City College," a government report on New York's immigrants observed, "is practically filled with Jewish pupils, a considerable proportion of them children of Russian or Polish immigrants on the East Side." *The New York Evening Post* reported in 1905 that "the thirst for knowledge . . . fills our city colleges and Columbia's halls with the sons of Hebrews who came over in steerage. . . ." In 1910 a survey of New York's slums found more Jews above age sixteen still in school than any other ethnic group. By 1916 Jewish enrollment in New York City's colleges had soared. At Adelphi College they made up 8 per cent of the student body; at Columbia, 13 per cent; at Fordham, 21 per cent; at Brooklyn Polytechnic, 30 per cent; at Hunter, 44 per cent; and at City College they constituted a whopping 73 per cent of the student body.[57]

The *Bolletino della Sera* in a 1907 editorial, "Let us do as the Jews," pinpointed the difference between the two ethnic communities. The article began by telling of the Jewish "conquest of this country" in the economic sphere:

> They are the owners of businesses, banks, and affairs. Israelites are the lawyers, judges, doctors, professors, teachers, managers of theaters, the monopolists of the arts. . . . Their schools are the most frequented and most active. What wonder if they

audaciously proclaim themselves the owners, the conquerors of this country! . . . But we must do as they do; we must thus invade the schools, teach ourselves, have our children taught, open to them the social paths by means of the hatchet of knowledge and genius. . . .

But instead of this what a contrast! The schools where the Italian language is taught are deserted. The Italian families falsify even the ages of their children in order to send them to the factories, instead of the schools, showing thus an avarice more sordid than that of the traditional Shylock. There is not a young Italian girl who knows to typewrite in both languages, and our men of affairs must employ Jewish girls or Americans for lack of Italians.[58]

In a period when city bureaucracies, businesses, and the professions were expanding, education became an economic commodity with market value. The fact that Jews were more literate and better educated enhanced their position in a society that valued such credentials highly. Italian offspring were, by 1905, moving up the blue-collar ladder, and they developed industrial skills which helped launch some of them in business careers, but their progress was slower, in part because of their values.[59]

IMMIGRANT LODGERS

As the Immigration Commission reported in 1911, the immigrant household commonly extended beyond the nuclear family:

One of the most significant features in connection with the households, the heads of which were of recent immigration, as compared with the households of the older Americans or native Americans, is the almost entire absence of a separate or independent family life. The system of living . . . in the southern and eastern European households . . . in any section of the country is that of the boarding group . . . numbering from 2 to 20, pay[ing] a fixed amount monthly for lodging, cooking

and washing. . . . This group system of living, which causes
congestion and unsanitary conditions, and renders impossible
any satisfactory form of family life, is made possible by the low
standards of the recent immigrants and by their desire to live
as cheaply as possible, or, in the case of families, to supplement the earnings of the head. . . .[60]

Lodgers represented the closest of neighbors and immigrants
were careful to choose those of similar ethnic origin and religious
background. These boarders became part of the immigrant household.

[T]he male boarder occupied a unique position. . . . Once he
moved in he quickly became a familiar. He even had the authority to spank misbehaving children. Wherever the family
went, the boarder went, too. He could often step between a
quarreling husband and wife. Families with a marriageable
daughter picked a boarder with the idea of marrying her
off. . . .[61]

Jacob Gordin, the leading writer of the contemporary Jewish
theater, fashioned an adaptation of *A Doll's House* called *Minna,*
which centered on a boarder, "a young man, whom they have
been forced to take into their house because of their poverty."
Both mother and daughter fall in love with the boarder. The
tragedy ends with the older woman, who is disgusted with her
arid husband, pedestrian life, and guilt, drinking carbolic acid.[62]

The conventional estimation of boarders was that such outsiders disrupted the normal flow of family life. The situation so
agitated social reformers that a number of them worked to pass
laws restricting the practice. But the economic role of these lodgers, aside from the rent they paid, remains largely ignored.[63]

The 456 Italian families surveyed in 1880 housed, in addition
to the nuclear family, 500 lodgers, virtually all of them Italian,
and most of them unrelated boarders who had lived in the United
States fewer than four years. Of the 367 who were gainfully employed some owned their own businesses, and over 12 per cent
occupied white-collar positions (see Table 9). A large majority

TABLE 9 OCCUPATIONAL DISTRIBUTION FOR ITALIAN AND RUSSIAN JEWISH LODGERS, BY PER CENT, NEW YORK CITY, 1880 AND 1905

| | Italian | | Jewish | |
	1880	1905	1880	1905
I	1.4	.3	1.6	.9
II	10.9	5.9	27.8	14.4
III	13.4	24.0	53.9	46.7
IV	7.1	20.0	15.9	35.6
V	67.3	49.6	.8	2.4
Total Working Lodgers	367	391	126	418
Total Lodgers	500	560	171	506
Percent of Total Who Are Related	28.6	49.8	42.7	29.2
Per Cent of Total Who Are Unrelated	71.4	50.2	57.3	70.8
Total Households Sampled	456	1,029	536	1,008

Source: Sample Data from Federal Census of 1880 and New York State Census of 1905.

however, did unskilled labor (if relative-lodgers are excluded close to 75 per cent of working boarders were unskilled).

Many of the men were "birds of passage," passing through the city for a season's wages, forming the rag-picking crews * that so affronted Jacob Riis:

> Bred to even worse fare, he takes both [the padrone and low pay] as a matter of course, and applying the maxim that it is not what one makes but what he saves that makes him rich, manages to turn the very dirt of the streets into a hoard of gold, with which he either returns to his Southern home, or brings over his family to join in his work and in his fortunes the next season.[64]

* Originally New York City followed the practice of paying gangs of rag pickers to trim the garbage heaps on the ash-scows before they went to sea. But as this turned into a very profitable business the city stopped paying $1.50 a day plus findings, and sold the garbage franchise. In 1889 this franchise brought in $80,000. Italian padroni were often the holders of such franchises and used their contracted Italian labor to pile through stinking mounds of the city's refuse. [Jacob Riis, How the Other Half Lives, 38–41.]

By 1905 the proportion of lodgers among the Italians had dropped to half the 1880 figure. Moreover, half of all lodgers in 1905 were relatives, a drop in nonrelated boarders of 62 per cent. The occupational distribution for Italian lodgers changed over the 25 years in much the same way as it did for other Italians. The white-collar class diminished (reflecting a decline in peddling) while blue-collar occupations were upgraded as the unskilled level dropped to a still very large 50 per cent.

Thus each segment of the Italian working population—head, offspring, and lodgers—underwent the same general rearrangement over the years, despite the specific differences between them. From 1880 to 1905 the blue-collar class for heads of family rose from 73 to 80 per cent; for offspring, from 85 to 87 per cent; and for lodgers, from 88 to 94, but within this class the distribution, reflecting expanded opportunities for Italians, was upgraded.

In contrast to the Italian experience, the proportion of boarders among the Jewish families almost doubled in the generation after 1880. Indeed, the figure for Jewish lodgers in this period exceeded the figures for black Harlem during the twenties, which was notorious for its boarders. The panic emigration from Russia after 1903 helped fill the ghetto with people who could neither find nor afford individual apartments. For the short term they moved in with others, often hoping to save enough to send *shifskart* (steamship tickets) back home to bring the rest of their families.[65]

As a consequence of this desperate emigration, the occupational distribution shown in Table 9 was downgraded between 1880 and 1905. The white-collar class dwindled from 29 to 15 per cent. Of all elements in either the Jewish or Italian households, Jewish boarders were the only ones who showed no gain in status.[66]

In sum, ethnic differences had clear economic consequences. Aware of the commercial mechanism, fortunate in their industrial connections and the quickness with which these ties could be used to effect, ambitious for education and its perquisites, Jews moved into a higher level of the New York City economy from the start and sustained this higher position over the years from 1880 to 1905.

V

American Time: Individual Career Mobility

Individuals have been speculating too much [about mobility]
and studying the facts too little. It is time to abandon specula-
tion for the somewhat saner method of collecting the facts and
studying them patiently.

Pitrim A. Sorokin, Social Mobility

In the years after 1870 many apologists for the free-wheeling age
of enterprise and the patent misery that attended its progress
made extravagant claims for America's promise of mobility. Some
suggested that success was so readily available to those who
worked for it that the unsuccessful must be lazy and intemperate.
They were society's unfit, being sloughed off in a sharp but fair
struggle for survival. Disturbed by some of these claims and their
unfortunate implications, Richard T. Ely, reformist founder of
the American Economic Association, wrote *Social Aspects of
Christianity* in 1889, offering his estimate of the chances for a
Horatio-Alger-type rise from rags to riches:

> If you tell a single concrete working man on the Baltimore and
> Ohio RR that he may yet be the president of the company, it
> is not demonstrable that you have told him what is not true,
> although it is within bounds to say that he is far more likely to
> be killed by a stroke of lightning.[1]

Laborer to corporate president is one example of mobility.
Placing the two markers so far apart is a valid way of testing a
Horatio Alger myth or a Carnegie gospel. If, however, one wishes
to turn to other questions that require a finer analysis of mobility,
more sensitive scales are necessary.

One such question involves the social and political implications of mobility. If a democratic society is to maintain comity and balance it cannot afford to produce a class of permanently immobile workers, immigrant or native. Certainly the Ely test for mobility does not address this issue, for very few people expected to achieve the type of progress he spoke of, and few would have turned to revolution because they could not achieve a corporate presidency. In testing for mobility it is probably better to employ Stephan Threnstrom's formulation:

> . . . the viability of a class system in which some citizens enjoy prestige, power and affluence while others are poor and powerless depends in considerable measure on the extent to which inequality is structured and permanent. Whether classes are 'fixed' or open, whether there are 'middle rungs' on the social ladder that are accessible to men on the bottom, are crucial questions. . . .[2]

In previous chapters the job patterns of Italians and Jews between 1880 and 1905 were compared, showing that both groups enhanced their economic status over time. Group mobility is, however, quite a different issue from individual mobility. That is, the fact that Italians in 1905 held down more attractive occupations does not indicate that Italians living in New York City in 1880 successfully climbed America's vaunted ladder of opportunity. Given the fact that the 1905 Italian community was not simply the 1880 group plus 25 years, improved status in 1905 might reflect a variety of possibilities having nothing to do with the mobility of Italians living in the United States in 1880. Conceivably an upgraded job profile might have resulted from the immigration of many skilled or wealthy Italians after 1880, or from the repatriation of large numbers of unsuccessful Italians, or from the disproportionate mortality of poor and unskilled Italians. Many more explanations are possible, but the point is sufficiently clear: individual mobility is not the necessary cause of group mobility. Consequently, patterns of individual mobility cannot be inferred from group progress, and must be studied separately.

At heart, the issue of mobility concerns the effect of time on occupational status; not time in general, for that becomes a simple query into the bearing of age on achievement, but rather "American time." This chapter focuses on the correlation between occupational status and time spent in the United States. The central hypothesis is that in a mobile society longer exposure to its opportunities will result in gradually escalating status.

The traditional approach has been to choose a sample of individuals at one point in time and trace the group over a period of years, usually a decade, while holding a finger to its occupational pulse. This methodology presents formidable obstacles, however. The most important problem stems from the difficulty of tracing individuals. Too many subjects are lost sight of along the way and sometimes this wreaks havoc on the sample's credibility. Nevertheless, the trace method remains important and necessary in the study of mobility.[3]

Fortunately it is possible in the present study to supplement the conventional methodology with another approach. For every individual that it listed, the New York State Census provided information on both occupation and length of residence in the United States, permitting us to explore the connection between American time and occupation level, the nub of the mobility issue. Thus in this chapter two methods of mobility analysis are applied to the census data, first the more general probing of the relationship between economic status and years in the United States, and then the tracing of individual immigrants over time.

A sample drawn from the 1905 Census was divided into four cohorts—0–6 years, 7–14 years, 15–25 years, and 26 years or more—representing length of residence in the United States. The resulting distribution for New York Italians is presented in Table 10, and points to a certain ambivalence in their patterns of progress. Two status levels, low white-collar and skilled blue-collar, were quite active, one waxing and the other waning in direct relation to American time. But the other three strata were far more sluggish, maintaining a regular percentage of the total, regardless of length of residence.[4]

TABLE 10 OCCUPATIONAL DISTRIBUTION FOR NEW YORK CITY ITALIANS BY LENGTH OF RESIDENCE IN THE UNITED STATES

	1–6 Years	7–14 Years	15–25 Years	26 to 99 Years	Total
I	.5	1.9	1.9	13.5	1.5
II	8.1	14.3	21.6	25.0	13.1
III	29.5	27.4	18.9	11.5	26.2
IV	20.0	20.4	21.4	11.5	20.0
V	42.0	35.9	38.3	38.5	39.2
Sample Size	881	565	378	52	1,876
Per Cent of Total Sample	47.0	30.1	20.1	2.8	100

Source: Sample Data from New York State Census for 1905.

Whether he had been in the country for two, three or twenty-five years, the likelihood that an Italian immigrant would land in the upper white-collar category did not exceed 2 per cent. Disdain for education and the large proportion originally anchored to unskilled jobs made it unlikely that even after 25 years a significant number of Italians could soar to the highest occupational levels.

Only in the last grouping, composed of Italians who had lived in the United States over 26 years, did the upper white-collar fragment climb sharply. Indeed, this entire cohort differed markedly from the three others. The anomaly stems from the fact that these Italians, who arrived in the country before 1879, were mostly from the more advanced northern part of the kingdom. Northerners coming to the United States brought along more money, were more literate, and included more professionals than the later-arriving southerners. Hence their occupational history differed from the stolid pattern of their southern compatriots.[5]

The one occupation stratum showing consistent time-related expansion was the lower white-collar grouping. It grew from

8 per cent of those in the United States less than six years, to 22 per cent of the 15–25 cohort, and 25 per cent of the northern-dominated old-timers who settled before 1879. A close analysis of this class's progress reveals the sector responsible for this headway. While office and sales-related occupations did not increase in step with the American-time variable, and peddling did so only slightly, the number of blue-collar Italians crossing into white-collar retailing neatly correlated with length of residence.

The Italian built his progress slowly. He saved his blue-collar earnings until he could invest them in a store and then worked for the best. Such shorter routes to the white collar as the professions and office work were closed to him. His way of moving up was by a hand-over-hand climb out of manual labor into a grocery store, a barber shop, or a saloon. "For we must remember," noted a contemporary commentator on the Italian condition, "that many general laborers, miners, and others are tempted to enter 'bisinesse,' and that they can do so by learning fifty words of English and buying a fruit stand. . . . In New York many men have begun with a pushcart, then got the privilege of a stand, then a concession to sell garden produce . . . and finally have set up a shop of their own." Of the 22 per cent of the 15–25 cohort who achieved lower white-collar status, all but 5 per cent did so as shopkeepers.[6]

In sketching a design for immigrant advancement one might outline a neat process of mobility where classes move up step by step, over time. As length of residence rises, concentrations increase at the higher echelons with corresponding decreases at the lower levels. Ideally the bottom class would deplete itself first, then the next lowest and so on. As Table 10 demonstrates, this was not true of New York Italians. The only blue-collar "feeder" class that declined in rhythm with upper-class increase was the skilled category. Levels four and five show no appreciable decline over the first three age brackets (the over 26 group which accounted for less than 3 per cent of the total again offers an exception; its semiskilled class was considerably smaller than either of the previous cohorts).

To account for this we must turn back to the historical particulars of the Italian experience in New York. Until after the 1890s Italians had not yet penetrated most skilled trades. Those who arrived earlier, therefore, primarily settled into unskilled and semiskilled occupations. When skilled jobs did become available, longer settled Italians had no special advantage in landing these jobs. And if they were already employed they generally stuck to familiar patterns. Therefore, newly arrived Italians often found it possible to be trained into skilled jobs, with little competition from their longer tenured compatriots. Consequently the lower blue-collar classes did not feed the skilled class.

One example that illustrates this point is the larger number of barbers among earlier settlers. Apparently later immigrants found a wider range of options and avoided this occupation, but those who had landed earlier and taken to barbering originally did not choose to give it up and move into another field which might rate higher status on some objective scale of occupations.

Moreover, the persistent significance of the large unskilled class across all cohorts is a very significant factor in Italian sluggishness. All laborers, skilled and less skilled alike, had problems making ends meet, witness the numerous descriptions of working-class poverty in this era. But no group had it harder than the unskilled laborer. Not only was his type plentiful, but he compounded his weakness by being illiterate and an easy mark for preying bosses and middlemen. Thus he had to rely on a working wife and children to make ends meet, especially, as often happened, when he was out of work. It was seldom possible for such a laborer to string together a sufficient number of work days to save money and invest it in a business.[7]

Patterns of Jewish progress over American time contrast with the Italian experience, as Table 11 shows. The changes are far more dramatic and activity is apparent on a wider scale, affecting four of the five classes. Only the unskilled class languished as if it bore no relation to the issue, which is precisely the case.

Jewish expansion in both upper and lower white-collar classes correlates neatly with the amount of time spent in the United

States. The upper class increased by a steady increment of 5
or 6 per cent in passing from cohort to cohort, starting as 4
per cent of the most recent settlers and finally swelling to 21 per
cent of the longest-resident group.

Jews produced a larger professional class than did the Italians.
With the passage of time in America, Jewish attorneys, physicians,
and teachers proliferated, as they translated this time into schooling and professional training. The major thrust for upper white-
collar expansion, however, came from rapid strides in upper-level
enterprise, as Jews moved into garment manufacture, real estate,
and the building industry.[8]

TABLE 11 OCCUPATIONAL DISTRIBUTION FOR NEW YORK CITY
RUSSIAN JEWS BY LENGTH OF RESIDENCE IN THE UNITED STATES

	1–6 Years	7–14 Years	15–25 Years	26 to 99 Years	Total
I	4.0	10.7	14.8	21.4	8.9
II	15.2	32.1	39.5	46.4	26.8
III	46.7	31.5	29.1	17.9	37.3
IV	32.6	24.1	15.3	10.7	25.4
V	1.5	1.6	1.2	3.6	1.5
Sample Size	854	619	481	28	1,982
Per Cent of Total Sample	43.1	31.2	24.3	1.4	100

Source: Sample data from New York State Census for 1905.

The low white-collar series exhibited even greater growth. The
role played by this class doubled to 30 per cent in going from the
first cohort to the second. Of the recent settlers in such positions
most worked as peddlers and shopkeepers, with a smaller number
in sales and clerical work. But peddling declined sharply over the
four groupings, while sales and clerical work increased slightly.
Retailing, was the major factor in lower white-collar growth,
which eventually amounted to 46 per cent after 26 years. As with
the Italians, such enterprise served as the mainspring for rapid
white-collar progress. The Industrial Commission commented on
this:

Economic advancement comes to . . . poverty stricken Hebrews with surprising rapidity. There is no way of telling definitely what proportion of the very poor eventually rise out of that condition, or how long it takes for them to do so. General observation, however, seems to indicate that the proportion is considerable and the rate rapid.[9]

Italian mobility was confined to an interplay of only two neighboring status levels and therefore limited in range. Jewish mobility proved broader because it involved all four of the occupational levels. Both skilled and semiskilled sectors declined as the two upper divisions expanded. Of the most recent settlers, 47 per cent were skilled laborers. For the next cohort, skilled labor decreased in concentration to 32 per cent *at the same time* that semiskilled labor decreased from 33 to 24 per cent. "Every year," observed one scholar, "large numbers [of Jews] desert the clothing industry to go into such occupations as small shopkeepers, insurance agents and clerks." Jewish tailors often found themselves replaced by other nationalities, but this seldom provided cause for despair, as they moved up to contracting or manufacturing and small business.[10]

Both New Immigrant groups redeemed the American promise of mobility. Progress *was* a function of time. But it was also a function of ethnicity. Jews experienced more progress than Italians. It was not that Jews came with more money, or even that they saved more money—both groups were thrifty—but rather that the "middlemen of Europe" brought more entrepreneurial savvy and "middle class" values. Moreover, they did not suffer the sharp braking force of stagnant low-skill sectors which held back Italian progress.[11]

INDIVIDUAL MOBILITY BY TRACING

The study of mobility through tracing is the most straightforward attack on the issue. It requires no special methodology,

dealing directly with individuals of known occupation and ob-
serving the changes in their status after a period of time. Unfortunately, because some people die, some move out of the city,
and others who do neither are nonetheless missed by the record,
the tracing approach is open to a potentially crippling bias.

Consider the following hypothetical example. The occupational distribution for New York's Italians in 1890 as determined
from the census shows 30 per cent white collar and 70 per cent
blue collar. The sample is then "traced," by using the city directory for 1900 and searching for the individual names from the
1890 sample. But, after the tracing is completed only the 30 per
cent white-collar segment could be followed. The others did not
appear in the directory. Jews in the 1890 sample showed 50–50
distribution, but in their case only the lower class could be traced
to 1900. As a result:

1. Trace attrition has destroyed the validity of the sample.
No longer does it represent a sample of New York's Italians but
only a sample of *upper-class* Italians. The sample may have
been painstakingly constructed to reflect all neighborhoods and
income levels, but the mechanics of tracing these people, by
forcing them through a selective sieve like the directory, imparted its own bias.

2. Any comparison between the two groups on the basis of the
after-trace mobility data would be misleading, since it would
compare the mobility patterns of rich Italians and poor Jews.[12]

Not all traces will suffer this distortion, but the effect of trace
attrition must be considered. Table 12 below does this, by comparing the initial distribution for both groups as determined
from the census, with the initial distribution for those immigrants
who could subsequently be traced through the directories. The
difference between these two shows the slant of the second sample away from true representativeness, the first potential problem
listed above. To test for point two, it is necessary to see if the
trace-induced bias falls in similar fashion on both groups, or
favors one group above the other.

TABLE 12 REAL OCCUPATIONAL DISTRIBUTION FOR ITALIAN AND RUSSIAN
JEWISH HEADS OF HOUSEHOLD COMPARED WITH THE OCCUPATIONAL
DISTRIBUTION OF THOSE WHO COULD BE TRACED,
NEW YORK CITY, 1880–1915

| | Italian | | Jewish | |
	Real	Trace	Real	Trace
I	2.3	3.8	10.8	11.2
II	18.9	27.2	31.1	35.3
III	19.0	15.7	43.9	40.7
IV	12.5	14.1	11.6	11.4
V	46.2	38.5	1.6	.9
*	1.2	.6	1.0	.4
Total:	1,822	312	1,784	533

* This category includes those who were in school or not gainfully employed at the time the census was taken.

Source: Sample data from 1880 Federal Census, 1892, New York State
Census, and 1905 New York State Census; *Trow's Directory for New York
City*, 1890, 1915, and *Uppington's General Directory of the Borough of
Brooklyn* 1905, 1913.

The margin of difference between real and trace distributions
is, in both cases, relatively slight. The bias is upward for both
groups. This slant means that the mobility data are based on a
sample that included slightly more white-collar and somewhat
fewer blue-collar workers than actually existed in the two immigrant communities. The distortion is, however, sufficiently
slight to avoid a situation where white-collar workers are traced,
most laborers are ignored, and the findings passed off as a study
of mobility.

The results of this trace study go beyond the relationship between time and occupational status to quantify the *rate* of mobility, indicating how really fluid New York's economic system
was. Close to half of New York's Italians who could be traced
changed not merely jobs but class levels within a decade. The
Jewish situation too showed significant fluidity, although in their
case, with 34 per cent changing class, the figure is less striking.

Little wonder that Gotham's dynamic bustle caught the eye of visitors.

TABLE 13 MOBILITY CROSSTABULATION * OF ITALIAN AND RUSSIAN JEWISH HEADS OF HOUSEHOLD: AGGREGATE DATA, NEW YORK CITY

Italian

Original Class	I	II	III	IV	V	**	Summary Data Before Trace	After Trace
I	58.3	8.2	4.1	2.3	2.5		3.8	6.4
II	8.3	76.5	26.5	38.6	24.2	50.0	27.2	40.4
III	16.7	7.1	55.1	2.3	17.5		15.7	18.3
IV	8.3	2.3	4.1	40.9	15.0		14.1	13.1
V	8.3	5.9	10.2	15.9	40.8	50.0	38.5	21.8
**							.6	
Total Sample							312	312

Jewish

Original Class	I	II	III	IV	V	**	Summary Data Before Trace	After Trace
I	90	9.2	6.9	9.8			11.2	17.3
II	10	81.6	32.7	27.9		50.0	35.3	46.7
III	0	5.9	55.3	27.9	60.0	50.0	40.7	28.5
IV	0	1.6	3.7	31.1	20.0		11.4	5.8
V	0	1.6	1.4	3.3	20.0		.9	1.7
**							.4	
Total Sample							533	533

* Columns are original class, rows are subsequent class, and underlined percentages are rates of persistence in class.
** Includes heads of household who were either in school or otherwise not employed initially.

Source: Sample data from Federal Census of 1880 and New York State Census of 1892, and of 1905, traced in New York and Brooklyn directories.

The high rate of movement was even more noteworthy, because it showed far more up-mobility than down-mobility. Of all

Italians who changed class more than three in four enhanced their status over a decade; a striking rate of progress for such poorly equipped new immigrants. Their Jewish partners showed less proclivity for change, but among those who did trade classes those moving up outnumbered backsliders by four to one.

Contemporaries like the Reverend Newman Smyth, who were concerned for the laborer, often feared that mobility was foreclosed. As the clergyman put it in a sermon to workingmen:

> The man at the bottom of the social ladder leading up to the social heavens may yet dream there is a ladder let down to him; but the angels are not seen very often ascending and descending; one after another, it would seem, some unseen yet hostile powers are breaking out the rungs of the ladder.

From the example of New York's immigrants it would seem that this concern was overwrought.[13]

Or perhaps he was right. That there was mobility is indisputable. But what kind and what degree? Were the middle rungs of the ladder hacked out in order to prevent meaningful mobility of the kind that put a white-collar position within the blue-collar worker's reach? The analysis thus far does not differentiate between the mobility of laborer to longshoremen and laborer to corporate president; between a laborer who persists in his class, and a surgeon who persists in *his* class.

Among Italians the lower white-collar stratum showed the greatest stability. This class of mostly shopowners retained more than three-fourths of its members over the tracing period. Of the 23 per cent who left its ranks, 8 per cent rose to the upper white-collar class by dint of business success. These fortunate souls were outnumbered, however, by others who were less successful. Fifteen per cent of the lower white-collar class slipped into blue-collar positions, and 6 per cent dropped all the way to unskilled jobs (see Table 13 above).

Even fewer of the small upper white-collar class maintained their grip on the high-status positions. Eight per cent moved down one step, while 33 per cent fell back into manual labor occupations. One hapless individual took the path from apex to nadir and after a decade had to make his living as a day laborer.

While Italians held on to their white collars at a rate of 83 per cent, the Jewish white-collar class held on more tightly, 93 per cent surviving the tracing period with white collars intact. Upper white-collar Jews persisted in class at a rate of 90 per cent, and those who did slide applied the brakes quickly. None of those who originally sat atop the occupational hierarchy dropped below the low white-collar level. Eighty-two per cent of the lower white-collar Jews retained their status over the tracing period, while 9 per cent moved up and 9 per cent suffered decline into the blue-collar class. For Jews, too, mobility was a two-way street.

As might be expected, the blue-collar class experienced more change than the upper division. Among blue-collar Italians, 30 per cent found their way up to a white-collar berth. Interestingly the semiskilled stratum provided the largest proportion of all cross-overs into the nonmanual sector. That semiskilled Italians did not move into skilled occupations is apparent. Only 2 per cent took that modest step. Such jobs held no particular attraction; the pay was not much better, and immigrants conceived of America's promise in entrepreneurial terms, not in the fine honing of Old World crafts. Thus 39 per cent of the semiskilled Italians captured the cherished white collar, mostly as shopkeepers, and another 2 per cent ecalated to upper white-collar status. The drift was not always upward however, as 16 per cent fell back into unskilled labor.

Unskilled work—what Mario Puzo termed the great Italian-American beachhead into the middle class—did not generate as much progress as one might expect just because there was "no place to move but up." Peter Blau and Otis Duncan may argue

> The main factor that determines a man's chances of upward mobility is the level on which he starts. The lower the level

from which a person starts the greater is the probability that
he will be upwardly mobile simply because many more occupational destinations entail upward mobility for men with low
origins than for those with high ones.[14]

Nonetheless it was not easy to shake off the debilities of a rural
background, alien status, and a miserable education, as the 42-
per-cent persistence rate shows.

Unskilled jobs often prevented progress. The pay was low,
usually about $1.50 a day, and the work year seldom exceeded
250 days. Moreover, an unskilled worker did not build useful
experience or refine specific skills, he did what other men
avoided—rag picking, day labor, and railroad excavation.[15]

Despite these obstacles, 59 per cent of the unskilled Italians
moved up. Half of these workers kept their blue collars, showing gradual progress, as they latched on to occupations in skilled
and semiskilled categories. Another 27 per cent took the hurdle
into the white-collar class, mostly as entrepreneurs, and 3 per
cent made the great climb from bottom to top within a decade.
Three Italians of 312 traced, 1 per cent, could boast this version
of rags-to-riches ascent, while only one, 0.3 per cent, suffered the
agonizing descent.

Jewish blue-collar workers quit manual labor in larger proportion than the Italians (38 per cent v. 30 per cent). The skilled
worker accomplished this leap more easily than all others, especially because so many Jewish tailors fixed their ambition to
contracting and then manufacturing. But the semiskilled laborer
also glimpsed such opportunities quite often. Thus, 38 per cent
of this category found a decade sufficient time to acquire white
collars, and another 28 per cent stepped up to skilled labor.
Only 3 per cent fell behind into unskilled work. Less than one-
third remained in the semiskilled class.

Let us move back and look at the forest whole after having
analyzed the trees. Table 13 summarizes the development of
both groups. The Italian white-collar fraction grew by 16 per
cent as it expanded to 47 per cent of the total. As a result, the

number of Italians in blue-collar fields dropped from 68 to 53 per cent. The true picture was even more fluid than these totals imply, for 18 per cent of those originally in white collars dropped down to blue-collar occupations while 31 per cent of Italians in the manual class skipped over the threshold into white-collar positions.

Eastern European Jews began with a larger white-collar segment than the Italians, and they continued to expand this class from 47 to 64 per cent, with 17 per cent in the upper white-collar stratum. Manual labor, originally performed by more than one of every two gainfully employed heads of household, declined to only 36 per cent of the total. Fully 39 per cent of the blue-collar class attained higher rank, and white-collar regression, which accounted for 18 per cent of the Italian upper-class slipping into blue collars, affected only 7 per cent of the Jews.

Clearly no rungs were hacked out of New York's ladder. Whatever method is used to measure mobility there is convincing proof that America's promise was fulfilled in the dynamic immigrant city. As a 1920 study of New York business leaders concluded: "Very few of New York's optimistic philanthropists, much less the landlords, saw in the procession of prospective Italian citizens the many prosperous merchants, mechanics, professional men and bankers who now constitute so important a part of the City's life." [16]

One such success story was written by Guiseppe Tuoti, who opened a real estate office on Grand Street in 1885. Within the decade the number of Italians owning real estate went from fewer than 100 to 3,000, while leaseholders increased from 50 to 1,000, and Mr. Tuoti's activities in housing properties expanded and prospered. In 1887, he formed a company to develop the town of Woodridge in New Jersey, which provided suburban housing for his slum-dwelling countrymen. Soon thereafter he turned to colonization operations in other New Jersey areas, on Staten Island, and on Coney Island. He also helped erect modern tenements in the Bronx. In 1906, in recognition of his exhibit at the Milan Exposition which portrayed the progress of Italians in New York from 1885 on, Tuoti received a commendation from the Italian Government. By 1924, "million dollar transfers of property . . . [were] daily occurrences," for this leading realtor.[17]

Over a short span of time many Italians found economic success. "The tradespeople prosper rapidly," concluded a 1902 report on New York's Italians. "The Italian barber enlarges his shop, perhaps sells out, becomes a banker; the fruit peddler expands and may eventually become an importer." Having escaped the static world of absentee-owned *latifundia* where years followed each other in regular patterns of peasant poverty, Italians took advantage of a New World economy where patterns were far more dynamic and progressive.[18]

Jews made their move into business earlier than the Italians and as a result attained higher concentrations in the white-collar sector. To succeed they had to cut prices and costs, introduce new techniques and machinery. This helped them take control of the clothing business, and as the case of Isaac Goldman illustrates, it was put to use in other areas as well.

In 1876 Isaac Goldman was discharged from his position as a compositor in a printing shop. Opening a two-man printing shop on William Street, he experimented with the latest machinery. By 1888 the shop had moved three times, each time to larger and more modern quarters. In 1895 the Goldman Company boasted the first linotype machines in New York. Each of these machines could turn out more work in one day than four experienced printers. Goldman did not allow himself to rest on these innovations or settle for a stable business. In 1905 he sold all of his machinery, moved to a new factory, and installed new equipment, a process he repeated a decade later. By this time, Goldman's press was producing highly profitable business catalogues and a long list of periodicals.[19]

INTERGENERATIONAL PATTERNS

The Austrian immigrant Edwin Steiner published a book about his experiences, *On the Trail of the Immigrant*. He was especially interested in the New Immigrants' accommodation to their new surroundings:

> In my wanderings through the [Jewish] Ghetto I dropped into a pawnshop on Avenue C one day, and after I made some purchases the proprietor grew friendly and introduced me to his family. . . . 'What are you going to be Charles?' I asked. 'A businessman like my father'; and the keen look in his big eyes, the determination of his whole frame and face, showed that he would succeed even better than his father. . . . Charles T's father began life by buying rags on Houston Street; his sons will sell bonds on Wall Street.[20]

Steiner touched an important facet of immigrant mobility in this passage, the issue of intergenerational mobility. This topic, however, deserves closer scrutiny than Steiner could give it.

The questions are plain and direct. What effect did the status level of the household head have on his offspring's occupational niche? A very high correlation between the careers of fathers and sons might imply a society closed around a *de facto* class system where family wealth and status play a major determining role. On the other hand, a high degree of random associations where offspring differ from their parents implies a fluid, dynamic society.

A study of Boston's occupational structure concludes that the tendency toward intergenerational status inheritance "was not very strong." More precisely, less than half of the men made careers at their fathers' level. Moreover, this dissimilarity was not uniform across all classes. Upper-class sons were more likely to inherit occupational status than were lower-class offspring, one hallmark of an open economy. Between 52 and 63 per cent of manual laborers' sons landed in high-skilled or white-collar jobs.[21]

The data on New York's immigrants are not sufficient for a definitive conclusion about the degree of occupational inheritance, but the results indicate a resemblance to the Boston experience. Taking Italians and Jews together, only 39 per cent of the immigrant offspring listed the same types of occupations as their parents. Of the remaining group, 24 per cent latched onto higher status levels while 38 per cent occupied lower-level jobs, undoubtedly because the sample was taken at a point early in their careers.[22]

Table 14 assembles the data for 765 Italian offspring and their parents. The "Summary" table shows an interesting divergence between the parents and their children. The older generation was more heavily concentrated in both white-collar divisions and in the lowest blue-collar category while their sons and daughters zeroed in on the skilled and semiskilled jobs. This does not, however, speak directly to the issue. It does not relate the status of the specific lower-class worker to that of his child. It provides no clue to the question of intergenerational occupational inheritance.

The detailed table of cross-tabulations does this. It plots the status of the parent against that of his child. Thus by looking at the second column we learn that 75 per cent of low white-collar Italians had children in manual jobs. Admittedly, this did not mean that the offspring would remain blue-collar laborers for the rest of their careers, but it does indicate that, at least in their early working years, the sons and daughters of shopowners and peddlers often did manual labor. Parental status made little difference for them. The same, as the lower half of the table shows, was true for the Jews. Most offspring of white-collar parents took blue-collar jobs at first.

On the other hand, it was not unusual for blue-collar parents in the skilled and semiskilled categories to have their children step above them. Among Jews this was true in 25 per cent of the cases, and among Italians one in ten workers in classes III and IV was outranked by his offspring. Even among Italian families

TABLE 14 INTERGENERATIONAL OCCUPATIONAL PATTERNS * AMONG
NEW YORK'S ITALIAN AND RUSSIAN JEWISH IMMIGRANTS: AGGREGATE DATA

Italian

Household Heads	Offspring						Summary Household Heads	Offspring
	I	II	III	IV	V			
I	18.7	1.4	0	0	0		2.1	.7
II	18.7	24.7	10.4	10.3	8.9		19.1	12.5
III	12.5	28.1	55.2	29.9	23.6		17.5	30.5
IV	25.0	28.1	22.4	47.1	20.2		11.4	25.2
V	25.0	17.8	11.9	12.6	47.4		49.9	31.1
						Total Sample	765	765

Jewish

Household Heads	Offspring						Summary Household Heads	Offspring
	I	II	III	IV	V			
I	7.6	2.4	2.3	0	5.5		14.6	3.0
II	32.3	33.7	22.4	27.2	11.1		37.9	28.4
III	32.3	38.8	49.5	33.0	38.9		36.3	41.2
IV	26.6	24.4	23.5	37.9	27.8		9.5	25.7
V	1.3	.7	2.3	1.9	16.7		1.7	1.8
						Total Sample	1,081	1,081

* Columns are household heads; rows are offspring.

Source: Sample data from Federal Census of 1880 and New York State Census of 1892, and of 1905.

headed by unskilled workers such intergenerational mobility was evident. Nine per cent of their children landed positions as clerks, salesworkers, and storekeepers.

The lowest-status families, not surprisingly, produced the largest number of unskilled offspring. Poverty and low status were in part inherited, and to that extent the society was not totally open and free. But this legacy of low status was passed on in a minority of the cases. Most children of unskilled laborers, very early in their careers, landed better jobs than their parents.

The situation was flexible and open. Parental background undeniably exerted some influence. Nonetheless, 54 per cent of the Italian heirs and 64 per cent of the Jews occupied different levels from their parents. Parental occupation was clearly not deterministic. Other variables, ethnicity for instance, proved more important (as Table 14 suggests). Jewish scions numbered 31 per cent in the upper class, compared with 13 per cent for the Italians.

What emerges from this discussion is a sense of the flux that dominated New York's economy. It was better, no doubt, to be the son of a rich businessman than of a poor laborer. But that is not at issue. The central point is that in an increasingly urban and technological society the effect of parental status receded in importance. Relatively independent factors like education, entrepreneurial skill, and craftsmanship took precedence. This society could hand a businessman's heir a ditch-digger's shovel, or put a stethoscope and scalpel in the hands of a garment worker's son. In this type of swirling atmosphere the immigrant could hope to achieve success for himself and his children. And a society where success was guaranteed to a few, but ruled out for none, served him well.

The data on occupational inheritance point to an open society, but do not reflect the true prospects for progress among the second generation. Indeed, a close look at the previous tables shows the offspring occupying lower-level positions than their parents. Obviously this results from the sample's restriction to at-home immigrant offspring. A sense of the longer range opportunities available to these immigrant sons derives from a comparison of first- and second-generation mobility patterns.

The table printed below compares the occupational mobility for both generations among the sampled Italians and Jews. In both ethnic groups the second generation progressed up the occupational ladder at a quicker pace than the parents. Italian offspring showed a heavy blue-collar orientation at the outset, with approximately one-fourth of the group in each of the three blue-collar strata. Over a decade this group registered considerable progress, producing an upper white-collar class of equal proportion to their parents. The lower white-collar class also grew significantly and lessened somewhat the gap between the generations. The older generation still boasted a larger white-collar class but their offspring showed a larger increment of growth. In one

TABLE 15 OCCUPATIONAL DISTRIBUTION OF ITALIAN AND RUSSIAN JEWISH HEADS OF HOUSEHOLD AND OFFSPRING, BEFORE AND AFTER TRACING, BY PER CENT: AGGREGATE DATA, NEW YORK CITY

Italian

	Household Heads Original	Household Heads After Trace	Offspring Original	Offspring After Trace	Offspring Out of School	Total Offspring After Trace
I	3.9	6.4	2.5	6.3	5.0	5.8
II	27.4	40.4	18.8	33.8	32.5	33.3
III	15.8	18.3	23.8	16.3	22.5	18.3
IV	14.2	13.1	26.3	18.8	12.5	16.7
V	38.7	21.8	28.6	25.0	27.5	25.8
Total	310	312	80	80	40	120

Jewish

	Household Heads Original	Household Heads After Trace	Offspring Original	Offspring After Trace	Offspring Out of School	Total Offspring After Trace
I	11.3	17.3	6.0	22.1	31.0	24.6
II	35.4	46.7	39.6	40.9	39.7	40.6
III	40.9	28.5	35.6	28.9	22.4	27.1
IV	11.5	5.8	14.8	7.4	5.2	6.8
V	.9	1.7	4.0	.7	1.7	1.0
Total	531	533	149	149	58	207

Source: Sample data from Federal Census of 1880 and New York State Census of 1892 and of 1905, traced in Manhattan and Brooklyn directories.

respect, however, the younger group did not match their parents' progress. Among the senior Italians the unskilled segment declined from 39 to 22 per cent, but this sector contracted only 4 per cent for the second generation, leaving them with the larger unskilled class.

Like their Italian counterparts, Jewish offspring also showed a lower grade distribution than their parents in the initial comparison. The after-trace distribution, however, displayed sharp rearrangement. The upper white-collar class alone grew by 16 percentage points, comfortably overtaking the parental proportion in that class. Thus, second generation Jews were even more mobile than their parents, entering the professions and big business at a faster clip.

In Table 15 a separate column is devoted to offspring who were reported in school during the census enumeration and subsequently located in the directory search. The table displays the occupational spectrum for this special group a decade after they left school. The other offspring may or may not have had American schooling—there is no way of knowing—but this group had the benefit of such education for certain.

The Italian group shows no particular occupational dividend from the schooling. As a class they held fewer white-collar positions and more unskilled jobs than the other offspring. Italians who attended school at the outset did not fare as well as those who worked. Predominantly blue collar, their jobs provided little reward for schooling, and because they were younger and less experienced than the other cohort, they had not yet equaled it in achievement.

The Jewish scholars differed dramatically. Rather than falling behind their older brothers and sisters, this special group latched on to a disproportionate share of upper-level jobs. They had 31 per cent in upper white-collar professions and business positions. Another 40 per cent filled lower white-collar slots. Remarkably, over 70 per cent vaulted into the white-collar world within a decade of leaving school, and less than 30 per cent of the sample did blue-collar work. Schooling had utility for Jewish students beyond the knowledge it imparted, as J. K. Paulding observed: "It is not with the grade of scholarship attained by their students that criticism . . . need concern itself, so much as with the motive and spirit at work beneath their activity. That the motive of commercial advantage holds a very high place in the whole movement is the common testimony of teachers." [23]

As the totals show, Jewish offspring maintained the lead over Italians that had been established by their parents. The ethnic distinction did not diminish from the first to the second generation. This did not, however, obscure the fact that both groups found progress through occupational mobility.

Whatever the methodology and whichever generation it is applied to, immigrant mobility was far more than a literary device or an ideological weapon; it was a fair interpretation of the American reality. New Immigrants from Italy and Russia, with differing degrees of success, found it possible to better themselves in bustling New York. The City's swift industrial growth may have been built on the backs of its workers, many of whom were immigrants, but these newcomers did not fail to partake in the City's progress.

VI

The Residential Dimension

In the larger cities the population changes much more frequently than is generally thought. New immigrants are attracted to these poorer residential quarters by the presence of friends or relatives and the necessity of securing living quarters at the lowest possible cost, but as their economic status improves after living in this country for some time, they very generally move to better surroundings. The undesirable districts of the cities that are now inhabited largely by recent immigrants were formerly populated by persons of the earlier immigrant races. Few of these are now found there, and these remnants ordinarily represent the economic failures—the derelicts—among a generation of immigrants which, for the most part, has moved to better surroundings.

United States
Immigration Commission,
Reports

New Immigrants who landed in New York before 1892 disembarked from their stinking steerage compartments at Castle Garden off the Battery. If they knew enough to avoid the various boarding house "runners," competing hackmen, and the shady characters who preyed on immigrants in their own tongue, they made their way north beyond the Custom House and Trinity Church. They trekked through an area that housed most of Manhattan's factories and warehouses in the first three wards, moved past City Hall, and beyond it turned right. Here, about a mile and a half from the point of entry they put down their baggage and looked around at "their" neighborhood.[1]

James McCabe described this immigrant section in the 1870s:

> Here every surrounding is dark and wretched. The streets are narrow and dirty, the dwellings are foul and gloomy, and the very air seems heavy with misery and crime. For many a block

the scene is the same. This is the realm of poverty. . . . For
many blocks to the north and south of . . . Worth Street and
from Elm Street back to the East River, the Five Points presents a succession of similar scenes of wretchedness.[2]

Italian immigrants moved into the old Irish section in this area
and fashioned a "New Italy" between Pearl and Houston Streets,
east of Broadway. Unable to afford better, they moved into the
worst housing, in basements, garrets, converted stables, and rear
tenements. In most cases they were completely closed off from
sunlight and fresh air. Here, reported Jacob Riis, were "the bulk
of tenements stamped as altogether bad, even by the optimists
of the Health Department. Incessant raids cannot keep out the
crowds that make them their home. In the scores of back alleys,"
he continued, "they have such shelter as the ramshackle structures afford with every kind of abomination rifled from the dumps
and ashbarrels of the city." [3]

This neighborhood swarmed with Italian ragpickers, producing
an even shabbier environment. "The old rookeries in Baxter, Mulberry, Mott, Worth, Park and Centre Streets," the *New York
Times* reported in 1881, "are packed to suffocation with them
[*chiffonniers*], and a large number of the junk shops where they
dispose of their stocks, are situated in this section." These shops
were usually cellars packed with rags, cans, bones, and a pair of
scales. "They live on bread crusts and pieces of meat that they
pick out of the barrels," the article continued, explaining that the
refuse of the city, "furnishes food and raiment for thousands." [4]

Despite these pressing conditions there was little pauperism.
Contemporary records showed that Italians did not frequently re-
sort to charity, accepting the lowest types of labor in preference
to the dole. Noted for their industriousness and thrift, they
pressed savings out of meager subsistence-level wages. And the
slum landlord considered them desirable tenants who paid their
rent and seldom complained about conditions.[5]

Transplanted urban villagers, they made little concession to
new surroundings. Women wore picturesque peasant costumes,

and the men, too, dressed in the manner of the Italian *paese*. "Red bandanas and yellow kerchiefs are everywhere; so is the Italian tongue," wrote a contemporary. In a throwback to their days on the farm the Italian population took to the streets whenever they could, "carrying on its household work, its bargaining, its love-making on street or sidewalk, or idling there when it has nothing better to do, with the reverse of the impulse that makes the Polish Jew coop himself up. . . ." [6]

By 1880 Italians had established another settlement uptown, far from the central business district. As rapid transit extended into Harlem, developers put up rows of impressive brownstones for an upper middle-class clientele. "Italians," writes Gilbert Osofsky, "were the first New Immigrant group to come to Harlem." They did not, however, settle in the genteel Harlem of Stanford White houses, but rather filtered into the unattractive "common tenements" on a slum fringe of East Harlem between 109th and 111th Streets. "Little Italy's" colorful religious festivals, peasant customs, obiquitous organ grinders and ragpickers annoyed the brownstone dwellers. "Here," asserted *Uptown New York*, "can be found the refuse of Italy making a poor living from Harlem ashbarrels." Reflecting the paucity of industrial and commercial opportunity in this largely residential district, fully 84 per cent of working Italians in this ward were unskilled. [7]

The area of primary settlement for eastern European Jews was the old German section on the Lower East Side. In his classic novel of the Jewish ghetto Abraham Cahan described David Levinsky's arrival in New York.

> I led the way out of the Immigrant Station. . . . Then I led the way across Battery Park and under the elevated to State Street. . . . Where were we to go . . . ? I mustered courage to approach a policeman. . . . I addressed him in Yiddish,

making it as near an approach to German as I knew how, but
my efforts were lost on him. He shook his head. With a wither-
ingly dignified grimace he then pointed his club in the direction of Broadway. . . .

Everybody knew that was the way for a newly arrived Jew to go.
As another New Yorker tells the young immigrant, "Walk straight
ahead. . . . Just keep walking until you see a lot of Jewish
people." [8]

Jews huddled together even more closely than the Italians,
forming the densest settlements in the city. "Practically all Eastern European immigrants arriving after 1870," Moses Rischin
relates, initially found their way to the lower East Side. Virtually
penniless . . . they were directed to the Jewish districts by representatives of the immigrant aid societies, or came at the behest
of friends, relatives, or employers."

The Tenth Ward adjoining the Italian district carried the sobriquet of a private city "Jewtown." "Men with queer skullcaps,
venerable beard and the outlandish long-skirted Kaftan of the
Russian Jew . . . crowded out the Gentiles. . . . When the great
Jewish holidays come around every year, the public schools in
the district have practically to close up." Like other immigrants
they brought their European world with them and, to the extent
that it was possible, tried to continue living in their established
patterns, keeping out the rude discontinuities suggested by a new
environment. "To them," remarked Edward Steiner, "[Rivington]
Street is only a suburb of Minsk." [9]

And, as they did in Minsk and other *shtetl* communities, most
East Siders worked close to home. At the center of "Jewtown"
stood the inappropriately termed *Khazar Mark* (Pig's Market).
At eight o'clock every weekday morning this corner of Ludlow
and Hester Streets was probably the noisiest and most crowded
spot in the city as Jewish workers competed for day labor in
the garment industry. Other Jews, usually longer settled, held
regular jobs in the makeshift lofts that laced the area, while yet
another group took work into their tenements. The streets, too,

provided a livelihood, as the many peddlers who lined Hester and Orchard Streets knew. More conventional enterprise was carried on a few blocks away in the stores along Grand Street.[10]

These areas of primary settlement—both Italian and Jewish—exhibited the classic slum characteristics. The houses were old and rundown, the apartments were overcrowded, and the quality of life suffered. The 1880 *Report* of the Association for Improving the Conditions of the Poor described the wretched situation in some of these tenements. "In some cases, in these blocks, from five to ten adjoining houses can be seen . . . where the privies are reeking with filth, full to the seat with excrement, and both floor boards and yard in front covered with the most disgusting foulness." Horse stables could be found in some yards and a variety of animals often shared the cellar dwellings with slum inhabitants.[11]

Although the Council of Hygiene recommended that water be supplied to each tenement floor, "a hydrant in the yard" was often the only accommodation, and water pressure was often too low to supply the needs of those living above the second or third stories. Dirt and filth spread. "Floors, clothes and persons are unwashed no more water being brought up the many flights than is absolutely necessary for drinking purposes." [12]

Such apartments as were fortunate to have a water source often suffered from neglected plumbing. "Last February," reported an AICP investigator, "at No. 7 Mulberry Street, a tap leak on the second floor caused water to trickle day and night through the ceiling of the hall, where icicles, some of them three feet long hung pendant from the laths." [13]

As the New Immigrant wave climbed toward its peak over the next 25 years, these problems intensified. The immigrant population spiraled, and slum congestion reached unprecedented levels. The Jewish Tenth Ward had a population of 432 people per acre in 1880, the highest ratio in the city. One decade later the figure mounted to 524 and continued to grow to 652 by 1900.[14]

Housing expanded upward to accommodate the flood of newcomers. The authoritative 1902 Tenement Commission *Report* found that Italians and Jews, who by now dominated lower Manhattan, overwhelmingly occupied slum tenements. Table 16, based on the Commission's painstaking analysis of raw census data for 1900, indicates that for every ward shown the percentage of New Immigrants in tenements exceeded the average. Over 90 per cent of the Jews occupied these multiple dwellings, and the figure for Italians was only slightly lower, reflecting a tendency among some Italians to own their own homes, even in the slums.[15]

TABLE 16 PRIMARY NATIONALITY, POPULATION, DENSITY, AVERAGE FAMILY SIZE AND PERCENTAGE DWELLING IN TENEMENTS FOR SELECTED LOWER MANHATTAN WARDS, 1900

Ward	Primary Nationality	Total Population	Density Per Acre	Average Family Size	Percentage of Total Families in Tenements	Percentage of Total Primary Nationality Fam. in Tenements
4	Italian	18,344	202.2	4.8	70.8	73.7
6	Italian	18,929	187.2	4.9	86.0	87.3
7	Russian/Jew	89,206	433	5.3	91.3	93.2
8	Italian	28,777	162.5	4.7	81.5	92.0
10	Russian/Jew	71,041	651.7	5.3	87.6	89.3
13	Russian/Jew	64,164	588.6	5.3	92.9	93.6
14	Italian	33,595	311.1	5.0	83.3	86.1
15	Italian	22,845	101.1	5.0	65.4	79.0

Source: Computed from Tenement House Department *First Report* (2 vols., New York, 1903), I, 101–3, 227.

Probably the most notorious aspect of ghetto life was the congestion in these tenement districts. Between the two nationalities the Russian Jews lived in decidedly more crowded wards than the Italians, as Table 16 shows. One reason for this was that the Italians settled in older neighborhoods already covered with low capacity "front and rear" tenements. "Hebrews, on the other hand, are especially associated with the big 'double decker' or 'dumb-bell' tenement," Kate Claghorn explained. "These houses were erected in great numbers on the East Side which was not so fully taken up with the old type of tenement as the wards entered by the Italians. . . . And since 1892," she continued, "great numbers of the big 'dumb-bells' have been erected, replacing the smaller dwellings, which simply could not, by any degree of crowding be made to hold the incoming thousands." [16]

Even more to the point, Jewish areas were devoted to light industry, which meant that tenements doubled as factories and most real estate was utilized for residence. Italians settled in wards that had warehouse districts and large factories for heavy industry. A significant number of Italians could even be found in the almost exclusively industrial First, Second, and Third Wards. Industrial structures took much room but absorbed no inhabitants and therefore overall statistics for density per acre in such wards were lower.[17]

Living quarters in these lower-density wards, however, were not in better condition, nor were they less congested. Immigration Commission investigators who reported on visits to 472 Russian Jewish ghetto apartments in 1907–08 found 34 per cent in good condition and gave another 57 per cent a "fair" rating. Substandard conditions appeared in only 9 per cent of the housing. The statistics for 419 southern Italian dwellings were considerably different: 17 per cent good, 49 per cent fair, and 34 per cent bad. This difference in quality was confirmed by a corresponding variation in the rents. The Jews averaged a monthly rent of $16.59, while the average Italian household paid some three dollars less, $13.51. In sum, Jews with larger families were renting larger apartments (average size 3.55 rooms, average number of rooms for Italians 3.12), in better condition and paying higher rents.[18]

Between 1900 and 1905 congestion worsened as the population of the Lower East Side went up by 14 per cent. Close to 40 Manhattan blocks—most of them between Stanton, Rivington, and Delancey Streets in the Jewish Tenth Ward and between Madison, Monroe, and Cherry Streets in the Seventh—swarmed with over 1,000 people per acre, and some approached a choking 1,700 per acre. The Eighth Assembly District, carved out of the heart of the Jewish ghetto, averaged 730 persons to each acre.[19]

The overall picture drawn from these statistics is bleak. Brittle men and women uprooted from their homelands for various reasons found that their slum environment often hampered the good fortune and decent style of life they came to seek. Some of these people were overwhelmed by the adversity, and many sad stories came out of these downtown neighborhoods. Jacob Riis reported on a young East Side couple who "took poison together . . . because they were 'tired'." The environment had defeated them. Another couple he visited suffered the death of a child from measles. The father, overcome by futility and despair, hushed his trembling wife, "If we cannot keep the baby, need we complain —such as we?" Perhaps the saddest commentary is that these melancholy situations became almost commonplace and the phrase, "taking the gas" was sufficiently common to elicit comprehending nods when word of the latest suicide passed through the streets.[20]

Such emphasis on the negative aspects of ghetto life, accurate as it may be, nonetheless obscures the important point that the urban subcommunity was often best suited to help provide the newcomers with a place that was hospitable in the broadest sense. By meeting many of the immigrants' varied and unique needs it made their adjustment possible.

To be sure, the difficult residential situation that greeted the New Immigrants in the slums often disappointed them. But they were not shocked by what they saw. They had known worse. European poverty and persecution had tempered them to toughness; few were so delicate that they fell to pieces when they confronted the piercing reality of slum life. They realized that elsewhere the terms of settlement were even harsher.

Much of downtown Manhattan's attraction for these immigrants was directly due to the heavy concentration of immigrants. The ethnic neighborhood, congestion and all, served constructive

functions. Newcomers needed friends, countrymen, and relatives
to help ease their way into a new society. They sought a way
station where the portable heritage they carried made at least
some comforting connections with reality; where they could consider the desirability of that heritage and nurture it or gradually
discard it. Moreover, they required help with the mundane matters of everyday life: the law, a job, the language.

The ghetto * supplied the social context which the immigrant
sought. As the Industrial Commission noted:

> The newly arrived Russian Jew is kept on the crowded East
> Side not only by his poverty and ignorance, but by his ortho-
> doxy. In this district the rules of his religion can most certainly
> be followed. Here can be found the lawful food, here the or-
> thodox places of worship, here neighbors and friends can be
> visited within a "Sabbath day's journey." [21]

Moreover, it protected him from ridicule. The organ grinder, ragpicker, or peddler could work at his lowly occupation without the
added burden of being the only one in the neighborhood.

For all of its drawbacks the system of house rental as opposed
to ownership was functional. The Irish in Newburyport, Massachusetts, focused their aspirations on home ownership, because it
was within grasp. Savings were hoarded with this one goal in
mind. But because home ownership in Manhattan was a rarity
most New York immigrants were willing to hope for better apartments in lieu of private homes. Consequently savings were available for other uses including business investment.

Moreover, the immigrant community did not consist of lines
of unvarying and decayed tenements. It provided a staged pat-

---

* The term "ghetto" is used with Robert E. Park's definition: " 'Ghetto'
. . . is no longer a term that is limited in its application to the Jewish people. It has come into use . . . as a common noun—a term which applies to
any segregated racial or cultural group. The ghetto, as it is here conceived,
owes its existence, not to legal enactment [as it did in Europe], but to the
fact that it meets a need and performs a social function. The ghetto is, in
short, one of the so-called 'natural areas' of the city." [Louis Wirth, *The
Ghetto* (Chicago, 1928), vii–viii.]

tern of housing. The well-off merchant or professional could
choose to live in the stately brownstones on East Broadway while
the newly arrived immigrant with modest resources could rent a
fraction of a room as a boarder. And the constant building that
was going on meant that a broad selection of apartments in various conditions was available.

Ghetto housing was functional in other respects as well. The
immigrant laborer could not afford the luxury of living on the
outskirts. He had to be close to sources of job supply—the docks,
warehouses, factories, and business streets—to take advantage of
sudden openings and opportunities. Uncertain employment, long
hours, and low wages also made commuting impractical. He had
to live where he worked, and slum housing placed him at the
industrial-commercial core of the city. The streets were dirty, un-
safe, and unhealthy; the style of life was unattractive, but this
housing placed him at the pulse of the job market for which he
qualified. Ghetto streets were a grapevine of information that
could be converted into opportunities. Few immigrants hesitated
to stop strangers and ask for advice or help. Chance meetings
and conversations, so important a part of the "good luck factor"
in business, were very common on the packed streets.*

Congestion also produced economic dividends. The peddler,
for instance, prospered as a result of the large concentrations;
so did the many specialty shops that catered to an ethnic clientele. Moreover, the narrowly confined pattern of settlement made
the "sweating system" possible. In fact, a careful analysis of
three Jewish Assembly Districts in 1905, shows that a spiraling
density of population per acre, usually taken to show increasingly pressing slum conditions, corresponded with a rise in the
proportion of people in the higher occupation levels. In the 12th
Assembly District with a population density per acre of 465,

* Moreover, "a commercial district, a business street, or a rooming house
area puts up notoriously slight resistance to the intrusion of a new group."
[Ernest W. Burgess, "Residential Segregation in American Cities," *Annals of
the American Academy of Political and Social Science*, CXXXX (Nov.
1928), 109.]

52 per cent were in the top three classes. The 4th A.D. recorded
a 548 p.d.a., and 66 per cent of its people filled these upper
strata. The super-saturated 8th A.D., with an average of 728 persons crammed into each of its 98 acres, boasted the largest grouping in the white-collar and skilled classes. It is, therefore, at
least conceivable that density and congestion, so long considered
negative standards—measures of propensity to disease, ill health,
and job competition—bore more than an incidental relationship
to opportunity, especially where the residents were predisposed
to petty retailing and light manufacture.[22]

Although the quality of life undeniably suffered in the slums,
many of the worst tenements were bulldozed and replaced with
new buildings. The slum was no stagnant backwater; new housing kept going up. Even before the new century, the *New York
Times* disclosed that

> Substantial, and in some instances, handsome new tenement
> houses, five and six stories high, everywhere abound, and in-
> stead of the erstwhile, miserably lighted, poorly ventilated,
> cramped quarters there may now be seen apartments and flats
> at once commodious and comfortable.
> . . . New schools have been built and are building. . . .[23]

In 1898 Henry Street absorbed half a million dollars in new
housing. Monroe Street was rejuvenated with $400,000, while
neighboring Madison Street took a $350,000 investment in hand-
some stride. An additional $625,000 refurbished Pitt, Pike,
Stanton, and Eldridge Streets. And Cherry Street underwent a
$400,000 rehabilitation. A total of $6,373,000 was spent on new
housing in this district. Such building and investment continued,
providing jobs, investment opportunities, and fresh housing.[24]

At the same time that new tenements went up the most lugubrious aspects of slum life were cleared away. Mulberry Bend
Park (Paradise Park) replaced the dangerous "abode of vile-
ness," Mulberry Bend. Out with the filthy tenements went the
underground beer dens, which served as inlets to "Ragpicker's
Row," "Bottle Alley," and "Bandit's Roost."

> Gone [the *New York Tribune* reported in July of 1899]. . . .
> and in its site now a playground for children and a breathing
> space for older people . . . is what was the worst strip of the
> ghetto. . . . There may have been worse blocks in the city
> than those bounded by Norfolk, Suffolk, Hester, Jefferson, Rut-
> gers, East Broadway and Canal, but if there were the writer
> never knew of them.
>
> . . . . Huge malodorous "barracks" . . . fronted these streets.
> In these blocks is said to have been the most overcrowded spot
> in the world. . . . Every room at one time was a workshop as
> well as a sleeping and living apartment. . . . factories honey-
> combed them all. . . . And now? Where these festering tene-
> ments were, a broad field stretches itself . . . instead of the
> many score of tenements.[25]

Probably the single most effective housing reformer was the
tough-minded Lawrence Veiller, whose tenement house exhibit
in February 1900 effectively focused attention on slum housing.
Referring to New York as "The City of Living Death," he argued
that "the working-man is housed worse than in any other city in
the civilized world, notwithstanding the fact that he pays more
money for such accommodations than is paid elsewhere." Gov-
ernor Theodore Roosevelt was moved by this crusade to assure
Veiller's associate Robert DeForrest, "Tell me what you want
and I will help you get it." What they wanted and eventually
achieved was a curb on dumb-bell tenements and a series of
safety reforms.[26]

The downtown slum met many of the immigrants' needs so
directly that many felt little urge to go beyond their ethnic enclaves for anything. Al Smith, "Urban America's" candidate for
the Presidency in 1928, recalled that when he grew up in the
Irish Fourth Ward on the Lower East Side, he seldom ventured
above Canal Street and almost never went beyond 14th Street.*
Such provincialism was common not just for the Irish but for the

* "When Salvatore Cotello, the first Italian elected to the State Assembly
from East Harlem, left to take his seat in Albany, he had never before, since
arriving in New York as a boy, ventured beyond the borders of the city."
[Nathan Glazer and Daniel P. Moynihan, *Beyond the Melting Pot* (Cambridge, 2nd ed., 1971), 188.]

immigrants who followed them into lower Manhattan's old districts as well. This village-mindedness grew out of many antecedents but in part reflected the wide range of functions served by the community.[27]

It was not by chance, for instance, that poet-to-be Harry Roskolenko expressed his youthful rebellion against the Jewish ghetto by seeking a place with broad horizons and no boundaries. At the age of thirteen the sensitive lad charged out of the Lower East Side and ran off to sea. Nor was it coincidence that Mario Puzo saw in his vocation an avenue for escape; "I decided to escape . . . by becoming an artist, a writer. . . . I did not yet understand why these men and women were willing to settle for less than they deserved in life and think that 'less' quite a bargain." What he could not understand was the richness of the ghetto and how comforting it was for its Old World attachments.[28]

Early leaders who planned to build stable long-standing communities on the basis of these attachments would, however, fail. The concept of an ethnic colony bound together by proximate residence and Old World values was based on a static picture of the immigrant and his community. But the lock and key relationship between immigrant needs and ghetto functions was not lasting. As economic and residential opportunities expanded, reliance on the ghetto as a buffer and way-station faded. With time and economic mobility, immigrants moved toward the mainstream. Ethnic communities would persist but without the permanence of the European *shtetl* or *paese,* for in New York it was neither necessary nor usual to die in the same place where one was born.[29]

Immigration represented the quintessential residential mobility, involving the decision to sever ties to land, country, and culture in search of a better situation in a better place. But the long ocean journey which carried the immigrants to a New World was often only the first step in a process that took these up-rooted from dwelling to dwelling in quest of fresh air, better jobs, decent housing, and neighborhoods safe from disease and crime.

Landing in New York City, they came to a metropolis with a long tradition of residential fluidity. James Boardman, who visited the United States between 1829 and 1831, remarked in his book *America and the Americans* that despite "the declara-tion of the venerable Franklin . . . that 'three removes are as bad as a fire,' the inhabitants of New York are the most loco-motive people on the face of the earth." After February 1, when leases were customarily renegotiated, "it is common to see at least one-third of the houses and stores ticketed" with "To Let" signs. On the first of May, the traditional moving day, "no less than the entire city is turned topsy-turvy, thousands of persons being in the act of removal, the streets filled with carts laden with furniture, porters, servants, children, all carrying their respective movables. . . ." John Dubois, Catholic Bishop of New York, wrote to a friend in 1835, "at the first of May, half of the inhabitants of the city moved from one district of the city to another." [30]

Irish and German immigrants who settled in New York City in this period seldom remained stationary for long. A study by Jay Dolan traced a sample of these Old Immigrants between 1850 and 1875, and found that over 55 per cent left the city. Among those who persisted in the city, 71 per cent of the Irish and 75 per cent of the Germans changed addresses. A large seg-ment of this mobile group changed residences at least twice in the twenty-five-year period. [31]

The New Immigrants who succeeded the Irish and Germans in the downtown neighborhoods in the 1880s proved even more mobile. At first they piled into the Lower East Side but this old area was not sufficiently large or attractive to contain them. Many Italians and Jews, like the Old Immigrants who preceded them, decided to move west, or to other less crowded cities and towns. This tendency to use New York as a temporary stop-off point produced high rates of out-mobility from the city.

Those who remained behind to settle in Manhattan did not linger at any one address. Where they moved depended on the transportation system and the availability of compatible job opportunities. Thus, at first they largely restricted their settlement to the central business district, but after the Brooklyn Bridge and then the other connecting spans were built and rapid transit opened yet other areas, they expanded their locus of settlement.

"Within the year," Trow's *Directory for New York City* reported in 1881, "there have been more changes in the homes of people than ever before recorded. . . . It has been from poorer ones to better ones." The congested slums, infested with "bucket shops," decrepit housing, and new but inappropriate dumb-bells, were the source of many of those seeking newer residences in better circumstances.[32]

It is not possible to calculate precisely how many ghetto dwellers changed address. But by using the available city directories it is possible to trace the residential patterns of those immigrants canvassed by the *New York Directory*. Unfortunately, by its own account the directory was not as comprehensive as one might wish.

> None but those who have tried it can form an idea of the trouble and annoyance experienced in obtaining the requisite information from our mixed and foreign population. In many instances visions of the sheriff haunt the reluctant householder and information is either absolutely denied or . . . willfully misleading. There are certain persons who are unwilling to have their names appear in the Directory . . . because they wish to avoid jury duty or payment of taxes on personal property. Even in the uptown fashionable districts the canvassers had no easy task owing on the one hand to the sublime indifference of the wealthy residents and on the other to the gross stupidity of their servants.[33]

Although the data drawn from directory traces must be taken with proper skepticism, such information is useful as a guide to residential turnover. Thus, of 974 Omaha residents sampled in 1880, 60 per cent are reported to have left the city by 1891. Another study of 692 Atlanta residents reveals that over 55 per cent left the city between 1870 and 1880 (the figure for immigrants is even higher). Of all Newburyport laborers who were traced over three separate decades, 1850–1860, 1860–1870, and 1870–1880, considerably more than half disappeared from city rolls. This same procedure produces staggering out-mobility rates for New York City. Of 449 Italian families sampled in 1880, only 8 per cent of the household heads could be located a decade later. For Jews the rate of persistence among 531 families was 33 per cent.[34]

Despite the directory's shortcomings, these figures are revealing. There is no reason in the present case to assume that the directory's exclusionary bias worked differently among the slum dwelling non-English-speaking Jews than among the slum dwelling non-English-speaking Italians. Whatever the objective rate of New York City persistence for the New Immigrants the ratio of persistence of 1 : 4 between Italians and Jews is probably essentially accurate.

The low levels of persistence are not surprising. As the major port of entry for New Immigrants it was natural that New York should be the city with the largest out-mobility rates. Of Italian arrivals to the United States in 1900, no less than 97 per cent landed at New York, but only 55 per cent of the total gave New York State as their destination. The differential persistence between Italians and Jews is also understandable in view of the greater transiency among Italians.[35]

Clearly the conventional picture of stagnant Italians bound to their "turf" by a strong village-mindedness is not accurate. The search for jobs took Italians to work sites across the nation and high repatriation rates carried many back to Europe, undercutting the kind of neighborhood stability that has been taken as a characteristic of Italians. Between 1880 and 1890 Italians set down roots less frequently than Jews. Consequently it took them longer to build the sophisticated community infrastructure that characterized Jewish areas.[36]

The original 1880 sample was augmented to provide a significant sample of Italians who could be located in the 1890 Directory. Then both groups were traced for residential change, and the results are presented in Table 17. It shows that for those *who remained in New York City*, a larger proportion of Italians persisted at the same address than Jews. That did not, however, mean that New York Jews left the ghetto behind at a quicker pace than their Italian neighbors. A comparison between the two in-

TABLE 17 RESIDENTIAL TRACE OF ITALIAN
AND RUSSIAN JEWISH HEADS OF HOUSEHOLD,
MANHATTAN, BY PER CENT, 1880–1890

Location in 1890	Italian	Jewish
No Change	26.2	17.2
Below 14th Street	52.4	65.5
14–41	8.8	4.0
42–71	5.5	4.0
72–99	1.4	5.2
Above 100th Street	3.4	2.9
Other	2.1	1.2
Total	145	174

Source: Sample data from 1880 Census Traced in Trow's *Directory* for Manhattan, 1890.

dicates that while 79 per cent of all Italians were traced to addresses below Fourteenth Street, 83 per cent of the Jews remained in this area. Thus, four of five New Immigrants who lived in lower Manhattan in 1880 *and persisted in the city until 1890* could be found within a one-mile radius of City Hall a decade later. Familiar for their institutions and still the major source of industrial and commercial jobs, the downtown neighborhoods continued to hold a tight grip on their immigrant constituents.[37]

But, as the figures suggest, the vast majority of New Immigrants did not remain in New York City. Many moved inland to smaller cities and towns. Others, however, remained in the metropolitan area, escaping the tracing net by a short move to Brooklyn, which was still known as "Manhattan's bedroom." Between 1880 and 1890 the Brooklyn population rose 40 per cent to 840,000, easily outpacing Manhattan's 24 per cent rate of expansion. The New Immigrant increment in Manhattan grew by a factor of 4.4 for Italians and 6.0 for Russians while in Brooklyn both colonies multiplied tenfold over the decade.[38]

David McCullough overstates the case when he argues that *The Great Bridge* "put Brooklyn on the map," but undeniably the Brooklyn Bridge did play an important role. Embodying the aspirations of assorted boosters, land developers, businessmen, prophets of a Greater New York, and urban reformers, the bridge was meant to dissolve congestion on lower Manhattan by directing settlement toward Brooklyn. Supported by two massive towers and leading directly from the center of the immigrant sector on the Lower East Side to Brooklyn its suggestion of escape to better conditions was obvious.

After opening in 1883 the bridge achieved many of the original goals; it stimulated growth, raised property values, and opened the other side of the East River to intensive immigrant settlement. Bridge trains began running in September (the bridge opened in May) and within a year carried 37,000 passengers daily, almost matching the work of the full ferry fleet before the bridge was opened. With the completion of the Brooklyn Elevated to Fulton Ferry in 1885, the trains handled nearly 20 million passengers annually, and before the close of the decade this figure—largely composed of people commuting from homes in Brooklyn to jobs in Manhattan—topped 30 million. By 1890, Brooklyn had more homes than Manhattan.[39]

Residential patterns in rapidly industrializing Brooklyn resembled the Manhattan model. Each of the groups carved out its own neighborhood, generally in run-down tenement areas which were previously inhabited by Old Immigrants. Italians followed the Irish, and Jews settled in German areas. And as in Manhattan the Jews were more tightly concentrated. In 1890 considerably more than half of Brooklyn's Russian Jews could be counted in four wards, while the four wards with heaviest Italian concentrations held only 42 per cent of Brooklyn's Italian population.[40]

The early Italian colonies developed in Red Hook and Williamsburg. In both cases a long line of waterfront docks and warehouses was supplemented by a sizable factory district, providing Italians with the job opportunities they sought. Living conditions in these old neighborhoods were often primitive. Some idea of the conditions they inherited can be gained from this *New York Times* description of Irish Red Hook in 1866:

> There are certain wards . . . in Brooklyn where . . . dirt and filth and poverty reign triumphant—quarters which in misery, squalor and wretchedness, in noisome lanes, streets plastered with offal and houses dirty . . . equal the lowest quarters of New York. . . . Here homeless and vagabond children, ragged and dirty, wander about; . . . and here accumulate all the causes of pestilence and disease; decaying garbage, dead animals, filthy and unclean privies . . . and houses badly arranged for ventilation.[41]

The German Sixteenth Ward in Williamsburgh was only slightly better. Over 30,000 foreign-born Germans lived in this dense ward which also housed the largest number of east Europeans in Brooklyn. "Scores of tenements," wrote the *New York Tribune,* "contain little manufacturing industries, . . . that require deft fingers and no implements besides a needle and a sewing machine. In addition there are scattered all over the district scores of manufacturers employing many men, women and children." This environment spawned the conventional Jewish occupational profile dominated by craftsman with a significant element in white-collar pursuits. A larger fraction than usual, however, worked at common labor.[42]

Breaking with the general pattern of residential succession

(as had the Italians in Harlem), east European Jews also put in their claims to a relatively new neighborhood at the western end of Brooklyn. In 1886 the small village of Brownsville in the 26th Ward had a population of 4,000 in one- and two-family frame houses. To the east of Rockaway Avenue almost all of Brownsville was farmland, and one could watch farmers plow their fields while orchards blossomed with fruit trees. The streets were unpaved and without sewers or street lights. This quiet rural area was a far cry from Williamsburgh or lower Manhattan, yet within a generation it competed with the Lower East Side as the center of American Jewry. This growth lay in the plans of developers who glimpsed attractive returns on the strength of the steam and elevated railroads which reached the area.[43]

In 1886 Aaron Kaplan, an East Side real estate agent, and his partner Samuel Phillips invested $1,000 in seven lots in Brownsville. The following year they added 13 more lots for $2,400 dollars, paying $300 down and securing a mortgage for the remainder. After an East Side tailor, Isidore Krupitsky, established a clothing factory with six machines in his Brownsville home, Kaplan saw his opportunities and persuaded Elias Kaplan (no relation) to bring his clothing factory to the area. For slightly more than $5,000 the industrialist was promised a two-family residence, a separate cottage, and a two-story shop. For his workers, the developers planned a row of frame houses which would sell for $1,000, $100 down and installments of $10 a month.[44]

Others quickly followed this vanguard, building a solid Jewish community east of Rockaway Avenue. In 1890 the census reported 784 Russsians and Poles, less than 3 per cent of the ward. Two years later the figure shot up to 4,000. By 1896, the *New York Tribune* dismissed Brownsville as "a land of sweatshops and whirring sewing machines, of strange Russian baths, of innumerable dirty and tiny shops, of cows which are milked directly into the pitchers and pails of customers at eventide, of

anarchists, of Jew dancing schools and of a peasant market." *
In short, except for the rural aspect, it already resembled the
Lower East Side community.[45]

The large number of Jews who moved to Brownsville were
not ready to leave their traditions behind, only the slum housing and its fetid environment. They established the synagogues,
settlement houses, and local institutions that are generally associated with areas of primary settlement. Rather than escaping
the ghetto they brought much of it with them. "Brownsville was
a completely Jewish world," Alter Landesman writes in his study
of the Brownsville community, "it came closest to the life of the
European *shtetl* most of them had known. The language in the
home was Yiddish, the newspapers that came into the home were
Yiddish and the store signs were in Yiddish." And the clothing
industry, even more than in Manhattan, dominated the occupational horizon with 76 per cent of the Jewish working population
in 1892 doing skilled work, generally as tailors, while most of the
rest of Brownsville's Jews wore white collars.[46]

A second residential trace of Manhattan's New Immigrants between 1905 and 1915 indicates a significant change in patterns
of dispersion. Between 1880 and 1890 fully 92 per cent of all
Italians disappeared from New York rolls. A generation later,
despite soaring repatriation, the rate of persistence within the
city more than tripled to 28 per cent. Better off than ever before,
many Italians rejected lonely railroad and construction jobs across
the continent in favor of New York's opportunities.

* *The Brooklyn Eagle* in 1898 wrote: "The village was at one time a very
desirable place for residence . . . but since the annexation, it has very
much deteriorated by the settling of a low class of Hebrews who have dis-
figured many of the dwellings by converting them into small business
places." [Alter Landesman, *Brownsville* (New York, 1969), 58.]

Another set of statistics illustrates one cause of this greater persistence. In the earlier trace 79 per cent of all Italians who remained in New York still lived below Fourteenth Street after a decade. Between 1905 and 1915, however, residential alternatives expanded and much fewer Italians restricted themselves to the downtown ghettos. Consequently 42 per cent of the traceable 1905 sample—a high figure, but nonetheless 37 per cent less than the earlier one—lived at downtown addresses in 1915.

Among Jews the proportion who remained in the city appreciated slightly to 36 per cent. But the tendency to leave the ghetto even outpaced the Italian example. In the 1880–1890 case 83 per cent of the Jews located in 1890 directories gave downtown addresses. The vast majority as yet found few uptown areas hospitable. But in the subsequent analysis, two-thirds of a 1905 sample had moved *outside* the downtown district by 1915.

New uptown areas beckoned the New Immigrants, causing many to disperse from the city core and, as the concomitant increases in city persistence imply, also having the effect of keeping many more of these newcomers in the city. This was made possible by an expanding transportation system, new housing, and the spread of commerce and industry away from the downtown centers.

As early as 1872, Charles McCabe argued, "Did the city possess some means of rapid transit between its upper and lower extremities. . . . There can be no doubt that the tenement sections would soon be thinned out." Reformer Charles Loring Brace predicted that such a system would permit workers to settle in "pleasant healthy suburban villages" which would provide children and adults with a healthful and moral environment.[47]

By 1881 New York had its first elevated transit system stretching from the Battery to Harlem.* In apparent confirmation of

* The trip from Battery to Harlem was scheduled to take only 40 minutes, but the elevated was not an unmixed blessing. "The dropping of oil, grease, water, coals, scraps of iron, tools and other liquid or solid substances . . . is

the rapid transit concept, rows of new houses and apartments quickly went up, straddling the routes. Soon cable cars and then electrically powered vehicles were introduced and ridership continued to grow. By 1890 New Yorkers averaged over 270 rides annually for each city dweller.[48]

Early plans for a subway had been dismissed as too costly, but by 1904 the Interborough Rapid Transit Line ran a tunnel from City Hall Park to 145th Street. A line connecting Brooklyn and Manhattan was inaugurated the following year. This expanding network opened new districts for settlement and helped distribute a large number of people uptown and in the surrounding boroughs.[49]

Such developments permitted businesses to move out of the downtown area, which was growing terribly expensive. Precisely because immigrants flocked to these areas and tenements were profitable, industry and commerce had to compete with landlords for real estate, pushing land values steadily upward. In 1910 an average acre of Manhattan property was valued at $222,526; below Fourteenth Street, however, an acre was worth $326,403. Large factories which outgrew crowded and costly downtown properties moved either a portion or all of their work elsewhere, maintaining only a sales office or a showroom downtown. This was especially true of the clothing industry, which dispersed from lower Manhattan into new lofts in the Brownsville and Wallabout areas of Brooklyn. Other businesses including sugar, meat, baking, confection, coffee, silk, tobacco, knit goods, fur, millinery, hat, cap, boot, shoe, jewelry, and produce also spread uptown from the central business district.[50]

Despite these trends, which produced new business centers around the city, the central business district continued to be the most significant source of manual occupations. The warehouses, docks, and factories that ringed this area produced many blue-

a source of . . . annoyance, damage, and even, . . . danger." [Robert C. Brooks, "History of Street and Rapid Transit Railways of New York City," (doctoral dissertation, Cornell, 1903), 164–77.]

collar opportunities. In 1906, 67 per cent of all factory jobs in the city were concentrated below Fourteenth Street. "Little Italy" in the Sixth A.D. accounted for 9.1 per cent of the city's industrial occupations on less than 1 per cent of its acreage.[51]

And jobs determined residence. Edward E. Pratt's 1907 study of over 10,000 industrial workers in Manhattan found that the tendency to cluster around the downtown area varied inversely with wages and directly with hours of work. Those immigrants who had to walk to their jobs and toiled long hours had little choice but to live in the vicinity. Only 13 per cent of workers with an eight-hour day lived below Fourteenth Street, as compared with 48 per cent of those who labored over nine and one-half hours a day.[52]

This explains the tendency among Italians to remain in the downtown area longer than the Jews. Since more Italians held low-paying positions, more Italians than Jews walked to work— 55 per cent versus 44 per cent—and more Italians traced short journey-to-work patterns (49 per cent of all Italian workers lived within twenty minutes of their factories; for Russian Jews the figure was 40 per cent). Jews obviously did not escape these pressures. In busy periods the clothing industry demanded 70- and even 80-hour work weeks. Nonetheless the Jewish population on the Lower East Side began to decline by 1910, but the Italian portion of the total population in the area grew from 5.8 per cent in 1910 to 8.4 per cent in 1920. Only after 1930 did this trend abate.[53]

Nonoccupational considerations also helped rivet Italians to their homes and neighborhoods more tightly than the Jews. Herbert Gans has described the dominating influence of the peer-group society among American Italians and its effect on in-dividual decision-making. Where job requirements did not in-terfere, Italians often preferred to keep their ties with the com-munity and sacrificed newer neighborhoods as a tradeoff for the amenities of "Little Italy." * Walter Firey, who studied Boston's

* Gans found that West End Italians did not generally leave the area in-dividually, waiting for an entire group move. Facing the redevelopment of

North End Italians, likewise emphasized the influence of social factors in explaining neighborhood persistence.[54]

Moreover, many Italians put off moving to new neighborhoods until they could buy a house surrounded by land. Edward Corsi, who came to the United States as a child and later was appointed Commissioner of Immigration by President Franklin Roosevelt, recalled how the Harlem tenement his family occupied in 1907 put his newly emigrated mother into a deep depression. She craved land, a house, and quiet. This despondency never wore off, and after a while she just got up, left her family, and went back to the land she remembered. This was not an isolated sentiment. "One of the chief objectives of the Italian in this country," Phyllis Williams has concluded, "is to own his own home. He lives under the most cramped and sordid conditions to save the money necessary." And Chicago social worker Sophonisba P. Breckinridge noted that the purchase of housing was very important to Italians who "bend every energy to this end." While successful New York Jews were said to move to Lexington Avenue, the Industrial Commission wrote of the Italians: "The more ambitious and successful among them move to the suburbs and become *property owners* in Long Island City, Flushing, Corona, Astoria, etc." [55]

Obviously many Italians in the slums knew that a house surrounded by property was beyond immediate possibility, especially if they had to live close to the factory district. Home ownership was not common in Manhattan. But many of them did put off moving to save money for the day when they could settle in one of the other boroughs and realize their dreams. In a survey of pensioned clothing workers, Leo Grebler found that 20 per cent of the Italians said they moved out of the ghetto to buy a house; only 9 per cent of the Jews gave the same reason. This differential preoccupation with home ownership meant that many

the West End and a forced relocation, one Italian sadly exclaimed: "I wish the whole world would end tonight! I'm going to be lost without the West End. Where the hell can I go?" [Herbert Gans, *The Urban Villagers* (New York, 1962), 290.]

of those Italians who did not return to Italy or leave the city in search of other opportunities would often rather delay moving out of the slums until they could afford to buy a house, while fewer Jews had these ambitions and therefore moved more readily.[56]

For some Jews, leaving the ghetto became a compulsion. Louis Wirth's famous study of Chicago, *The Ghetto*, found that many Jews sought to leave the ghetto image behind and hoped to achieve this by moving to more "American" neighborhoods. Thus the characteristics which made the ghetto a comfortable way station for the newly settled Jew rendered it offensive to the *arriviste*. For him it was a handicap, particularly if he had no deep regard for Old World traditions and sought to assimilate. This was especially true of those Jews who sought white-collar careers at a time when image and conformity to conventions in dress, speech, and comportment were important. Gilbert Osofsky has written that for some Harlem Jews the mere mention of their former residence on the Lower East Side provoked painful embarrassment.[57]

Other Jews sought to follow the clothing industry, which was moving to the Wallabout, Williamsburgh, and Brownsville sections of Brooklyn. Under way by 1900, this trend gathered momentum in the aftermath of the Triangle Fire of 1911, which resulted in stricter factory safety laws. Union and city officials applied pressure for the enforcement of these laws and the aging downtown lofts simply could not pass muster. The enforcement of Tenement Laws also brought the decline of homework. Between 1900 and 1915 the number of licensed homeworkers dropped from 21,000 to 5,700.

But above all, Jews moved in order to escape poor conditions and secure better housing. In the Grebler survey of clothing workers, respondents were asked to describe their reasons for moving from the Lower East Side. Most of the Jews played the same theme:

> . . . to get away from the congestion, filth and lack of open space.

> I lived on the East Side all those years . . . because my earn-
> ings were too small to afford higher rental. As soon as my chil-
> dren started to work I looked for an apartment with at least
> the toilet in the apartment. . . .

> . . . to acquire a higher grade of living so our children could
> grow up in better conditions than we did.[58]

The variations in sentiment and outlook between Italians and
Jews help explain some of the differences in their patterns of
residential movement. These differences should not, however, obscure the fact that large numbers in both groups were moving
out of the downtown area. In the earlier period between 1880
and 1890, 80 per cent of the New Immigrants who remained in
Manhattan clung to the downtown region. One generation later
this was no longer true.

TABLE 18 RESIDENTIAL TRACE OF ITALIAN AND RUSSIAN
JEWISH HEADS OF HOUSEHOLD AND OFFSPRING,
MANHATTAN, BY PER CENT, 1905–1915

| Location in 1915 | Italian | | Jewish | |
	Head of Household	Offspring	Head of Household	Offspring
No Change	13.4	12.1	5.4	3.7
Below 14th Street	34.4	36.4	28.1	20.1
14–41	7.0	6.5	1.7	3.0
42–71	4.3	3.7	2.5	1.8
72–99	4.8	4.7	5.8	9.1
Above 100th Street	23.6	28.0	28.1	28.7
Bronx	6.4	5.6	21.1	23.2
Other	6.0	2.8	7.4	10.3
Total	186	107	242	164

Source: Sample data from 1905 State Census for New York County, traced
in 1915 *Directory of Manhattan and the Bronx*.

Table 18 provides some clues about where this movement led.
Unfortunately the great difference in reliability between the
Manhattan and Brooklyn directories, and the fact that the latter
ceased publication in 1913, limited the tracing of Manhattan's

1905 cohort to the 1915 *Directory* for Manhattan and the Bronx. Within these limits (and those imposed by the attrition of the sample in the tracing process) the table shows that 16 per cent of the Italians moved to non-Italian sections between 14th and 99th Streets. However, less than half of this number originally lived in lower Manhattan. The percentage of downtown Jews moving into this same area was 8 per cent, seemingly too slight a base to support the United States Industrial Commission's assumption that "from Hester Street to Lexington Avenue is a journey of about ten years. . . ."[59]

The road out of the ghetto, if one wanted to stay in Manhattan and the Bronx, led all the way uptown to Harlem and beyond. Thus 20 per cent of the downtown Jews moved to Harlem, prompting the longer-settled Germans to leave the area, although some stood fast, putting their finger in the dike with such signs as *"keine Juden und kein Hunde,"* on their apartment houses. Another 17 per cent moved even further uptown to the Bronx.

Harlem also continued to attract Italians, who had established a "Little Italy" there as early as 1880. Only 3 per cent, however, chose to settle in the Bronx.[60]

As Table 18 demonstrates, Italian offspring matched the residential patterns of their parents fairly closely, with over 40 per cent located at lower Manhattan addresses in 1915. Indeed 12 per cent of the younger generation who could be traced in 1915 lived at the same address they shared with their parents a decade earlier. This ability to keep the second generation in the neighborhood was partly responsible for keeping the Italian population on the Lower East Side growing into the twenties. Conversely the flight of Jewish offspring from the ghetto, apparent from Table 18, helped set the Jewish population there on a declining course earlier.

Many of the immigrants who could not be located in 1915 and therefore are not accounted for in the table were nonetheless not far away. The trend of immigrant settlement was shifting to Brooklyn and other boroughs. In 1900, 71 per cent of New York

City's foreign-born Italian population (145,433) resided in Manhattan and the Bronx; only one-fourth settled in Brooklyn. One decade later Brooklyn's share moved up to 30 per cent, and by 1920 it stood at 35 per cent. Manhattan's proportion by this time had declined to less than half (see Table 19).

TABLE 19 PERCENTAGE OF ITALIAN AND RUSSIAN POPULATION IN THE BOROUGHS OF NEW YORK CITY, 1900–1920

	Italians			Russians [**]		
	1900	1910	1920	1900	1910	1920
Manhattan	71.4 [*]	58.6	47.2	81.7 [*]	58.9	40.4
Brooklyn	25.6	29.5	35.3	17.6	33.2	39.5
Bronx	[*]	7.4	10.1	[*]	5.7	18.2
Queens	2.1	3.3	5.1	.4	1.7	1.6
Richmond	1.0	1.3	2.2	.3	.5	.3
Total Number	145,433	340,765	390,832	178,568	484,189	479,797

[*] In 1900 Manhattan and Bronx data were not given separately as The Bronx did not become a separate county until 1904.
[**] Data for Russians in 1900 include Russian Poles.
Source: Federal Census for 1900, 1910, and 1920.

The shift in Jewish settlement was even more striking. From 82 per cent in 1900, the percentage of Russians living in Manhattan skidded 42 points to 40 percent in 1920, while Brooklyn's share climbed correspondingly from 18 to 40 per cent. The Bronx in 1920 held 18 per cent of the Russian Jewish population, a larger share than lived in Brooklyn in 1900.

As early as 1905, newly landed immigrants were bypassing Manhattan for Brooklyn. A sample of immigrant Italians and Jews discloses that 15 per cent of Italians living in Manhattan were recent newcomers with less than three years in the United States. The percentage of fresh settlers in Brooklyn was only slightly lower at 13 per cent. Clearly the functions that had been served exclusively by the downtown colonies in 1880 were now available elsewhere. As immigrants moved into Brooklyn the rate of growth of its industrial work force comfortably outdistanced that of Manhattan.

In fact, a comparison of occupational distributions for both boroughs in 1905 indicates that Italians and Jews in Brooklyn were more successful, with a larger white-collar class. A close look at these figures reveals, however, that this upper class was largely made up of longer settled immigrants who probably achieved their high status in Manhattan and then moved out. Thus Brooklyn's larger white-collar class did not indicate that New Immigrants were more successful in Brooklyn so much as it suggested that more successful immigrants resided in Brooklyn.

In his famous article on "Population Succession in Chicago: 1898–1930," Paul Frederick Cressey proposed a general scheme for explaining the process of immigrant dispersion:

> Immigrant stocks follow a regular sequence of settlement in successive areas of increasing stability and status. This pattern of distribution represents the ecological setting within which the assimilation of the foreign population takes place. An immigrant group on its arrival settles in a compact colony in a low-rent industrial area usually located in the transitional zone near the center of the city. If the group is of large size several different areas of initial settlement may develop in various industrial sections. These congested areas of first settlement are characterized by the perpetuation of many European cultural traits. After some years of residence in such an area, the group, as it improves its economic and social standing, moves outward to some more desirable residential district, creating an area of second settlement. In such an area the group is not so closely concentrated physically, there is less cultural solidarity, and more American standards of living are adopted.[61]

This analysis and the set of principles espoused by the Chicago school of urban sociologists have set the tone for subsequent discussions of immigrant settlement.

More recent examinations of immigrant settlement patterns question some aspects of this neat outline. Howard Chudacoff argues that "The Omaha experience revises Paul Frederick Cressey's model," because no mass collection of any single "nationality developed in the core, and those small clusters that did form underwent rapid turnover." A new study of Chicago by Humbert Nelli also questions the extent of immigrant concentration and tacks on a list of specific qualifications to Cressey's general theory of population succession.[62]

The New York experience resembles the Cressey model to a limited extent. Immigrants settled in dense ethnic communities around the industrial core, (rents, however, were not low). Ward data may show a variety of nationalities in any given district, but a look at the manuscript census demonstrates that these different nationalities were not randomly mixed. They formed definite ethnic enclaves, unlike the Omaha case. Thus, for example, in 1905, Election District Eight in the Fourth Assembly District was all Jewish except for one block in the Pike Slip area.[63]

It did not take the New Immigrants long to establish other colonies far from the industrial core. Outlying districts away from the "transitional zone," like Harlem and Brownsville, grew almost from the start of the new influx. These neighborhoods lacked any significant industrial capacity and should probably be considered "areas of secondary settlement" according to the Cressey design. Such areas therefore should show different social, economic, and cultural characteristics from the "primary area." The process of Americanization should be further along and residents should be longer settled with better jobs. That was not the case in Brownsville, Harlem, or many of the subsequently settled immigrant communities.

The problem with Cressey's model is that he presented immigrant settlement as a process of development from the core to other areas. Thus, he ignored much of the movement within the ghetto that other investigators did notice. "Hardly two months are they in the same room," Lillian Betts wrote in 1905. "They can move as silently as Arabs, a residence of one year for a[n

Italian] tenant is remarkable." But even more significantly he overlooked the great amount of out-mobility among the unsuccessful. His analysis made it seem that immigrants, once settled, stay in the primary areas until success permits them to infiltrate more desirable regions. Stephan Thernstrom, Clyde Griffin, and others have shown that residential mobility was often more typical of the unskilled than the other classes. They formed a "floating proletariat" and roamed American cities in search of jobs. The New York data confirm this thesis. In four separate sample traces —New York, 1880–1890, Brooklyn 1892–1902, Manhattan 1905–1915, and Brooklyn 1905–1913—it was the white-collar class which persisted in the city in higher proportion than the blue-collar class, which moved out in large numbers.[64]

The Cressey model, based on looking at immigrant communities as static settlements wherein all immigrants of a specific nationality settle together at one time, is too simple. In New York the process was far more complex. Newly settled immigrants did not invariably cluster around the central business district in downtown Manhattan. They did in the 1880s, when transportation, housing, and industry conspired to pull them there. And when the transportation system, with its great bridges as the centerpiece, opened new routes, immigrants and industry fanned out to newer neighborhoods.

But at the same time that these developments were taking place, new settlers continued to arrive. And they, with their immigrant culture intact, often ignored the Lower East Side, filing into these other districts. They did not come to fresher neighborhoods in Harlem or Brownsville by way of dispersal from the industrial core, nor had they assimilated or climbed the occupational ladder; they were as "green" as those immigrants who had previously settled downtown, but nonetheless they settled in "secondary settlements." These neighborhoods were often no further along the road to assimilation and occupational progress than the Lower East Side, where schools and settlement houses abounded.

Focusing on the ethnic group as a distinct unit, Cressey lost sight of the fact that this unit was not at any time a static, fully formed group. It was constantly losing people to other cities and absorbing large increments of Old World newcomers. The picture then was far more dynamic and variegated than Cressey shows. Areas of "secondary settlement" constantly attracted not inconsiderable numbers of recent immigrants, who brought their outlook and made their demands in a "primary settlement" way. Thus, in discussing the Russian Jews, Cressey notes that they dispersed from the core more than "any other group of recent immigrants," but were nevertheless "concentrated in rather definite settlements." He explains this apparent deviation by referring to the "bonds of a common religion and culture and the external prejudice of gentile culture." If the New York case is any indication, he ignored the major cause: a steady influx of newly arriving Jews who settled in these newer areas.[65]

On the basis of Census Tract data Cressey concluded that Italians "were even more compact and immobile than the Poles." Students of urban mobility are, by now, familiar with the ecological distortion introduced by relying on gross figures like those given for Census Tracts. Thus, Humbert Nelli disputes Cressey's findings because "a district might contain a sizeable Italian element over a period of years but within that group there operated a continual turnover of individual residents." The apparently high rates of Italian turnover for New York support these arguments. Italians moved out of the city at a very rapid pace, indicating much residential mobility. It is true that even after the Jewish population on the Lower East Side began to decline, the Italian community continued to grow. But this growth derived from the great number of newly arriving Italians who flocked towards the industrial center. Moreover, Census Tract data for the Lower East Side show that Italians were less clustered than the Jews in both 1910 and 1920, which by Cressey's criteria indicate greater dispersion from the core.[66]

Cressey's colleagues Robert E. Park and Ernest W. Burgess were concerned about this great flux that typified American cities.

Mobility, they feared, "leads to change and therefore to loss of continuity"; it destroyed contacts with church, neighbors, and local institutions. In their opinion, "the total effects of forces like . . . mobility . . . seem to be subversive and disorganizing." Jacob Riis also feared the implications of constant movement, and declared that unless this constant flow out of established communities closed, "we perish." [67]

Notwithstanding such theoretical reservations, New York's immigrants welcomed the opportunity to escape their neighborhoods, leaving others to express qualms and weigh the cosmic implications. Indeed, as mobility within the city increased and new areas opened to the immigrants, a greater percentage remained in the city. Flexibility added to rather than detracted from stability.

VII

The New York Experience

When we possess rather detailed knowledge about . . . New-buryport, Massachusetts, in the late nineteenth century but lack comparable observations about . . . New York City, it is risky to generalize. . . .

> Stephan Thernstrom,
> "Reflections on the New
> Urban History"

Americans have long celebrated their nation as a land of unique opportunity for all men. Few other societies place such emphasis on the qualities of self-made men or the significance of social mobility. So important was this idea of a distinctive social fluidity that very early in American history it took an important place in the national ideology. Writing in 1782, the French immigrant Michel Guillaume St. Jean de Crèvecœur explained his adopted country's uniqueness by pointing to the even-handed opportunity it offered to all comers, winning them away from the Old World and its ways.

> What attachment can a poor European emigrant have for a country where he had nothing? The knowledge of the language, the love of a few kindred as poor as himself, were the only cords that tied him: his country is now the country which gives him land, bread, protection, and consequence: *Ubi panis ibi patria* is the motto of all immigrants. . . .
> . . . Here the rewards of his industry follow with equal steps the progress of his labor, his labor is founded on the basis of nature, *self interest;* can it want a stronger allurement? Wives and children, who before in vain demanded a morsel of bread, now, fat and frolicsome, gladly help their father to clear those

fields whence exuberant crops are to arise and to feed and to clothe them all. . . . The American is a new man. . . . From involuntary idleness, servile dependence, penury, and useless labor he had passed to toils of a very different nature, rewarded by ample subsistance—This is an American. . . .

. . . After a foreigner from any part of Europe is arrived, and become a citizen; let him devoutly listen to the voice of our great parent, which says to him, "Welcome to my shores. . . . If thou wilt work I have bread for thee: If thou wilt be honest, sober, and industrious, I have greater reward to confer. . . . Go thou, and work and till; thou shalt prosper, provided thou be just, grateful and industrious.[1]

Those who accepted this bright picture have been assailed as too complacent, too willing to accept abstractions instead of spending the time and effort to investigate the issue rigorously. Thus Robert Foerster complained that Americans dismissed gritty questions on mobility by reasoning simply that "it is Eldorado that lures and is found." Concluding his own brilliant survey of Italian settlement in America, Foerster put the question directly: "Have they profited by coming? Has the game for them been worth the candle?"[2]

His response was far less sanguine than Crèvecœur's. He reported pessimistically in 1919 that Italians were scarcely better off than their predecessors had been twenty-five years earlier. Foerster dismissed such items as the $85,000,000 in savings shipped back to Italy in a single year with this basic lesson in statistics: "Wherever Croesus lives, though the mass go naked, the average wealth, strictly speaking, is high." Others may point to the Delmonicos, Gianninis, and DiGiorgios who achieved enormous success, but for the average Italian immigrant, however, "the pictures that cut across the years are somber."[3]

Recently other scholars have reopened this question that touches the core of American ideology, and have attempted to measure immigrant progress in the United States. The first iconoclastic reports concluded that mobility was mostly a myth "more conspicuous in American history books than in American history."

William Miller's 1949 study of Progressive Era business elites found rich native American Protestants atop the corporate structure. Their offspring, he contended, inherited the inside track on these high positions. The sons of immigrants did not glide into corporate chairs. Not more than 3 per cent of the business leaders were drawn from either immigrant or poor farm backgrounds.[4]

Stephan Thernstrom's pioneering 1964 study of *Poverty and Progress* in Newburyport, Massachusetts, focused on mobility from the bottom up and reported that the laboring class did not experience substantial occupational mobility between 1850 and 1880. Only one in ten laborers worked himself up the ladder to a skilled craft. Moreover, being foreign born handicapped Newburyport's Irish in the occupational competition. Based on his analysis, Thernstrom believed that "the barriers against moving more than one notch upwards were fairly high." America was better for them than Europe had been, and they did make slight progress, but this sober gradual mobility bore no relationship to the mesmerizing plots that spilled from Horatio Alger's confident imagination. "This was not the ladder to the stars that Horatio Alger portrayed and that later writers wistfully assumed to have been a reality in the days of Abraham Lincoln and Andrew Carnegie."[5]

Since 1964, a number of historians have quarrelled with Thernstrom's prematurely general dismissal of American mobility. They contend that the sluggish Newburyport economy was not the proper place to test the issue. Herbert Gutman's study of thirty-odd iron, locomotive, and machine manufacturers in Paterson, New Jersey, between 1830 and 1880 convinced him that the rags-to-riches theme was appropriate. "So many successful manufacturers who had begun as workers walked the streets . . . that it is not hard to believe that others . . . could be convinced by personal knowledge that 'hard work' resulted in spectacular material and social improvement."

Clyde Griffen studied "Craft and Ethnic Differences in Poughkeepsie," and also found that social fluidity in that city was suffi-

cient to confirm "the national faith that merit sooner or later was
rewarded by success." Howard Chudacoff emphasized residential
over occupational change as an indicator of social mobility in his
study of Omaha, Nebraska. Nonetheless, he concluded similarly
that "a large number of men improved their condition in a gen-
uine, though limited, way."

Humbert Nelli's recent history of Chicago's Italians treats the
issue of mobility in more conventional terms, eschewing the
quantitative methodology employed by Griffin and Chudacoff,
but he too argues that the idea of mobility was pronounced
"myth" too hastily. "Whether through legitimate business activities, criminal actions or politics, Chicago's Italians made substantial headway [by 1920] in an effective economic adjustment to
urban America."

Focusing on Southern cities, Richard Hopkins and Paul Worthman have detailed the same sort of steady progress. In Atlanta,
Georgia, Hopkins discovered greater mobility than Thernstrom
described in Newburyport and stated flatly that "the achievement of some degree of success or improvement in occupational
status was fairly common [for native and immigrant] white At-
lantans in the later nineteenth century." And the Worthman study
of Birmingham, Alabama, which analyzed a sample of 1,500 individuals uncovered "significant rates of upward occupational
mobility," and "extensive" movement from blue collar to white
collar positions among whites.[6]

More recently Thernstrom has admitted that his "early work—
on the laborers of Newburyport—was misleading in its emphasis
on the barriers to working class occupational achievement. . . .
In other communities . . . the occupational horizon was notably
more open." His study of Boston produced a more conventional
conclusion than his Newburyport analysis. "The American class
system . . . allowed substantial privilege for the privileged and
extensive opportunity for the underprivileged." Even the oft-
maligned Horatio Alger, straw man for debunking mobility stud-

ies, is resurrected as a sober social commentator. "If Horatio Alger's novels were designed to illustrate the possibility, not of rags-to-riches but of rags-to-respectability, as I [now!] take them to have been, they do not offer widely misleading estimates of the prospects open to Americans." [7]

The present study of the two largest immigrant groups in the nation's most important and most populous metropolis provides additional evidence that mobility was not restricted to a select few well-born individuals. Social mobility was both rapid and widespread even for immigrants who came from the peasant towns of southern Italy and the Russian Pale. At first they qualified only for jobs as laborers, tailors, and peddlers, but with time and effort they found in New York ample opportunities for themselves and their children.

Indeed, despite the contention by Peter Blau and Otis Duncan that "the opportunity to achieve occupational success in the course of one's career is not so good in the very large metropolis as in the city of less than one million inhabitants," New Yorkers outpaced all others in climbing the economic ladder. In fairness to these authors and their distinguished study of the *American Occupational Structure,* their conclusions are based on recent data and may well be valid for the modern period; it was not the case, however, between 1880 and 1915. The nation's major metropolis offered exceptional possibilities for progress out of the manual classes.[8]

The highest percentage of blue- to white-collar mobility in Atlanta, Omaha, or Boston for the decade between 1880 and 1890, was 22 per cent, and that was the average achievement for all citizens, natives and immigrants alike. Gotham's New Immigrants, who began the decade at the bottom of the Promised City's social order, rose out of the manual class at a rate of 37 per cent in the same decade. One might expect that New York's great flux would produce deeper valleys to match such higher peaks, but that was not the case. In Boston between 1880 and 1890, 12 per cent of the white-collar class slipped into blue-collar occupations; only 10 per cent of New York's New Immigrants suffered such a decline.[9]

For the following decade mobility statistics for Brooklyn are even more striking. Between 1892 and 1902, 57 per cent of those who could be traced graduated out of the manual division. Subsequently over the eight-year period, 1905–1913, 49 per cent made the same climb. Admittedly the directory for Brooklyn was less extensive than the one for Manhattan. But the fact that immigrant occupations (which unlike mobility were not determined from directory sources but directly from the census) were more attractive in Brooklyn suggests that the higher mobility in this borough was more than a mere artifact of the measuring device.

Manhattan data for 1905–1915 are based on stronger evidence, nonetheless the findings are not significantly different. In a comparison with other cities after 1900, New York's mobility percentage stands highest. Between 1900 and 1910, 23 per cent of Omaha's working population switched blue collars for white. The figures for such mobility in Boston, Norristown, and Los Angeles between 1910 and 1920 were 22 per cent, 16 per cent, and 8 per cent, respectively. Among Manhattan's New Immigrants, 32 per cent managed this ascent between 1905 and 1915.[10]

Mobility was not restricted to any one group, both natives and immigrants climbed the class ladder. The amplitude and frequency of such progress were, however, functions of ethnicity. Despite the fact that Italians and Jews shared important characteristics—they came to the United States in the same years, settled in the cities in about the same proportions, formed similar ethnic enclaves in downtown Manhattan, and shared the burdens of alien language and religion—Jews from eastern Europe entered the economy at a higher level than the Italians and sustained a higher rate of cross-class movement over the entire period 1880–1915.

From 1880 on, Italian immigration was drawn primarily from the peasant towns of southern Italy, dominated by single males in their working years with few industrial skills. Almost half of these immigrants were illiterate and few brought with them significant sums of money. This made it difficult for them to qualify for anything but the lowest rung of the economy, and the transient character of the group as a whole helped keep them there.

Italians emigrated largely for short-term economic motives. As the unusually high repatriation rates demonstrate, few intended to sever ties with their mother country permanently. Even those who did not go back to Europe often failed to sink roots, flitting across the country behind the *padrone* and his promises. Consequently, ambitions were geared to the short range, foreclosing careers that were based on sustained effort and piecemeal development. Moreover, the large sums of money sent back over the ocean to Europe drained risk capital from investment and enterprise. Lacking the desperation of men without bridges behind them, Italians were often ready to return home if they gathered a sufficient bankroll or if the job market slackened.

Because the New York economy was expanding its housing, building new factories, extending its transit lines, and upgrading its port facilities, the Italian newcomer was not forced to learn a craft; he could trade on his muscles and his willingness to work hard. In short, the city did not force him to equip himself beyond his peasant origins. It stood ready to use his primitive skills as they were. Consequently three of four Italian household heads in 1880 did manual labor and more than half were unskilled.

Russian Jews took a different tack. They too included a large contingent of poor and illiterate males, but they came in family groups, brought urban skills, and settled in New York with the intention of remaining. With anti-Semitism on the rise in Europe, Jews who came to the United States did not look back so fondly at the mother country. Under such conditions they thought in terms of the long range and their settlement was more stable.

Jews in Europe had been marginal men. Precluded from owning land because of their religion and prevented from building power or prestige in the established ways, they were shunted into

less desirable jobs as innkeepers, peddlers, and dealers in second-
hand clothing. But this experience, so déclassé in Europe, fit the
dominant needs of their New York environment. "Jews, who were
commercial *faute de mieux* in manorial Europe were as peripheral as the first mammals among the dinosaurs, but fortuitously
advantaged later," Miriam K. Slater has written.[11]

However much their significant concentration in tailoring may
reflect previous experience, it was also directly related to the
emergence of New York City as the world's center of clothing
production. Their skills were very specific. Lacking American
education and money, they could not compete at the white-collar
level. They also would not compete for unskilled jobs. "The emigrants of other faiths coming here . . . are . . . able bodied
laborers who are willing to live on almost any kind of food, and
working on railroads, canals, and the like must endure considerable exposure and fatigue. To send our people to labor in that
way," a representative of the Russian Relief Fund in New York
explained to officials of the Alliance Israelite Universelle in 1881,
"would be cruel and *futile*." For Russian Jews to succeed there
had to be a clothing industry and the opportunity to peddle.
Their unique good fortune in New York derived from the fact
that the city provided both, permitting them to enter the economy at its middle rungs.[12]

By 1905, both groups upgraded their occupational patterns reflecting in part New York's own development, and in part their
own expanded connections and control. Italians entered the
needle trades and took work on the docks, displacing the Jews
and the Irish. Gradually they cut their heavy reliance on unskilled labor, avoiding such stigmatized pursuits as rag picking
and organ grinding. But they could not catch up to the Jews, who
continued to move one step ahead. Close to 45 per cent of the
Jewish immigrants claimed white-collar positions, including a
good number of professionals, manufacturers, retailers, investors,
and office workers.

Ethnic differences proved equally important for mobility. Both

Italians and Jews found the New York economy fluid and open, but Jews moved upwards more quickly and more often. This is apparent by comparing four separate cohorts, differentiated by length of residence in the United States. Italians and Jews showed enhanced occupation profiles as the number of years spent in the country increased. Taking the longest residing cohort of significant size, those who had lived in the country between 15 and 25 years, 24 per cent of the Italians achieved white-collar status, with only 2 per cent in the upper white-collar sector. Among the Jews, 54 per cent wore white collars and a significant 15 per cent reached the upper white-collar stratum. While Italian progress proceeded along one line, shopkeeping and self-employed artisanship, the Jews took more opportunities to move into both upper and lower white-collar positions.

In a second analysis of mobility, Italians and Jews were traced over three separate decades. When these data are aggregated they show that 32 per cent of all Italians who started in blue-collar categories crossed to the upper class within a decade. Considering the Italian reputation for sluggish mobility and Robert Foerster's gloomy conclusions about the rate of their advance, such growth is surprisingly impressive, indicating that almost one-third of a largely peasant group could leave manual labor behind within a decade.

The companion statistic, however, shows that fully 21 per cent of the Italian white-collar class dropped back into blue-collar categories, demonstrating how tentative their ascent was. This flux helps explain Foerster's dismal conclusions about the Italian experience in America. Looking out at the Italian-American community in 1919 he saw that they still inhabited poor houses and occupied low-paying jobs.

But he missed the interstitial changes within that community. Moreover, he was wrong to expect that a community which continued to absorb masses of incoming peasants would not show poverty. The proper question is, was there progress over time. And the answer is, yes. If an Italian immigrant remained in the city one decade his chance of proceeding from a blue-collar job to a white-collar position was 32 per cent—not bleak by any standard.

Russian Jews left the manual class at a rate of 41 per cent, and once they achieved the upper class they did not slip down as easily as the Italians. Only 9 per cent of the white-collar class dropped back to manual labor. If we sum the two percentages as a crude index of mobility Italians register 10.4, the Jews 31.6.

What accounted for these differences? Why did the Jewish group find it easier to navigate toward the economic mainstream? Interestingly, one important explanation of differential mobility, differential fertility, favored the Italians. According to Blau and Duncan men from smaller families achieve more, and more successful men have smaller families. They quote the *capillarité sociale* theory advanced by Arsene Dumont at the turn of the century: "Just as a column of liquid has to be thin in order to rise under the force of capillarity so a family must be small in order to rise on the social scale." They further speculate that men who are more successful achieve satisfaction from their careers, while less accomplished individuals "must find other sources of social support and gratification"; hence larger families.[13]

It is suggestive to note the size of Jewish and Italian families in this sample study of 16,191 New Yorkers. Italians averaged 2.62 offspring per family between 1880 and 1905 while Jews averaged 3.21. Calvin Goldscheider has pointed out that the conventional picture of lower Jewish fertility was largely based on American-born Jews and that the foreign-born generation had larger families, but he assumed that as a consequence the immigrant generation was not economically mobile ("*In contrast* most second generation Jews were economically mobile"). The data indicate that the first generation not only had large families but were also quite mobile.[14]

This is not the place for a full discussion of the issue nor do the data, based only on those immigrant offspring still living at home, permit a full analysis. But within these restrictions certain observations are in order. Russian Jews had larger families living with them than did Italian Catholics. Furthermore, since Jews were unusually mobile it does not seem that family size increased as a consequence of the need to compensate for stunted progress. In view of these findings, it may well be that the inverted birth rate (higher occupation-lower family size) that researchers have found is due less to the higher mobility of smaller-sized families than to the social-psychological disposition of families, once they achieved the upper level, to have fewer children.

Other matters proved more significant, with more direct effects. Obviously the fact that Italians came in at the very bottom of the occupational hierarchy while Jews entered at step three was important. Jews were able to move into the employer class while Italians were still trying to move into skilled and semiskilled employment. This helped Jews in the blue-collar class as well, as one Italian unionist pointed out with some bitterness:

> In general, . . , management was constituted of Jewish capitalists, who either because of the influence of the Rabbi of the synagogue, or because they were annoyed by the too-verbal insistence of their co-religionists, revealed themselves to be less cut-throat with the latter than they were with the Italian workers who besides not being able to express themselves in English, had a little disposition toward the niggardly characteristics of Jewish cloakmakers. And the salaries that the Italians received were very inferior to those that were realized by their fellow Jewish cloakmakers, for the latter if not inferior, at least were only equal in technical capacity to the Italians. From the wage earning viewpoint the Italian element remained several steps below the Jewish cloakmakers.[15]

Moreover, Russian Jews were driven by a demon, seeking the security that had constantly eluded them in Europe. If "ruthless underconsumption" could help one become a "sweater," a contractor, or a shopkeeper, it seemed a small price to pay for self-employment. Because of their past they did not trust outsiders, whom they considered fickle and untrustworthy. They placed great emphasis on independence, on being a *balabos far sich* (one's own boss). This ambition translated into an emphasis on professional positions, shopkeeping, and manufacturing. These had been their goals in Europe, and the fact that they were more easily achieved in New York made them no less attractive.

Persecution, marginality, and alienation from the outside Christian world in Europe made of the *shtetl* a close-knit community. Rather than the family allegiances of the Italian peasant community summed up in Edward Banfield's phrase "amoral familism," the Jews possessed an ethnic consciousness and interrelationship that provided jobs, built industries, and provided ghetto capitalists with handsome returns on investments. Isaac Rubinow long ago pointed out that "almost every newly arrived Russian Jewish laborer comes into contact with a Russian Jewish employer, almost every Russian Jewish tenement dweller must pay his exorbitant rent to a Russian Jewish landlord." Among Italians it took time to build an ethnic consciousness as an American minority group; they did not bring a wider ethnic self-image with them. As Max Ascoli noted, "They became Americans before they were ever Italians." [16]

Few southern Italians had the ambition to become big businessmen or professionals. Life in the peasant towns of the *mezzogiorno* squelched such dreams with an inescapable iron reality. No matter what one dreamed, one's lot was fixed to a life of peasant poverty. For the sake of his own equilibrium, as Herbert Gans has argued, the Italian peasant restricted his aspirations. Jews, even in the ghetto, had some mobility through commerce and education, and this kept ambitions flickering. Because Italians did not see such mobility at home, they brought to New York a truncated conception of their own possibilities; an outlook that placed self-imposed limits on ambition. "Their trip across the ocean took them from rural towns to urban villages." This peasant gestalt was kept alive in their narrowly drawn village neighborhoods. As late as 1962, Italians in Boston's West End looked upon white-collar people "as not really working." [17]

Much has been made of the different values regarding education. The specific consequences of these differences are more apparent among the second generation, but they did not fail to help first-generation Jews who were more appropriately educated for industrial America than the southern Italians. Not only were their specific skills more apt but also their exposure to a labor ideology and the inclusion of a secular intelligentsia permitted them to build a labor movement. As early as 1885 a Jewish workingman's union was formed. By 1892 the United Hebrew Trades boasted 40 affiliates. Italians did not enter the labor movement in large numbers until much later.[18]

Education in the narrower sense, literacy plus specialized knowledge, became increasingly important in the age of business bureaucracy. The expansion of corporations and the wider use of the corporate form as well as the expansion of government and municipal services demanded a larger supply of lawyers, clerks, teachers, accountants, and other educated white-collar workers. Education became an economic tool rather than merely an esthetic one. Here the Jewish respect for education gave them an economic advantage. Italians, based on their experience, considered education an irrelevant prolonging of childhood. In a perverse way this argument became self-fulfilling. Without schooling, they took blue-collar jobs. For such jobs formal education *was* irrelevant . . . and costly, by postponing entry into the job market. Only when one aspired to white-collar status could the argument be drawn that education offered pragmatic benefits.

The persistence of the Italian attitude among the offspring is evident from a number of indications: The second generation's occupational similarity with their elders, especially in the concentration of Italian sons in unskilled jobs; the persistence of Italian offspring in first-generation neighborhoods; the fact that American-born Italian offspring did not differ much from their Italian-born brothers in occupational interest; and the fact that attendance in American schools made no noticeable difference in occupational outlook.

Jewish offspring did not follow their parents so closely. They were reared to exceed their parents' achievements, and although this created tremendous tensions, as psychologists and novelists have gone to great pains to illustrate, it kept the issue before them constantly. They must succeed. They must be ambitious. They must aspire to do well. Thus by 1905 Jewish offspring were moving into white-collar positions as professionals, salespeople, clerical workers, and shopkeepers. Unlike the Italians, place of birth did make a difference. Jewish offspring born in America, open to its training and schools, did better than their European-born brethren and subsequently moved up the ladder more quickly.

Aside from fertility, ethnic background, education, and cultural differences, differential mobility has also been ascribed to the influence of the ghetto as a mobility barrier. Both groups settled tightly packed ghettos, with the Jews clustering together even more than the Italians, so that it would be difficult to show how the ghetto hindered one group more than the other. But the entire issue of the ghetto's retarding effect should be questioned. The tremendous rates of out-mobility demonstrate that New York's neighborhoods were very porous barriers. Lower Manhattan's ethnic colonies bore no resemblance to the European "ghetto." In Europe the term stood for enforced residential segregation within a regulated area of settlement, but the downtown community in Manhattan held few immigrants back from seeking better fortune elsewhere. Between 1880 and 1890, 95 per cent of the semiskilled and unskilled Italian work force left their neighborhoods and indeed the city. The ghetto, per se, cannot be charged with restricting occupational progress.

A more compelling argument can be drawn for the ghetto as a mobility launcher. It offered the immigrant hospitality of place. It provided jobs, business, and political contacts as well as investment opportunities. The local schools and settlement houses further aided the immigrant to assimilate and to acquire essential skills. The downtown neighborhood often provided him the best base for accumulating sufficient experience and capital to move elsewhere, if he wished. Of course many moved away from the ghetto no better off than when they first settled. This was especially true of unskilled and semiskilled Italians, who often joined the "floating proletariat" to search for jobs around the country.

Persistence in the city related inversely to class. Those who did not move into higher occupational levels found it rather easy to move to other cities. Unlike the present, when geographic mobility is more common to white-collar workers, in the period 1880–1915 such movement typified the blue-collar class. At first Italians were very mobile geographically, but by 1905–1915 as they achieved better positions the number leaving the city dropped dramatically. Persistence within neighborhoods, however, was not so clearly related to class or occupation. For both job and ethnic reasons Italians tended to remain in their original neighborhoods longer.

Residential mobility, like its occupational counterpart, symbolized the broad options open before the New Immigrants. They opened new ethnic neighborhoods in Harlem, South Bronx, Williamsburgh, South Brooklyn, and Brownsville. Some of the immigrants chose to disperse among the natives, away from their own group, others moved out of the Lower East Side to fresher ghettos, but the movement itself indicated a freedom that the *paese* and *shtetl* lacked.

The relationship between occupational and residential mobility is not a direct one. As Howard Chudacoff found in Omaha, "place utility [is] multidimensional, including economic, social, psychological, ethnic and . . . other components. Residential mobility [involves] relocation of an individual to a place of higher utility. Perceptions of utility, however, are not usually optimal . . . ," nor are they restricted to the ability to pay. Gradually, however, as immigrants could afford better, the old clearing house for New Immigrants on the Lower East Side was eclipsed by newer areas.[19]

Thus American society, at least so far as New York can bear witness for the nation, afforded immigrants and their children a comfortable margin of mobility. Immigrants who carried the burdens of European poverty and persecution and settled into slums and poor jobs as aliens, were nonetheless mobile. Clearly the statue standing in New York's harbor shined her symbolic torch for the poor as well as the rich and well born. To answer a question posed by an earlier investigator of immigrant mobility: Yes, the myth of an open American society with opportunity for the common man "squared with social reality." [20]

Certain aspects of mobility are beyond the ken of studies such as this one. Daniel Bell and others have discussed the role of crime in ethnic mobility, but studies that are based on census and directory samples inevitably miss such occupations as bank robber, prostitute, or gangster. Suffice it to say that given the levels of mobility uncovered in New York, crime was not the only way up.[21]

Another point, anticlimactic as it may be, should be made. Occupational mobility helps us judge the American promise by materialist standards. In that respect Jews assimilated more quickly, and rapidly climbed the economic ladder. But this merely scratches the surface. We can move away from the issue of mobility—it existed. But did the American system provide a better quality of life? As David Levinsky asks for all who came and were successful, "Am I happy?"

> There are moments when I am overwhelmed by a sense of my success and ease. I become aware that thousands of things which had formerly been forbidden fruit . . . are at my command now. . . . One day I paused in front of an old East Side restaurant that I had often passed in my days of need and despair. The feeling of desolation and envy with which I used

> to peek in its windows came back to me. It gave me pangs
> of self pity for my past and a thrilling sense of my present
> power. . . .
>
> I am lonely. . . .
>
> No I am not happy. . . .
>
> I can never forget the days of my misery. I cannot escape from
> my old self. My past and present do not comport well. David,
> the poor lad swinging over a Talmud volume at the Preacher's
> synagogue, seems to have more in common with my inner iden-
> tity than David Levinsky, the well known cloak manufacturer.[22]

As another immigrant son, Mario Puzo, has written,

> There is a difference between having a good time in life and
> being happy. . . . We are all Americans now, we are all suc-
> cesses now. And yet the most successful Italian man I know
> admits that though the one human act he could never under-
> stand was suicide, he understood it when he became a[n Amer-
> ican] success, . . . He went back to Italy and tried to live
> like a peasant again. But he can never again be unaware of
> more subtle traps than poverty and hunger.[23]

But then Horatio Alger never promised happiness.

Appendix A

The sample procedure employed in this study was constructed after lengthy consultation with the late Professor Steven Bever of the Center for Policy Research and discussions with Professor Donald Treiman, also with the Center, Professor Abram Jaffe of the Bureau for Applied Research, and Professor John Hammond of Columbia University.

The sampling technique for 1880 was straightforward. Heavily Italian or Russian Jewish districts were studied. These areas were located on the basis of contemporary and secondary accounts, as well as the more arduous method of perusing the census. The Jewish and Italian wards with large concentrations were selected and further broken down by election districts. Those election districts with fewer than ten families of either nationality were skipped.

The huge concentration of New Immigrants in lower Manhattan in 1880 made it rather easy to do this, especially because those areas which were not heavily Italian or Jewish had no, or almost no, Italians or Jews. They were still very tightly clustered, with heavy concentrations in some E.D.'s and almost none in others. Italians were also sampled in Harlem where they had established an ethnic community by 1880. The Brooklyn returns were also

scanned in areas which were reputedly Jewish or Italian neighborhoods, but where the numbers were small as yet.

The procedure employed was to select every fifth household
and copy all the data about that family and its members. If a
name was illegible or unclear it was skipped over and the next
one chosen in its place. In no case was it necessary to alter the
procedure to the extent that two families could not be drawn
from every ten.

The nationality of the household was usually common to all
members, but where it was not, for the purposes of the sample,
nationality was determined by the household head. In the case
of Russians and Poles there were some E.D.'s in Brooklyn that
were of this nationality but were clearly not Jewish, and they
were not sampled. This was true in the 13th, 14th, and 16th
Wards. They were easily identifiable by non-Jewish first names
such as Wladislav, Christina, and Catherine.

The manuscript schedules collected by federal government
census takers after 1880 were not accessible. Therefore, the source
employed for the 1892 and 1905 samples was the New York
State Census. For 1892 only the Brooklyn records exist, while
for 1905 enumerations are available for both Brooklyn and Manhattan. For 1892 a two-stage stratified systematic sample was
used. On the basis of ward-nationality data supplied in John S.
Billings, *Vital Statistics of New York City and Brooklyn, 1890*,
the first stage of the sample was to divide the Italian and Jewish population by ward into heavy, medium, and low concentration wards. Then a proportionate stratified sample was
taken from each of the three strata.

For 1905, the same procedure was used, with an added stage
which first divided the sampling between Brooklyn and Manhattan according to the proportion of their total population in
the two boroughs and then proceeded for the next two stages in
the same manner as was used for Brooklyn in 1892.

The occupation distribution for these samples by ward or
assembly district is given in Appendix B.

Appendix B

TABLE 20 OCCUPATIONAL DISTRIBUTION OF ITALIAN HOUSEHOLDS
(ALL MEMBERS) FOR SAMPLED WARDS IN MANHATTAN AND
FOR BROOKLYN, BY PER CENT, 1880

Ward	I	II	III	IV	V	Total
4	0	11.4	14.3	2.9	71.4	35
6	2.4	23.2	12.2	8.7	53.5	254
8	1.7	15.1	20.3	20.9	41.9	172
12	0	2.3	14.0	0	83.7	43
14	.9	14.9	13.1	3.3	67.9	336
15	2	22.4	30.6	22.4	22.4	49
Brooklyn	1.0	13.6	14.6	17.5	53.4	103
Mean Total	1.4	16.6	15.2	10.0	56.8	992

Source: Sample data from 1880 Federal Census for New York and Kings
Counties.

TABLE 21 OCCUPATIONAL DISTRIBUTION OF RUSSIAN JEWISH
HOUSEHOLDS (ALL MEMBERS) FOR SAMPLED WARDS IN
MANHATTAN AND FOR BROOKLYN, BY PER CENT, 1880

Ward	I	II	III	IV	V	Total
4	0	12.5	33.3	50.0	4.2	24
6	4.1	30.6	50.4	14.1	.8	121
7	4.2	41.2	43.3	10.0	.8	120
10	2.9	31.0	55.1	10.3	.7	554
13	2.6	26.3	57.9	12.5	.7	152

TABLE 21 OCCUPATIONAL DISTRIBUTION OF RUSSIAN JEWISH
HOUSEHOLDS (ALL MEMBERS) FOR SAMPLED WARDS IN
MANHATTAN AND FOR BROOKLYN, BY PER CENT, 1880 (*Continued*)

Ward	I	II	III	IV	V	Total
Brooklyn	7.1	28.6	28.6	35.7	0	14
Mean Total	3.2	31.2	52.3	12.5	.8	985

Source: Sample data from 1880 Federal Census for New York and Kings
Counties.

TABLE 22 OCCUPATIONAL DISTRIBUTION OF ITALIAN HOUSEHOLDS
(ALL MEMBERS) FOR SAMPLED WARDS IN BROOKLYN,
BY PER CENT, 1892

Ward	I	II	III	IV	V	Total
2	7	12.6	7.7	4.9	73.9	142
6	2.7	18.7	23.3	13.6	41.6	257
8	0	5.6	3.7	7.4	83.3	108
13	11.1	11.1	44.4	11.1	22.2	9
16	0	33.3	11.1	33.3	22.2	9
19	0	80.0	0	20.0	0	5
21	0	0	33.3	55.5	11.1	9
26	7.3	9.1	21.8	16.4	45.5	55
Mean Total	2.2	14.3	16.0	11.6	55.9	594

Source Sample data from New York State Census of 1892 for Kings County.

TABLE 23 OCCUCATIONAL DISTRIBUTION OF RUSSIAN JEWISH
HOUSEHOLDS (ALL MEMBERS) FOR SAMPLED WARDS IN
BROOKLYN, BY PER CENT, 1892

Ward	I	II	III	IV	V	Total
16	3.2	20.1	63.0	6.3	7.4	189
26	8.6	9.2	75.5	6.7	0	163
8	0	25.0	56.3	6.3	12.5	16
13	11.1	33.3	50.0	0	5.5	18
21	0	12.5	83.3	4.2	0	24
2	6.3	56.3	31.3	6.3	0	16
6	0	28.6	57.1	14.3	0	7
Mean Total	5.3	17.8	66.7	6.2	3.9	433

Source: Sample data from New York State Census of 1892 for Kings
County.

TABLE 24 OCCUPATIONAL DISTRIBUTION OF ITALIAN HOUSEHOLDS (ALL
MEMBERS) FOR SAMPLED ASSEMBLY DISTRICTS IN MANHATTAN AND
BROOKLYN, BY PER CENT, 1905

Manhattan A.D.	I	II	III	IV	V	Total
1	0	8.1	26.2	19.2	46.5	172
2	.4	13.7	28.1	17.5	40.4	498
6	.8	9.3	30.1	15.4	44.7	246
22	0	19.4	33.3	25.0	22.2	36
28	0	50.0	33.3	0	16.7	12
32	1.0	13.8	36.8	23.0	25.3	391
33	33.3	66.6	0	0	0	3
Manhattan Mean Total	.7	12.7	30.9	18.9	36.8	1,358

Brooklyn A.D.	I	II	III	IV	V	Total
2	4.9	14.6	24.4	9.8	46.3	82
3	2.1	13.8	23.2	38.4	22.5	289
7	3.2	14.7	15.3	14.7	52.1	190
11	0	17.3	9.6	23.1	50.0	52
18	2.5	28.2	23.1	15.4	30.8	39
21	1.4	10.8	20.3	8.1	59.5	74
Brooklyn Mean Total	2.5	14.9	20.0	23.6	39.1	726

| Mean Total Manhattan & Brooklyn | 1.3 | 13.5 | 27.1 | 20.5 | 37.6 | 2,084 |

Source: Sample data from New York State Census of 1905 for New York
and Kings Counties.

TABLE 25 OCCUPATIONAL DISTRIBUTION OF RUSSIAN JEWISH
HOUSEHOLDS (ALL MEMBERS) FOR SAMPLED ASSEMBLY DISTRICTS IN
MANHATTAN AND BROOKLYN, BY PER CENT, 1905

Manhattan A.D.	I	II	III	IV	V	Total
4	8.5	27.9	30.0	32.5	1.1	714
8	6.0	29.1	34.9	27.8	2.2	450
12	5.3	20.0	26.3	39.8	.5	186
14	0	45.8	33.3	20.8	0	24
28	10.3	58.8	23.5	7.4	0	68
32	3.0	33.7	52.5	8.9	2.0	101
33	18.2	31.8	36.4	0	13.6	22
Manhattan Mean Total	7.2	30.3	32.3	28.8	1.5	1,565

Brooklyn A.D.	I	II	III	IV	V	Total
5	29.2	33.3	16.7	4.2	16.7	24
6	0	71.4	28.6	0	0	7
7	33.3	58.3	8.3	0	0	12
14	33.3	66.7	0	0	0	3
18	30.0	15.0	30.0	25.0	0	20
21	11.1	24.3	46.0	17.2	1.5	470
Brooklyn Mean Total	13.1	25.9	42.7	16.2	2.1	536

| Mean Total Manhattan & Brooklyn | 8.7 | 29.2 | 34.9 | 25.6 | 1.7 | 2,101 |

Source: Sample data from New York State Census of 1905 for New York
and Kings Counties.

Notes

INTRODUCTION

1. Quoted in Jesse Lemisch, "Listening to the 'Inarticulate'," in Thomas N. Guinsburg, ed., *The Dimensions of History* (Chicago, 1971), 127–28.
2. The following three collections include many important articles by the new historians: Stephan Thernstrom and Richard Sennett, eds., *Nineteenth Century Cities: Essays in the New Urban History* (New Haven, 1969); Tamara K. Hareven, ed., *Anonymous Americans: Explorations in Nineteenth Century Social History* (Englewood Cliffs, 1971); Barton B. Bernstein, ed., *Towards a New Past: Dissenting Essays in American History* (New York, 1967).
3. Stephen Thernstorm, *Poverty and Progress: Social Mobility in a Nineteenth Century City* (Cambridge, 1964); Richard J. Hopkins, "Status, Mobility, and the Dimensions of Change in a Southern City," in Kenneth T. Jackson and Stanley K. Schultz, eds., *Cities in American History* (New York, 1972), 216–31; Howard Chudacoff, *Mobile Americans: Residential and Social Mobility in Omaha* (New York, 1972); Stephan Thernstrom, *The Other Bostonians: Poverty and Progress in the American Metropolis, 1800–1970* (Cambridge, 1973); Paul B. Worthman, "Working Class Mobility in Birmingham, Alabama, 1880–1914," in Tamara Hareven, ed., *Anonymous Americans*, 172–213; Clyde Griffin, "Workers Divided: The Effect of Craft and Ethnic Differences in Poughkeepsie, New York, 1850–1880," in Thernstrom and Sennett, eds., *Nineteenth Century Cities*, 49–97; Stephan Thernstrom, "Reflections on the New Urban History," in Felix Gilbert and Stephan Graubard, eds., *Historical Studies Today* (New York, 1972), 326. A more comprehen-

sive list of mobility studies, as well as a discussion of the theoretical and historical literature in this field is available in Edward Pessen, ed., *Three Centuries of Social Mobility in America* (Lexington, 1974), passim, and especially in an excellent bibliographic essay, 305–13.

4. Nathan Glazer and Daniel Patrick Moynihan, *Beyond the Melting Pot* (Cambridge, 1970), lv; Moses Rischin, *The Promised City* (Cambridge, 1962).

5. "And the fact is this . . . that there is no basis whatsoever for the suggestion that Jews monopolize United States business industry." Editors of *Fortune, Jews in America* (New York, 1933), 34.

6. Alexander DeConde, *Half Bitter, Half Sweet: An Excursion into Italian-American History* (New York, 1971), 333; Humbert Nelli, *The Italians of Chicago: A Study in Ethnic Mobility* (New York, 1970), passim.

7. Thernstrom, *Other Bostonians*, 143; Marshall Sklare, ed., *The Jews: Social Patterns of an American Group* (Glencoe, 1958), 43.

8. Peter Knights, *The Plain People of Boston, 1830–1860: A Study in City Growth* (New York, 1971), 4.

9. One thing that the exclusionary bias of the directory did not do is avoid the slums or lower class workers. For a discussion of city directories and their use in migration studies see Sidney Goldstein, *Patterns of Mobility, 1910–1950: The Norristown Study* (Philadelphia, 1958), 90–123; also Peter Knights, *Plain People of Boston*, 127–39.

10. Donald Treiman's work is contained in a full-length study, "Occupational Prestige in Comparative Perspective," which has not yet been published. A short version of the thesis was delivered before the Conference on International Comparisons of Social Mobility in Princeton New Jersey, June 1972, in a paper entitled "The Validity of the 'Standard Occupation Prestige Scale' for Historical Data."

11. "The Golden Door: Immigrant Mobility in New York City, 1880–1915" (Columbia U., 1975).

12. Oscar Handlin, "History: A Discipline in Crisis," *American Scholar*, XL (Summer 1971), 455; Richard Jensen and Charles Dollar, *Historian's Guide to Statistics* (New York, 1971), 30.

13. Robert William Fogel and Stanley L. Engerman, *Time on the Cross: The Economics of American Negro Slavery* (Boston, 1974). Many of the reservations expressed by critical reviewers are included in Herbert G. Gutman's spirited and debunking review, "The World Two Cliometricians Made," *Journal of Negro History*, LX (Jan. 1975), 53–227. Arthur Schlesinger Jr., "The Humanist Looks at Empirical Social Research," *American Sociological Review*, XXVII (Dec. 1972), 770.

CHAPTER I—The Immigrant City

1. John Maas, *The Glorious Enterprise: The Centennial Exhibition of 1876 in Philadelphia* (New York, 1973); James D. McCabe, *The Illustrated*

History of the Centennial Exhibition (Philadelphia, 1876). For the past few years an exhaustive study of Philadelphia, 1850–1880, has been under way. This study, the Philadelphia Social History Project, under the direction of Theodore Hershberg, has gathered voluminous data on the social and economic makeup of Philadelphia and has under way an in-depth mobility analysis of the entire city. A full description of the Project can be found in Theodore Hershberg, "The Philadelphia Social History Project: A Methodological History" (doctoral dissertation, Stanford U., 1973). Some of its findings are summarized in Theodore Hershberg, "Free Blacks in Ante-Bellum Philadelphia: A Study of Ex-Slaves, Free Born, and Socioeconomic Decline," *Journal of Social History*, V (Dec. 1971), 183–209; Bruce Laurie, Theodore Hershberg, and George Alter, "Immigrants and Industry: The Philadelphia Experience, 1850–1880," *Journal of Social History*, IX (Winter 1975), 219–67.

2. Emma Lazarus, "The New Colossus," *The Poems of Emma Lazarus* (2 vols., New York and Boston, 1889), I, 202–3.

3. *Ibid.*; Charles Morley, ed., *Portrait of America: Letters of Henry Sienkiewicz* (New York, 1959), 277.

4. Pete Hamill, "The Lost America," *New York Post*, Oct. 11, 1972, 32; Niles Carpenter, *Immigrants and Their Children* (Washington, 1927), 29.

5. United States Industrial Commission, *Reports*, Vol. XV, *Report on Immigration* (19 vols., Washington, 1901–2), 449; hereinafter cited as Indust. Comm., XV.

6. Bayrd Still, *Mirror for Gotham* (New York, 1956), 214, 213. "For Europeans New York is America, but for Americans it is the beginning of Europe," wrote Paul de Roussiers in the 1890s.

7. Robert Ernst, *Immigrant Life in New York City* (New York, 1956), 62; Jay P. Dolan, "Immigrants in the City: New York's Irish and German Catholics," *Church History*, XXXI (Sept. 1972), 357; Indust. Comm., XV, 462.

8. Jacob Riis, *How the Other Half Lives* (New York, 1957), 18–19. As late as 1905 in an article "The Jews of New York as Observed in Ten-Year Investigations," pioneer demographer Walter Laidlaw wrote: "New York is first of all a German City . . . ," *American Hebrew*, LXXVI (May 1905), 785–92.

9. Riis, *How the Other Half Lives*, 18–19.

10. United States Immigration Commission, *Reports*, Vol. XII, *Emigration Conditions in Europe* (41 vols., Washington, 1911), 17; hereinafter cited as Immig. Comm., XII. Figures are rounded off.

11. Maldwyn A. Jones, *American Immigration* (Chicago and London, 1960), 207; Immig. Comm., XII, 17.

12. United States Immigration Commission, *Reports*, Vol. I, *Abstract of Reports of the Immigration Commission* (41 vols., Washington, 1911), 148; hereinafter cited as Immig. Comm., I; A. L. Wayland, "A Scien-

tific Basis of Charities," *Charities Review*, III, No. 6 (1894), 266. The Rev. M. D. Lichliter complained to a Senate committee: "the moral fiber of the nation has been weakened and its lifeblood vitiated," by the New Immigration, which he labeled "oriental scum." He continued, "let us not unduly tax our assimilating powers." United States Immigration Commission, *Reports*, Vol. XXIII, *Statements of Societies Interested in Immigration* (41 vols., Washington, 1911), 17–18; hereinafter cited as Immig. Comm., XXIII.

13. Immig. Comm., I, 36.
14. Indust. Comm., XV, 510–11. On agricultural experiments and efforts at dispersal and resettlement, see *ibid.*, 495–507; Leonard G. Robinson, *The Agricultural Activities of the Jews in America* (New York, 1912). *The Jewish Communal Register of New York City: 1917–1918* (New York, 1918), 1245–48, reports that, between 1901 and 1912, 59,729 people were sent from New York to 1,474 different towns and cities. See also Mark Zbrowski and Elizabeth Herzog, "A Colony in Kansas 1882," *American Jewish Archives*, XVII (Nov. 1965), 114–39; Charles Bernheimer, "Jewish Agricultural Colonies," *Jewish Exponent*, Dec. 30, 1887; Zosa Szajkowski, "The Alliance Israelite Universelle in the U.S. 1860–1949," *Publications of the American Jewish Historical Society*, XXXIX (June, 1950), 389–443; Joseph Brandes, *Immigrants to Freedom: Jewish Communities in Rural New Jersey since 1882* (Philadelphia, 1971). For such efforts among the Italians see Humbert Nelli, *Italians of Chicago, 1880–1930: A Study in Ethnic Mobility* (New York and London, 1970), 16–20; Robert Foerster, *The Italian Emigration of Our Times* (Cambridge, 1924), 363–73; E. G. Meade, "The Italians on the Land," *United States Bureau of Labor Bulletin*, 70 (1907), 473–533; Andrew F. Rolle, *The Immigrant Upraised: Italian Adventurers and Colonists in an Expanding America* (Norman, Okla., 1968).
15. Margaret Myers, *The New York Money Market* (New York, 1931), 213–14, 238–366; Moses Rischin, *The Promised City: New York's Jews, 1870–1914* (Cambridge, 1962), 5; Thomas Adams, Harold M. Lewis, and Theodore T. McCrosky, *Regional Survey of New York and Its Environs, Population, Land Values, and Government* (8 vols., New York, 1929), II, 423.
16. Myers, *Money Market*, 332–33.
17. *Ibid.*, 296, 289–92.
18. United States Department of Interior, *Compendium of Tenth Census: 1880* (Washington, 1883), Part 2, 1070; United States Department of Interior, *Abstract of Eleventh Census: 1890* (Washington, 1892), 159; Robert M. Lichtenberg, *One-Tenth of a Nation: Natural Forces in the Economic Growth of the New York Region* (Cambridge, 1960), 17.
19. Still, *Gotham*, 218–19.
20. Theodore Dreiser, *The Color of a Great City* (New York, 1923), 4.
21. Still, *Gotham*, 208.

22. John A. Garraty, *The New Commonwealth* (New York, 1968), 138. The idea of rags-to-riches mobility is explored in Irwin G. Wyllie, *The Self-Made Man in America; The Myth of Rags-to-Riches* (New Brunswick, N.J., 1954). A selection of rags-to-riches literature is provided by Moses Rischin, ed., *The American Gospel of Success: Individualism and Beyond* (Chicago, 1965). Several important essays on the non-raggedy background of America's rich are included in William Miller, ed., *Men in Business: Essays on the Historical Role of the Entrepreneur* (New York and Evanston, 1962). Stephan Thernstrom, *Poverty and Progress: Social Mobility in a Nineteenth Century City* (Cambridge, 1964), has a chapter on "The Promise of Mobility." The classic distillation of this thought, voiced as early as 1622 by Virginia's Peter Arundle—"Yea. I say that any honest laborious man may in a shorte time become riche in this country"—is quite readably illustrated by Horatio Alger's short novels. See also Louis B. Wright, "Franklin's Legacy to the Gilded Age," *The Virginia Quarterly Review*, XXII (1946), 268–79; Richard B. Morris, *Government and Labor in Early America* (New York, 1946).

23. Harry E. Resseguie, "A. T. Stewart and the Development of the Department Store, 1823–1876," *Business History Review*, XXXVI (1965), 301–22; "Alexander Turney Stewart," *Dictionary of American Biography* (20 vols., New York, 1936), XVIII, 3–5; Louis Windmiller, "The Commercial Progress of Gotham" in Charles Conant, ed., *The Progress of the Empire State* (New York, 1913), 318; George T. Borrett, *Letters from Canada and the United States*, in Still, *Mirror for Gotham*, 190.

24. Russell Conwell, "Acres of Diamonds" in Oscar Handlin, ed., *Readings in American History* (2 vols., New York, 2nd ed., 1970), II, 90–91.

25. Dreiser, *Color of a Great City*, 13; Garraty, *New Commonwealth*, 15; James D. McCabe, *New York by Sunlight and Gaslight: A Work Descriptive of the Great American Metropolis* (Facsimile of an 1872 Edition, New York, 1964), 174; Peter Casill, *New York: Memories of Yesteryear* (New York, 1964), 219–20; Still, *Gotham*, 228.

26. Robert E. Park and Herbert A. Miller, *Old World Traits Ttransplanted* (New York and London, 1921), 42, 46; Foerster, *Italian Emigration*, 331; Anzia Yezeirska, *How I Found America*, 265, quoted in Henry Feingold, *Zion in America* (New York, 1974), 123.

27. Dreiser, *Color of a Great City*, viii.

28. George C. Booth, "Tenement House Inspection," *Thirty-Sixth Annual Report of the New York Association for Improving the Conditions of the Poor* (1879), 64.

29. Kate H. Claghorn, "The Foreign Immigrant in New York City," *United States Industrial Commission Report* (19 vols., Washington, 1901), XV, 472–73.

30. Of the 1,464 Italians in 1860, 926 were men. Ernst, *Immigrant Life in New York City*, 97, 199, 214–17; Indust. Comm., XV, 472; Foerster, *Italian Emigration*, 323.

31. Jacob Riis, *How the Other Half Lives*, 41; Claghorn, "Foreign Immi-

grant in New York City," 457; Charles Loring Brace, *The Dangerous Classes in New York City* (New York, 1880), 194.

32. Italian emigration and its many causes are masterfully studied by Robert Foerster, *Italian Emigration*, especially Books II, III, and IV. Other sources include: Immig. Comm., XII, Part II, "The Emigration Situation in Italy;" Denis Mack Smith, *A History of Sicily: Modern Sicily after 1713* (New York, 1968); Luigi Villari, *Italian Life in Town and Country* (New York and London, 1902); Leonard Covello, *The Social Background of the Italo-American School Child* (Leiden, 1967), 34–63. An important article on the topic is J. S. McDonald, "Italy's Rural Social Structure and Emigration," *Occidente: An International Review of Politics and Society*, XII (Sept.–Oct. 1956), 437–57.

33. Indust. Comm., XV, 473.

34. Foerster, *Italian Emigration*, 327.

35. Charlotte Adams, "Italian Life in New York City," *Harper's Monthly*, LII (April 1881), 676–84.

36. Park and Miller, *Old World Traits Transplanted*, 146–47; Virginia Yans McLaughlin, "Immigration and the Social Order," *The Study of American History* (2 vols., Guilford, 1974), II, 126; George E. Pozzetta, "The Italians of New York City, 1890–1914" (doctoral dissertation, U. of North Carolina, 1971), 102–7. For a description of localism and some of its effects in Chicago see Rudolph Vecoli, "Contadini in Chicago: A Critique of *The Uprooted*," *Journal of American History*, LIV (Dec. 1964), 404–17.

37. Andrew R. Rolle, *The American Italians, Their History and Culture* (Belmont, 1972), 71; Nelli, *Italians of Chicago*, 15–16; Indust. Comm., XV, 497, 495.

38. Nelli, *Italians of Chicago*, 15; United States Department of Commerce *Fourteenth Census: State Compendium for New York* (Washington, 1924), 62. Foreign-born Irish totaled 203,400 and Germans 194,100.

39. Arthur Hertzberg, *The Zionist Idea* (Philadelphia, 1959), 180; Immig. Comm., XII, 274–79; Howard Morley Sachar, *The Course of Modern Jewish History* (New York, 1958), 240–46. On Jewry in Russia and their problems see Simon M. Dubnow, *A History of the Jews in Russia and Poland* (3 vols., Philadelphia, 1946), especially Vol. III; Salo Baron, *The Russian Jew Under Tsars and Soviets* (New York, 1964); Israel Friedlander, *The Jews of Russia and Poland* (New York and London, 1915); Mark Vishniak, "Anti-Semitism in Tsarist Russia," in Koppel Pinson, ed., *Essays on Anti-Semitism* (New York, 1946); John B. Weber and Walter Kempster, *A Report of the Commission of Immigration Upon Causes Which Incite Immigration to the United States* (Washington, 1892), esp. 35–57.

40. Samuel Joseph, *Jewish Immigration to the United States, 1881–1910* (New York, Reprint of a 1914 Columbia University doctoral dissertation, 1969), 57–69; Amos Elon, *Israelis: Founders and Sons* (New York,

1971), 68. President Benjamin Harrison decried "the revival of anti-Semitic laws," in a letter to the Russian government.

41. Sachar, *Course of Modern Jewish History*, 246. Joseph, *Jewish Immigration*, 66–68; Weber and Kempster, *Report*, 38–40; Elon, *Israelis*, 134.

42. Ernst, *Immigrant Life in New York City*, 253; Indust. Comm., XV, 471; quote from *Asmonean* is in Ernst, *Immigrant Life*, 85.

43. *Ibid.*, 215–18; Rischin, *Promised City*, 55; Allon Schoener, ed., *Portal to America* (New York, 1967), 53–101.

44. American immigration records did not provide information by religion and only after 1899 was "Hebrew" included as a racial category. Russian and Polish totals *in the cities and especially New York* have been used as proxies for Jewish figures. See Indust. Comm., XV, 475–76 ("The Russians and Poles, practically all Hebrews . . . ,"). Evidence to back up this substitution rests on more than impressionistic accounts. The outstanding demographer of Jewish settlement, Nathan Goldberg, has gone to some length in his article "Occupational Patterns of American Jews," *The Jewish Review*, III (April 1945), 3–24, to show the statistical undergirding for this assumption. His data indicate that for New York City, especially until after 1900, "Russian" can safely be taken to mean "Jewish."" A lengthier and more detailed discussion of the same point can be found in Joseph, *Jewish Immigration*, 87–104. See also Ernst, *Immigrant Life in New York City*, 225. For a tabular analysis of Russian immigration and its Jewish component see Joseph, *Jewish Immigration*, 93–94, 164; Rischin, *Promised City*, 270; Mark Wischnitzer, *Visas to Freedom* (Cleveland, 1956). These tables confirm the Immigration Commission assertion in *Emigration Conditions in Europe*, p. 280, that "although we have only figures for the total immigration (including non-Jews) from Russia to the United States, those figures fluctuate *according to the difference in position of the Jews in Russia*" (italics in original).

45. Indust. Comm., XV, 476; Edward E. Pratt, *Industrial Causes of Congestion of Population in New York City* (New York, Reprint of 1911 ed., 1968), 35; *Fortieth Annual Report of the New York Association for Improving Conditions of the Poor* (1883), 19; New York State Legislature, *Report of the Tenement House Commission, 1895* (Albany, 1895), 11; Still, *Mirror for Gotham*, 208; Rischin, *Promised City*, 79.

46. Zosa Szajkowski, "The Attitude of American Jews to Eastern European Jewish Immigrants (1881–1893)," *Publications of the American Jewish Historical Society*, XL (Sept. 1950–June 1951), 221–80; Brandes, *Immigrants to Freedom*, 29, 5; *Fortieth Census: New York State Compendium*, 62.

47. Garraty, *New Commonwealth*, 187; Riis, *Other Half*, 3. For an interesting conceptual treatment see David Ward, *Cities and Immigrants: A Geography of Change in Nineteenth Century America* (New York, 1971), 5, 26–33, 92–102, and passim. See also Thomas Adams, Edward

Bassett, et al., *Regional Survey of New York and Its Environs: Buildings, Their Uses and Spaces about Them* (New York, 1931), 32, 210; Indust. Comm., XV, 453–55; Riis, *Other Half*, 5–14.

48. The *New York Times* felt that, if the winning plan represented the best possible, then the slum problem was beyond solution. Perhaps, the paper sarcastically continued, "the gentleman who offered the prizes really desired to demonstrate this [the impossibility of solution] to the public before proposing any other scheme." Roy Lubove, *The Progressives and the Slums: Tenement House Reform in New York City, 1890–1917* (Pittsburgh, 1962), 29–32; Rischin, *Promised City*, 81–86.

49. Robert C. Brooks, "History of Street and Rapid Transit Railways of New York City" (doctoral dissertation, Cornell U., 1903), 177.

50. See Cecyle Neidle, "The Foreign Born View America: A Study of Autobiographies Written by Immigrants to the Uniited States" (doctoral dissertation, New York U., 1962), and Cecyle Neidle, ed., *The New Americans* (New York, 1967).

51. Abraham Cahan, "Yekl," in Milton Hindus, ed., *The Old East Side: An Anthology* (Philadelphia, 1969), 27.

52. W. H. Auden, *Epistle to a Godson and Other Poems* (New York, 1972), 3.

53. Riis, *Other Half*, 21.

CHAPTER II—The Immigrant Context

1. Immig. Comm., I, 14, 24.

2. Oscar Handlin, *Race and Nationality in American Life* (New York, 1950), 78–80.

3. Edward A. Saveth, *American Historians and European Immigrants* (New York, 1948), 142. John Higham discusses the social climate toward immigration in *Strangers in the Land: Patterns of American Nativism 1860–1925* (New York, 1968), especially Chs. 6–7. Oscar Handlin's *Race and Nationality in American Life,* 57–135, offers a pungent analysis of the Immigration Commission's racism and forced reasoning.

4. In addition to this central role in the work of the Commission, Jencks, together with W. Jett Lauck, authored *The Immigration Problem: A Study of American Immigration Conditions and Needs* (New York, 1911), which was actually a distillation of the forty-one-volume Immigration Commission Report. This work, frequently reissued, proved quite influential.

5. Kenneth M. Stampp, *The Peculiar Institution: Slavery in the Ante-Bellum South* (New York, 1955), vii–viii. Stampp's point, admirable though his intent may have been, understated the importance of differences accruing to race and nationality.

6. W. B. Bailey, "Birds of Passage," *American Journal of Sociology,* XVIII

(Nov. 1912), 392–93; Andrew F. Rolle, *The American Italians, Their History and Culture* (Belmont, 1972), 3; Immig. Comm., XII, 47–48.

7. *Ibid.;* W. Jett Lauck, "The Vanishing American Wage Earner," *Atlantic Monthly*, CX (Nov. 1912), 694.

8. Jencks and Lauck, *Immigration*, 29–30; Bailey, "Birds," 392–93; Immig. Comm., I, 47–48.

9. Immig. Comm., XII, 39.

10. Leone Carpi, *Delle colonie e dell'emigrazione d'Italiani all'estero* quoted in Betty Boyd Caroli, *Italian Repatriation from the United States, 1900–1914* (New York, 1973), 32; Robert Foerster, *Italian Emigration of Our Times* (Cambridge, 1919), 41; Giovanni Florenzano in Caroli, *Repatriation*, 32.

11. Foerster, *Italian Emigration*, 31.

12. *Ibid.*, 39; Diomede Carito, *Nella terra di Washington; Le mie visioni della psiche Nord America* in Caroli, *Italian Repatriation*, 77.

13. *Ibid.*, 48.

14. Hertzberg, *The Zionist Idea*, 180.

15. Immig. Comm., XII, 40, 42; Immig. Comm., I, 16; Joseph, *Jewish Immigration*, 133–39, 184–85.

16. *Ibid.*, 98; United States Immigration Commission, *Reports*, Vol. III, *Statistical Review of Immigration, 1819–1910—Distribution of Immigrants, 1850–1900* (41 vols., Washington, 1911), 88; hereinafter cited as Immig. Comm., III.

17. Immig. Comm., III, 34–44. These figures were based on the annual figures compiled by the Commissioner General of Immigration.

18. Treasury Department Bureau of Statistics, *Tables Showing Arrivals of Alien Passengers and Immigrants in the United States From 1820 to 1888* (Washington, 1889), 78; U. S. Commissioner General of Immigration, *Annual Reports* (Washington, 1889, 1890); Immig. Comm., III, 89–91. Between 1880 and 1899 age records were compiled for "under 15 years," "15 to 40 years," "40 years and over," while after 1899 the three categories were "under 14," "14–44," and "over 44."

19. Edwin Steiner, *On the Trail of the Immigrant* (New York, 1906), 263.

20. United Hebrew Charities, *Report*, in Joseph, *Jewish Immigration*, 176, 127; Immig. Comm. III, 34–44.

21. Hebrew Charities, *Report* in Joseph, *Jewish Immigration*, 177; Immig. Comm., III, 89–91.

22. Foerster, *Italian Emigration*, 330–31.

23. Indust. Comm., XV, 474; Foerster, *Italian Emigration*, 330–31.

24. *Ibid.* For an impression of early Italian opera in New York City see Howard Mariano, "Italians in New York in the 1850s," *New York History* (April 1949), 30–35.

25. Immig. Comm., XII, 170–73; Booker T. Washington, "Naples and the Land of the Emigrant," *The Outlook*, CVIII (June 1911), 295, 297. Washington was especially surprised by the primitive tools available to

Italian farmworkers, comparable in his opinion to slave tools in the ante-bellum southern United States.

26. Foerster, *Italian Emigration*, 352; Immig. Comm., III, 131–34, 176–78.
27. Immig. Comm., XII, 181.
28. "Opinion of Rev. N. Walling Clark" in Immig. Comm., XII, 182. See also testimony of Joseph H. Senner before the Industrial Commission, XV, 167–74.
29. Immig. Comm., XII, 292–93.
30. *Premier Recensement général de la population de l'empire de Russie* in Indust. Comm., XII, 286.
31. Charles S. Liebman, "Orthodoxy in American Jewish Life," *American Jewish Yearbook*, LXVI (New York, 1965), 19. He points out that those Jews who settled America were not drawn from the elite of "learning, piety or money."
32. Joseph Lopreato, *Italian Americans* (New York, 1970), 38–39.
33. Immig. Comm., I, 98.
34. Mario Puzo, "Choosing a Dream," Thomas C. Wheeler, ed., *The Immigrant Experience* (New York, 1971), 36–37.
35. Immig. Comm., III, 84–87.
36. *Ibid.*, 355–59; *ibid.*, I, 102–3.
37. *Ibid.*
38. Bailey, "Birds," 395.
39. Stephan Thernstrom, *The Other Bostonians: Poverty and Progress in the American Metropolis, 1880–1970* (Cambridge, 1973), 163. "On the whole neither the immigrant agricultural workers nor the immigrant skilled workers follow their former occupation to a large extent after coming to the United States. . . . Immigrants choose an occupation without much regard to their previous training and experience." Louis Bloch, "Occupation of Immigrants Before and After Coming to the United States," *Journal of American Statistical Association*, XVII (June 1921), 762–63.

CHAPTER III—Immigrant Occupational Distribution 1880–1905

1. Berthold Brecht, "A Worker Reads History," *Selected Poems*, translated by H. R. Hays (New York, 1947), 109. Some examples of efforts at building a historical portrait of the past on the basis of folk tales are: Sterling Stuckey, "Through the Prism of Folklore; The Black Ethos in Slavery," *Massachusetts Review* (Summer 1968), 417–37; J. D. Elder, "Color, Music, and Conflict: A Study of Agression in Trinidad with Reference to the Role of Traditional Music," Ronald Frucht, ed., *Black Society in the New World* (New York, 1971), 315–24; George Korson, *Black Rock: Mining Folklore of the Pennsylvania Dutch* (Baltimore, 1960).
2. Dreiser, *Color of a Great City*, 3.

3. The biographical information for this family and the three others is drawn from the 1880 Federal Census of the Population, manuscript schedules for New York and Kings Counties.
4. Foerster, *Italian Emigration*, 343.
5. Dreiser, *Color of a Great City*, 113–15.
6. One scholar who considers the importance of immigration for New York's progress is Ira Rosenwaike, *Population History of New York City* (Syracuse, 1972), 92, and passim.
7. The two most popular occupation groupings were clerks, bookkeepers, storeworkers: 45,312, and tailors, dressmakers, milliners: 43,546, respectively, United States Department of the Interior, *Population of the United States at the Tenth Census, 1880* (Washington, 1883), 892.
8. The census provides the following information for Manhattan in 1880:

	Native Born	Foreign Born
Total Number Working	240,076	273,301
Per Cent in Agriculture	.3	.6
Professional/Service	26.6	35.2
Trade/Transportation	31.7	22.6
Manufacturing/Mechanical/Mining Industries	41.4	41.6

9. *Tenth Census of the United States*, 892.
10. The 1880 samples were assembled by surveying the following wards: In Manhattan for Italians—4, 6, 8, 12, 14, 15; for east European Jews—4, 6, 7, 10, 13. In Brooklyn the following wards were surveyed: 2, 6, 8, 12, 13, 14, 16, 18, 25. These districts contained the preponderant majority of both groups. In these wards, every fifth reported household was included in the sample. Although researchers have cavilled about the reliability of census data, it should be noted that the 1880 census was taken under more careful conditions than its predecessors. It employed a larger staff of supervisors and attempted to minimize distortions and exclusions. Moreover, the law provided penalties for false information, and unlike the 1970 census the enumerator was required to visit personally every house and each family dwelling therein. Carrol D. Wright with William C. Hunt, *The History and Growth of the United States Census* (Washington, 1900), 61–66.
11. For an explanation of the classification system used by the federal census "to refer every specification of occupation to some grand division of industry," and a frank discussion of some of its shortcomings, see United States Department of the Interior, "Remarks upon the List of Occupations and Upon the Numbers Returned Under the Several Titles," *Compendium of the Tenth Census*, 1350–55.
12. Alba M. Edwards, "A Social Economic Grouping of the Gainful Workers of the United States," *Journal of the American Statistical Association,*

XXVII (1933), 377–87; Alba M. Edwards, *Comparative Occupation Statistics for the United States, 1870–1940* (Washington, 1943), 87–89. A discussion of the classification system used in this study can be found in Stephan Thernstrom, *The Other Bostonians*, 289–302. Michael B. Katz elaborates on some weaknesses of occupational scales in "Occupational Classifications in History," *Journal of Interdisciplinary History*, III (Summer 1972), 63–88. More recently three scholars associated with the Philadelphia Social History Project, Bruce Laurie, Theodore Hershberg, and George Alter in "Immigrants and Industry: The Philadelphia Experience, 1850–1880," *Journal of Social History*, IX (Winter 1975), 219–67, question the validity of such scaling because of the fluidity of status *within* specific occupations over time. Their concern, however, is with an earlier period, and they admit that the status of specific occupations underwent far less change as we approach the twentieth century. David L. Featherman and Robert M. Hauser, for instance, argue that although "some individual titles apparently have shifted their relative position . . . the overall transformation of the hierarchy in the last fifty years has been glacial in nature," quoted in *ibid.*, from Featherman and Hauser, "On the Measurement of Occupation in Social Surveys," *Sociological Methods and Research*, II (Nov. 1973), 241. Donald Treiman disputes the idea that occupational variance prevents a hierarchical scaling system in "Occupational Prestige in Comparative Perspective" unpublished MS, and in his paper "The Validity of the 'Standard International Occupational Prestige Scale' for Historical Data," delivered before the Conference on International Comparisons of Social Mobility in Past Societies, Princeton, New Jersey, June, 1972. Clyde Griffin's "Comment" on this paper at the same conference should be consulted for a critical appraisal of the Treiman argument, although many of his reservations are relevant to pre-1880 and fall away for the period after that. Griffin's article "Occupational Mobility in Nineteenth Century America," *Journal of Social History*, V (Spring 1972), 310–30, is also helpful.

13. In 1880 peddlers were a major portion of the low white-collar class; they represented 12.0 per cent of the total Italian sample. By 1905 they represented only 2.1 per cent. If they are subtracted, the 1880 low white-collar division would read 12.9 per cent; 1905 would be 15.7.

14. Confectioners equaled 19, shoemakers and masons 17, and tailors 14 per cent of the skilled group.

15. Adolfo Rossi, quoted in Robert Foerster, *Italian Emigration of Our Times*, 326.

16. Charlotte Adams, "Italian Life in New York," *Harper's Monthly*, LXII (April 1881), 676–84.

17. Louise C. Odencrantz, *Italian Women in Industry* (New York, 1919), 3–5; John Mitchell, "Immigration and the American Laboring Classes," *Annals of the American Academy*, XXXIV (July 1909), 125–29;

Mary K. Reely, ed., *Selected Articles on Immigration* (New York, 1917), 13.

18. For the 1905 survey, a weighted sample of the Italian community in New York City was assembled. The data were drawn from the manuscript schedules of the 1905 New York State Census which are housed in the various County Clerks' offices. The sampled assembly districts for Manhattan: 1, 2, 3, 6, 22, 28, 32; for Brooklyn 2, 3, 7, 11, 18, 21. The total number of households sampled was 1,029. The sampling technique is discussed in Appendix A.

19. *Report of the Mayor's Pushcart Commission* (New York, 1906), 17. The Commission was chaired by the famous housing reformer Lawrence Veiller.

20. Jesse Eliphalet Pope, *The Clothing Industry in New York* (Columbia, Mo., 1905), 53–54; Indust. Comm., XV, 326; Indust. Comm., XIV, p. xxvi; Joel Seidman, *The Needle Trades* (New York, 1942), 35–36, 43–47.

21. Charles B. Barnes, *The Longshoremen* (New York, 1915), 5–7.

22. *Ibid.*, 67–68, 102–6; Foerster, *Italian Emigration*, 356.

23. *Ibid.*, 336.

24. *Ibid.*, 354; Federal Writers' Project, *The Italians of New York* (New York, 1938), 61. In 1898 the New York Bureau of Labor Statistics reported that of the 15,000 workers hired to enlarge the Erie Canal 13,500 were Italians earning $1.20 to $1.50 a day. See Indust. Comm., XV, 435. Although Public Works employment was supposed to be restricted to American citizens, this was often circumvented: United States Industrial Commission, *Reports*, Vol. VII, *Capital and Labor* (19 vols., Washington, 1901), 94; Twelfth Census of the United States, *Special Report on Occupations* (Washington, 1904), 634–35.

25. Constantine Panunzio, *The Soul of the Immigrant* (New York, 1928), 76–78. "Thirty years ago," mused Robert Foerster in 1919, "when rag pickers and street musicians seemed to many the quintessence of Italian Immigration, the pick and shovel workers were silently being carried to the remote places and set to work on the railways," *Italian Emigration*, 357–58.

26. Mario Puzo, "The Italians, American Style," *New York Times Magazine* (Aug. 6, 1967), 26; Federal Writers' Project, *Italians of New York*, 61; Foerster, *Italian Emigration*, 360; Indust. Comm., XV, 441. Most Italian laborers earned $1.50 a day, or at least that is what they remembered. "He recalled that whatever kind of labor he performed he earned $1.50 a day, the *exact* amount mentioned by all returnees in discussing their pre-1914 experiences in the United States," Caroli, *Italian Repatriation*, 86.

27. They also provided 288 of 298 barbers, 30 of 30 organ grinders, 97 of 100 rag pickers, and 1,799 of 1,921 laborers. The survey, however, was not equally distributed among all immigrant groups and had a particu-

larly heavy representation of Italians. See Carrol D. Wright, *Seventh Special Report of the Commissioner of Labor: The Slums of Baltimore, Chicago, New York and Philadelphia* (Washington, 1894), 187–95. See also Indust. Comm., XV, 473; Rocco Corresco, "Biography of a Bootblack," in Eli Ginzberg and Hyman Berman, *The American Worker in the Twentieth Century* (New York, 1963), 82–85; Twelfth Census, *Report on Occupations*, 634–35.

28. Treiman Scores which provide a simple numerical mean for occupation status confirm this apparent upgrading. The mean rating for 1880 was 24.8 and rose to 27.9 by 1905.

29. Foerster, *Italian Emigration*, 362.

30. The size of the peddling fraction was even larger among the Jews. In 1880, 23.1 per cent of the total peddled, but as with the Italians this dropped by 1905 to 5.7 per cent.

31. Ande Manners, *Poor Cousins* (New York, 1972), 216.

32. "East Side Street Vendors," *New York Times*, July 30, 1893; "Thursday on Hester Street," *New York Tribune*, Sept. 15, 1898.

33. Samuel Joseph, *Jewish Immigration*, 44; Pope, *Clothing Industry in New York*, 47; Indust. Comm., XV, p. xxvi. The Babylonian Talmud, *Tractate Kiddushin*, 82b, discusses desirable occupations that a father should teach a son, and mentions tailoring or weaving.

34. Seidman, *Needle Trades*, 37.

35. Indust. Comm., XV, 322–25, 345.

36. Riis, *How the Other Half Lives*, 88–89.

37. *Compendium of Tenth Census*, 1,071; United States Department of Commerce and Labor, *Census of Manufacturers, 1905*, Part II (Washington, 1907), 746, 770.

38. Pope, *Clothing Industry*, 47.

39. Riis, *How the Other Half Lives*, 94.

40. Heywood Broun and George Britt, *Christians Only: A Study of Prejudice* (New York, 1931), 231–32.

41. Treiman scores encapsule the progress, 1880: 35.0; 1905: 39.1.

42. Alexander DeConde, *Half Bitter Half Sweet* (New York, 1971), 100.

43. *Compendium of the Tenth Census*, 1,038–41, 1,071; *Census of Manufacturers, 1905*, 778–81.

44. Thernstrom, *Other Bostonians*, 49–51; Blau and Duncan, *American Occupational Structure*, 420–31; Natalie Rogoff's suggestive study, *Recent Trends in Occupational Mobility* (Glencoe, 1953), makes much of this point, ch. 3.

45. Five professions—clergy, dentist, lawyer, physician, teacher—totaled 2.2 per cent of the 1880 work force and dropped to 2.0 per cent in 1900. Traders, dealers and peddlers dropped from 9.9 to 8.1 per cent. Masons and cabinetmakers decreased from 3.1 to 2.3 per cent. Tailors increased from 3.8 to 5.5 per cent. Managers and manufacturing officials also went up, from .98 to 1.9. Clerks, typists, salesmen, bookkeepers, and accountants, as a group, increased from 11.5 to 13.8. These comparisons

are based on *Tenth Census of the United States,* 892 and *Twelfth Census Special Report on Occupations,* 634–41. One of the difficulties with such comparisons is the fact that the 1880 census data for occupations is incomplete, listing only the most prominent occupations.

46. Thernstrom, *Bostonians,* 49–51.

47. Nathan Reich "Economic Trends," in Oscar Janowsky, ed., *The American Jew* (New York, 1942), 163.

48. Treiman readings are the best short measure of these changes. In 1880, Jews outpointed Italians by 10 points. By 1905 Italians advanced by three points, Jews by four, and the difference stretched to 11 points.

49. C. Bezalel Sherman, *The Jew Within American Society* (Detroit, 1965), 162–66; Seidman, *The Needle Trades,* 84–88; Rudolf Glanz, *Jew and Italian, Historic Group Relations and the New Immigration (1881– 1924)* (New York, 1970), 38–42; Melech Epstein, *Profiles of Eleven* (Detroit, 1965), 61–64, 113–30, 191–99, and passim; Immig. Comm., I, 417–18; Isaac A. Hourwich, *Immigration and Labor* (New York, 1912), 325–30. See also Melech Epstein, *Jewish Labor in the United States of America: An Industrial, Political and Cultural History of the Jewish Labor Movement* (2 vols., New York, 1950–53); Edwin Fenton, "Immigrants and Unions: A Case Study, Italians and American Labor, 1870–1920" (doctoral dissertation, Harvard, 1958); Edwin Fenton, "Italians in the Labor Movement," *Pennsylvania History,* XXVI (April 1959), 133–48; Foerster, *Italian Emigration,* 402; Luciano J. Iorizzo and Salvatore Mondello, *The Italian Americans* (New York, 1971), 76–85; Nathan Glazer and Daniel P. Moynihan, *Beyond the Melting Pot* (Cambridge, 1963), 191–93; George E. Pozzetta, "The Italians of New York City, 1890–1914" (doctoral dissertation, U. of North Carolina, 1971), chapter X.

50. Abraham Cahan, *The Rise of David Levinsky* (New York, 1917), 464; Milton Reizenstein, "General Aspects of the Population," in Charles S. Bernheimer, ed., *The Russian Jew in the United States* (Philadelphia, 1905), 46–47.

51. Indust. Comm., XV, 474. As late as 1950 more than 80 per cent of New York's Italian working men were in unskilled or semi-skilled work. See Colin Greer, *The Great School Legend: A Revisionist Interpretation of American Public Education* (New York, 1972), 86.

CHAPTER IV—The Immigrant Household and Its Occupations 1880–1905

1. The role of the entire family as contributors to household earnings can be seen in United States Immigration Commission, *Reports,* Vol. XXVII, *Immigrants in Cities* (41 vols., Washington, 1911), Tables 307 and 308, p. 323–24; United States Bureau of Labor, *Report on Condition of Woman and Child Wage Earners in the United States,* Vol. II, *Men's*

Ready Made Clothing (19 vols., Washington, 1911), 842–59; hereinafter cited as *Woman and Child Wage Earners* II.

2. This, and other early views on woman factory labor are in Edith Abbott, *Women in Industry* (New York and London, 1924), 49, 52, 321.

3. Mary Van Kleeck, *Artificial Flower Makers* (New York, 1913), 116, 90;
Odencrantz, *Italian Women in Industry*, 13, 27.

4. *Ibid.;* Robert Foerster, *Italian Emigration*, 347, 330–81; United States
Department of Labor, *Summary of the Report on Condition of Woman
and Child Wage Earners in the United States* (Washington, 1916), 97–
103.

5. Foerster, *Italian Emigration*, 347; Mabel Hurd Willet, *The Employment
of Women in the Clothing Trade* (New York, 1902), attributes the
decline of women in other garment jobs to the rise of the task system,
36, 68; Pope, *Clothing Industry*, 53; Indust. Comm., XV, 326.

6. Van Kleeck, *Artificial Flower Makers*, 30, 1, 91–97, 116–17; Odencrantz,
Italian Women, 45; United States Bureau of Census, *Census of Manufacturers, 1905* (Washington, 1906), 780–81.

7. Van Kleeck, *Artificial Flower Makers*, 94–95, 230–35.

8. Leo Grebler, *Housing Market Behavior in a Declining Area* (New York,
1952), 113–14.

9. Theodore Dreiser, *Color of a Great City*, 95–96.

10. Grebler, *Housing Market Behavior*, 113–14; *Woman and Child Wage
Earners*, II, 11, 71, 98–100.

11. Immig. Comm., I, 414; Odencrantz, *Italian Women*, 60; *Woman and
Child Wage Earners*, II, 67, 71; Immig. Comm., XXVII, 322–25.

12. Odencrantz, *Italian Women*, 38–39, 43–44; *Woman and Child Wage
Earners*, II, 217–18, 221. Herbert Gans reported in his study of West
End Italians in 1962 that women did not expect to work, except under
duress, *The Urban Villagers* (New York, 1962), 129.

13. Pope, *Clothing Industry*, 50; Abbott, *Women in Industry*, 230; Indust.
Comm., XV, 325; United States Immigration Commission, *Reports*, Vol.
XI, *Immigrants in Industries* (41 vols., Washington, 1911), 556–57;
Woman and Child Wage Earners, II, 221; Robert A. Woods and Albert
J. Kennedy, eds., *Young Working Girls; A Summary of Evidence From
Two Thousand Social Workers* (Boston and New York, 1913), 22–23.

14. *Woman and Child Wage Earners*, II, 221. In 1880, 58 per cent were in
skilled occupations. In 1905, reflecting the same sort of upgrading exhibited by male Jews, over 50 per cent were in white-collar jobs.

15. Jacob Riis, *How the Other Half Lives*, 91.

16. Joel Seidman, *The Needle Trades*, 62–63; Pope, *Clothing Industry*, 57,
155–60.

17. *Woman and Child Wage Earners*, II, 53, 221; Immig. Comm., I, 752.

18. See Oscar Handlin, *The Uprooted* (New York, 1951), especially his
poignant chapter on "Generations"; Joseph Lopreato, *Italian-Americans,*
56–87. A number of essays in Thomas C. Wheeler, ed., *The Immigrant
Experience* (Baltimore, 1972), also describe the difficulty of trying to

grow up between two worlds. For a statistical study see United States Immigration Commission, *Reports*, Vol. XXVIII, *Occupations of the First and Second Generations of Immigrants in the United States* (41 vols., Washington, 1911).

19. The sample is restricted to those living with their immigrant parents, because that is the only way to ascertain their status as immigrant offspring. The census did not ask place of birth of parents.. Therefore once the children moved away, if they were born in the United States, there would be no indication that they were immigrant offspring. Although the sample is therefore restricted to a young universe, the census did not record part time jobs which would render the data presented here far less useful. Instead, all of the occupational data represent bona fide full time jobs. For discussion of the significance of career beginnings see Peter M. Blau and Otis Dudley Duncan, *The American Occupational Structure* (New York, 1967), 48–55.

20. For samples of anti-Italian prejudice see Charles Barnes, *The Longshoremen*, 9; Alexander DeConde, *Half Bitter Half Sweet* (New York, 1971), 98–117; John Higham, *Strangers in the Land*, 48; 90–91, 169, 180, 184, 264, 160, 183.

21. Odencrantz, *Italian Women*, 45.

22. *Charities*, XII (1904) 462; John H. Mariano, *The Italian Contribution to American Society* (Boston, 1921), 13; Herbert Gans, *Urban Villagers*, 213; Leonard Covello, *The Social Background of the Italo American School Child* (Leiden, 1967), 65–102, 350–60.

23. Lillian Brandt, "A Transplanted Birthright," *Charities*, XII (1904), 494–96. Unless schools were doing markedly better than their reputation would have it, this charming letter was touched up by Miss Brandt.

24. Treiman readings for 1880: 23.8, for 1905: 29.4.

25. United States Immigration Commission, *Reports*, Vol. XXVIII (41 vols., Washington, 1911), 279, 369.

26. Van Kleeck, *Artificial Flowers*, 85–86.

27. Brandt, "Transplanted Birthright," 494; Odencrantz, *Italian Women*, 205, 249–51, 256.

28. Van Kleeck, *Artificial Flowers*, 36; Odencrantz, *Italian Women*, 280; Brandt, "Transplanted Birthright," 497.

29. Covello, *Italian School Child*, 192–238; Lopreato, *Italian Americans*, 56–87.

30. As with the Italians, Jews faced a good deal of prejudice. See Moses Rischin, *Promised City*, 261–62; Judd L. Teller, *Strangers and Natives* (New York, 1968); 97; John Higham, "Anti Semitism in the Gilded Age," *Mississippi Valley Historical Review*, XLIII (1957), 559–78; John Higham, *Strangers in the Land*, 26–27, 66–67, 92–94, 160–61; Oscar Handlin, "American Views of the Jew at the Opening of the Twentieth Century," *Publications of the American Jewish Historical Society*, XL (1951), 324–35.

31. Jesse Pope, *The Clothing Industry*, 106; Indust. Comm., XV, 325.

32. *Ibid.*, 388.
33. If the entire sample of the second generation is considered, professionals accounted for 2.6 per cent while the professional increment of the older generation was larger, 3.5 per cent. But the narrow restrictions placed on the offspring sample make it reasonable to assume that a survey of the *entire* second generation, *including those who were older and living away from their parents,* would yield a much larger upper white-collar class. And this class would be divided between professionals and entrepreneurs in the same ratio as found in the sample described in the text. The state census for 1900 supports such an assumption by showing that 2.5 per cent of the first generation Russians in New York State took professional occupations while 4.3 per cent of the second generation did professional service. United States Immig. Comm., XXVIII, 280, 370.
34. A convenient summary of many views on the connection between Jewish educational values and mobility is Miriam K. Slater, "My Son the Doctor: Aspects of Mobility among American Jews," *American Sociological Review,* XXXIV (June 1969), 359–73. The individual authors and their work: Talcott Parsons, "The Sociology of Modern Anti-Semitism," in Isacque Graebler and Stewart H. Britt, eds., *Jews in a Gentile World* (New York, 1942), 106, 113; Will Herberg, *Protestant, Catholic, Jew* (Garden City, 1960), 9; Thorstein Veblen "The Intellectual Preeminence of Jews in Modern Europe," in Max Lerner, ed., *The Portable Veblen* (New York, 1948), 469; Louis Wirth, "Education for Survival: The Jews," *American Journal of Sociology,* XLVIII (May 1943), 682–91; Abraham Cahan, "The Russian Jew in the United States," in Charles S. Bernheimer, ed., *The Russian Jew in the United States* (Philadelphia, 1905), 38, emphasis added.
35. Judd Teller, *Strangers and Natives,* 79; see also Mark Zborowski and Elizabeth Herzog, *Life Is with People: The Culture of the Shtetl* (New York, 1962), 355; Miriam K. Slater, "My Son the Doctor."
36. Nathan Glazer, "The American Jew and the Attainments of Middle-Class Rank: Some Trends and Explanations," in Marshall Sklare, ed., *The Jews: Social Patterns of an American Group* (Glencoe, 1958), 140; Isaac Rubinow, "Economic and Industrial Condition of Russian Jews in New York," in Charles S. Bernheimer, *The Russian Jew,* 106; Indust. Comm., XV, 478; Herberg, *Protestant, Catholic, Jew,* 10, 178.
37. Teller, *Strangers and Natives,* 97; Higham, *Strangers in the Land,* 161, 278. "Sons and daughters of eastern European Jews," writes Higham, "were edging into the white collar world and finding office managers unwilling to employ them."
38. The 7 per cent figure combines upper and lower white-collar businessmen. Higham, *Strangers in the Land,* 278; Glazer, "American Jew," 140.
39. Van Kleeck, *Artificial Flower Makers,* 38, 86; Immig. Comm., XXVIII, 370.

40. Woods and Kennedy, *Young Working Girls*, 11.
41. Van Kleeck, *Artificial Flower Makers*, 34.
42. *Ibid.*, 34–37.
43. Stephan Thernstrom, *The Other Bostonians*, 168. For a discussion of fertility and mobility see Blau and Duncan, *American Occupational Structure*, 361–99; Sidney Goldstein and Calvin Goldscheider, *Jewish Americans: Three Generations in a Jewish Community* (Englewood Cliffs, 1968), 115–35; two articles by Calvin Goldscheider explore various aspects of Jewish fertility and their implications, "Socio-Economic Status and Jewish Fertility," *The Jewish Journal of Sociology*, VII (Dec. 1965), 228–33; "Ideological Factors in Jewish Fertility Differentials," in *ibid.* (June 1965), 92–105. See also A. J. Jaffe, "Religious Differentials in the Net Reproduction Rate," *Journal of the American Statistical Association*, XXIV (June 1939), 335–42, and John S. Billings, "Vital Statistics of the Jews in the United States," *Census Bulletin No. 19* (Dec. 30, 1889), 4–9.
44. Covello, *The Social Background*, 150–92, quote from 152; Rudolph Vecoli, "Contadini in Chicago," *Journal of American History*, LIV (Dec. 1964), 405–7; Foerster, *Italian Emigration*, 51–105.
45. Zborowski and Herzog, *Life Is with People*, 412, 420.
46. Edward C. Banfield, *The Moral Basis of a Backward Society* (Glencoe, 1958), passim.
47. Zborowski and Herzog, *Life Is with People*, 295–320, quote is from 297; Nathan Hurvitz, "Sources of Motivation and Achievement of American Jews," *Jewish Social Studies*, XXIII (Oct. 1961), 217–34. See also Miriam K. Slater, "My Son the Doctor"; Fred L. Strodtbeck, Margaret R. McDonald, and Bernard C. Rosen, "Evaluation of Occupations: A Reflection of Jewish and Italian Mobility Differences," *American Sociological Review*, XXII (Oct. 1957), 546–53; Fred L. Strodtbeck, "Family Interaction, Values and Achievement," in Marshall Sklare ed., *The Jews: Social Patterns of An American Group* (Glencoe, 1958), 147–68.
48. Covello, *Social Background*, 224.
49. Gans, *The Urban Villagers*, 122–30, 198–99, 210–12, quote is on 198.
50. Covello, *Social Background*, 43–44, 330–89, 402–6, 467, quotes from 404, 467, and 402; Van Kleeck, *Artificial Flower*, 205, 244–50; Edwin Steiner, *On the Trail of the Immigrant*, 271. For a wide-ranging bibliography on education for immigrants see Colin Greer, *The Great School Legend: A Revisionist Interpretation of American Public Education* (New York, 1972), 186–202.
51. *Ibid.*, 124; Indust. Comm., XV, 475–477.
52. *Ibid.*, 475.
53. Diane Ravitch, *The Great School Wars: New York City, 1805–1973* (New York, 1974), 178; Colin Greer, *School Legend*, 123. Selma Berrol's "Immigrants at School, 1898–1914" (doctoral dissertation, City U.

of New York, 1967) is an important study of New Immigrant schooling.
54. Jacob Riis, "The Children of the Poor," in Robert A. Woods et al., *The
    Poor in Great Cities* (London, 1896), 102.
55. Indust. Comm., XV, 478.
56. Park and Miller, *Old World Traits Transplanted,* 7. For an interesting
    discussion on the "Jewish mind" see Louis Wirth, *The Ghetto* (Chicago,
    1928), 75–95; also Werner Sombart, *The Jews and Modern Capitalism*
    (New York, 1913), passim.
57. Indust. Comm., XV, 478; *The Two Hundred and Fiftieth Anniversary
    of the Settlement of the Jews in the United States* (New York, 1906),
    215. The Immigration Commission study of New York slums found
    33 per cent of the Russian Jewish household heads spoke English com-
    pared with 22 per cent of the Italians. Among those in the United
    States ten years or more, the figures stood at 46 and 35 per cent. In
    terms of general literacy, 81 per cent of the Russian Jews could read and
    write compared with 56 per cent for the Italians. Immig. Comm.,
    XXVII, 327–29; Charles K. Feinberg, "Census of Jewish Students for
    1916–1917," *Menorah Journal,* III (Oct. 1917), 252–53; John Higham,
    Strangers in the Land, 364.
58. Quoted in Park and Miller, *Old World Traits,* 239–40.
59. For an interesting discussion of white-collar developments see Robert H.
    Wiebe, *The Search for Order: 1877–1920* (New York, 1967), 111–32.
60. Immig. Comm., I, 422. See also Immig. Comm., XXVII, 322–26.
61. Hutchins Hapgood, *The Spirit of the Ghetto: Studies of the Jewish
    Quarter of New York* (New York, reprint of 1902 ed., 1972), 91. See
    also Maurice Fishberg, "Health and Sanitation: New York City," in
    Charles Bernheimer ed., *The Russian Jew,* 287; Harry Roskolenko, *The
    Time That Was Then* (New York, 1971), 41–51.
62. Hapgood, *Spirit of the Ghetto,* 143.
63. Woods and Kennedy, *Young Working Girls,* 55; Odencrantz, *Italian
    Women,* 184.
64. Riis, *How the Other Half Lives,* 38–41.
65. Gilbert Osofsky, *Harlem: The Making of a Ghetto* (New York, 1963),
    138.
66. This data is expressed in Treiman scores and illustrated in graphs in
    Thomas Kessner, "The Golden Door: Immigrant Mobility in New York
    City, 1880–1915" (doctoral dissertation, Columbia U., 1975), 163–65.

CHAPTER V—Individual Career Mobility

 1. Quoted in John G. Cawelti, *Apostles of the Self Made Man* (Chicago,
    1968), 125. See also Irwin G. Wyllie, *The Self Made Man in America:
    The Myth of Rags to Riches* (Brunswick, 1954); Sidney Fine, *Laissez-
    Faire and the General Welfare State* (Ann Arbor, 1956); Benjamin G.

Rader, *The Academic Mind and Reform: The Influence of Richard T. Ely in American Life* (Lexington, 1966); Richard Hofstadler, *Social Darwinism in American Life* (Philadelphia, 1944); Irwin G. Wyllie, "Social Darwinism and the Businessman," *Proceedings of the American Philosophical Society*, CIII (1959), 629–35.

2. Stephan Thernstrom, *The Other Bostonians*, 46.

3. For a discussion of some problems that mobility researchers encounter, and the liberties one such scholar took, see *ibid.*, 265–88.

4. Of New York's gainfully employed Italians in 1905, over 47 per cent lived in the country less than six years and only 3 per cent were in America before 1879, reinforcing the earlier point that the status of Italians in 1905 tells us little about the progress of the 1880 colony.

5. The professional fragment alone in the 26–99 cohort accounted for 6 per cent. Among the other cohorts the proportion of professionals never exceeded .9 per cent. Aside from the data in Table 10, this much-noted difference can be studied in the figures presented by the Immig. Comm., *Reports*, I–II, passim.

6. Robert Foerster, *Italian Emigration of Our Times*, 338; Indust. Comm., XV, 474.

7. On the laboring class see Robert Coit Chapin, *The Standard of Living Among Workingmen's Families in New York City* (New York, 1909); Eli Ginsberg and Hyman Berman, eds., *The American Worker in the Twentieth Century* (New York, 1963); Clarence D. Long, *Wages and Earnings in the United States: 1850–1890* (Princeton, 1960); United States Industrial Commission, *Reports* (19 vols., Washington, 1901–2); United States Senate, *Report on the Relations Between Capital and Labor* (4 vols., Washington, 1885); Robert H. Bremner, *From the Depths: The Discovery of Poverty in the United States* (New York, 1956); John A. Garraty, *The New Commonwealth: 1877–1890* (New York, 1968), 128–78; John A. Garraty, ed., *Capital and Labor in the Gilded Age* (Boston, 1968); Walter E. Weyl, "The Italian Who Lived on 26¢ a Day," *Outlook*, XCIII (Dec. 1909), 966–75.

8. Both Samuel P. Abelow, *History of Brooklyn Jewry* (Brooklyn, 1937), and Alter F. Landesman, *Brownsville: The Birth, Development and Passing of a Jewish Community in New York* (New York, 1969), devote considerable space to the Jewish building industry. See also Abraham Schepper, "The Jew as Builder and Landlord," *The Jewish Forum*, I (June 1918), 272–77.

9. Indust. Comm., XV, 477.

10. Jesse Pope, *The Clothing Industry*, 106.

11. The use of Treiman values is helpful here. The mean value for Italians over the series reads 27.4, 27.8, 28.7, and 32.8. For the first three groupings which involved 97 per cent of the sample and stretches over 25 years the increase was 1.3 points. The values for Jews read 34.1, 37.6, 39.9, and 41.9.

12. Peter Knights discusses some aspects of mobility research and its sources

in *The Plain People of Boston* (New York, 1971), passim, and especially in Appendix A and B, 127–43.

13. Reverend Newman Smyth, *Social Problems: Sermons to Workingmen*, quoted in Stephan Thernstrom, *Other Bostonians*, 45–46.
14. Peter Blau and Otis D. Duncan, *American Occupational Structure*, 401–2.
15. George E. Pozzetta, "The Italians of New York City, 1890–1914" (doctoral dissertation, U. of North Carolina, 1971), 318–20.
16. William Thompson Bonner, *New York, The World's Metropolis* (New York, 1924), 380.
17. *Ibid.*
18. Indust. Comm., XV, 474.
19. Bonner, *New York, The World's Metropolis*, 601.
20. Edward Steiner, *On the Trail of the Immigrant* (New York, 1906), 162.
21. Thernstrom, *Other Bostonians*, 84–85.
22. Because the information on offspring is limited to those still living with their parents it "is not sufficient for a definitive conclusion."
23. J. K. Paulding, "Educational Influences in New York," in Charles Bernheimer, ed., *The Russian Jew in the United States*, 190–91; Immig. Comm., XII, 330; Indust. Comm., XV, 325, 478.

CHAPTER VI—The Residential Dimension

1. Edwin Steiner, *On the Trail of the Immigrant*, 64–93; Andrew Rolle, *American Italians*, 58–59: Lawrence Guy Brown, *Immigration: Cultural Conflicts and Social Adjustments* (New York, 1933), 185–99; Peter Roberts, *The New Immigration* (New York, 1912), 18–48. On steerage conditions see United States Immigration Commission, *Reports*, Vol. XIX, *Steerage Conditions* (41 vols., Washington, 1911). For an account of the problems encountered by arriving immigrants, see Freidrich Kapp, *Immigration, and the Commissioners of Emigration* (New York, 1870). An account of a New Immigrant who became a United States Commissioner of Immigration and his attempts to meet some of these problems is in Constantine Panunzio, *The Soul of an Immigrant* (New York, 1928).
2. James D. McCabe Jr., *Lights and Shadows of New York Life or the Sights and Sensations of the Great City* (New York, reprint of 1872 ed., 1970), 398.
3. Kate Holliday Claghorn, "Foreign Immigration and the Tenement House in New York City," in Robert W. DeForrest and Lawrence Veiller, eds., *The Tenement House Problem* (2 vols., New York, 1903), II, 87; Andrew Rolle, *American Italians*, 60; Indust. Comm., XV, 472–73; Jacob Riis, *How the Other Half Lives*, 42.
4. "The Refuse of the City," *New York Times*, Dec. 4, 1881.

5. Indust. Comm., XV, 474; Robert Foerster, *Italian Emigration*, 325–26; Charlotte Adams, "Italian Life in New York City," *Harper's Monthly*, LII (April 1881), 676–84; George Pozzetta, "The Italians of New York City, 1890–1914," 318–20. For a short play set in "Little Italy" and portraying New York Italians' penchant for crimes of passion see Horace B. Fry, *Little Italy: A Tragedy in One Act* (New York, 1904).

6. Jacob Riis, *How the Other Half Lives*, 40–45.

7. Gilbert Osofsky, *Harlem: The Making of a Ghetto* (New York, 1963), 78–83. The occupational statistics are from the census sample for 1880.

8. Abraham Cahan, *The Rise of David Levinsky* (New York, 1917), 89–91.

9. Moses Rischin, *Promised City*, 78–80; Riis, *How the Other Half Lives*, 77–78; Steiner, *Trail of the Immigrant*, 175.

10. Ronald Sanders, *The Downtown Jews: Portraits of an Immigrant Generation* (New York, 1969), 40–45; Hutchins Hapgood, *The Spirit of the Ghetto* (New York, reprint of 1902 ed. with notes by Harry Golden, 1966), 3–75; Rischin, *Promised City*, 76–91; Riis, *How the Other Half Lives*, 76–87.

11. New York Association for Improving the Condition of the Poor, *Thirty-Seventh Annual Report* (1880), 18–20. These *Reports* offer valuable information on slum housing, most include a section written by an AICP investigator detailing slum conditions. *The Charities Review*, which appeared after 1891, is also a significant source. After January 1901 the name was changed to *Charities* and in 1905 became *Charities and Commons*. Finally in 1909 it took the title *Survey*. A convenient collection of articles excerpted from this journal is Lydio F. Tomasi, *The Italian in America: The Progressive View* (New York, 1972).

12. A.I.C.P., *1880 Report*, 18–20.

13. *Ibid.;* John A. Garraty, *The New Commonwealth*, 189–94; Roy Lubove, *The Progressives and the Slums* (Pittsburgh, 1962), 28–45, 94–107.

14. Edward Ewing Pratt, *Industrial Causes of Congestion of Population in New York City* (New York, 1911), 35.

15. The Commission "made an arrangement with tabulators of the United States Census . . . by which the department obtained, for the sum of $10,000—practically at cost of copying—certain important facts . . . drawn from the census schedules of 1900, and tabulated for each house in the city." New York State Tenement House Department, *First Report, 1902–1903* (2 vols., New York, 1902–1903), II, 25. In a survey of New York slums the United States Immigration Commission found 1.3 per cent of the Italian sample owning their own homes, while not one Jew fit this category, *Immig. Comm.*, XXVII, 305. Jews of course, did own houses on the East Side but generally this was a form of investment in tenements rather than purchase of a home. Abraham Schepper, "The Jew as Builder and Landlord," *The Jewish Forum*, I (June 1918), 272–77; Milton Reizenstein, "General Aspects of the Population: New York" in Charles Bernheimer ed., *The Russian Jew in the*

United States, 46–47. Home ownership, especially for lower-class workers, can often have adverse effects on mobility, by draining capital that
could be used for investment. This may have had an effect in hampering Irish mobility in Newburyport, Massachusetts; see Stephan Thernstrom, *Poverty and Progress*, 115–37, 139–52.

16. Claghorn, "Foreign Immigration and the Tenement House in New
    York City," 87.
17. John S. Billings, *Vital Statistics of New York City and Brooklyn: 1890*
    (Washington, 1894), offers short descriptions of wards and sanitary dis-
    tricts in Manhattan and Brooklyn. Land maps are very helpful in pro-
    viding a picture of city streets and the factories, warehouses, and housing
    on these blocks. See, for instance, Roger H. Pidgeon, *Atlas of the City
    of New York Lying South of Fourteenth Street* (New York, 1881).
    This atlas was published irregularly during this period. Also helpful are
    the Landmark Maps and neighborhood-block maps reproduced in
    I. N. Phelps Stokes, *The Iconography of Manhattan Island* (6 vols.,
    New York, Reprint of 1916 ed., 1967). They can be found in Volume II
    after page 452, and in Volume III, plates 174–80.
18. Immig. Comm., XXVII, 304, 286, 282, 280–81.
19. Leo Grebler, *Housing Market Behavior in a Declining Area* (New York,
    1952), 108; E. E. Pratt, *Congestion of Population*, 30–35.
20. Riis, *How the Other Half Lives*, 9, 34; Rischin, *Promised City*, 89; Ande
    Manners, *Poor Cousins*, 218.
21. Indust. Comm., XV, 477. Louis Wirth's classic study of *The Ghetto* is
    concerned with Chicago, but nonetheless is useful for New York. See
    also Park and Miller, *Old World Traits Transplanted*, passim; Lawrence
    G. Brown, *Immigration: Cultural Conflicts and Social Adjustments*, 200–
    260. For a modern view of the immigrant communities and the neigh-
    borhoods they settled, see David Ward, *Cities and Immigrants* (New
    York, 1971); Eugene P. Ericksen, Richard N. Juliani and William L.
    Yancey, "Emigrant Ethnicity: A Review and Reformulation," a paper
    prepared by the authors at Temple University (1974).
22. See Appendix B, especially Table 25.
23. "Change on the East Side," *New York Times*, July 8, 1899.
24. *Ibid.*
25. "Slums That Once Were," *New York Tribune*, July 30, 1899.
26. Roy Lubove, *Progressives and Slums*, 122–24. Housing attracted a
    good deal of attention in this period as reformers focused on the ills and
    threatened dire consequences. Henry George thundered at New Yorkers,
    paraphrasing English historian Thomas Macauley: "Whence shall come
    the new barbarians? Go through the squalid quarters of great cities and
    you may see, even now their gathering hordes," quoted in Alter F.
    Landesman, *Brownsville* (New York, 1969), 6. United States Commis-
    sioner of Labor, Carrol D. Wright, earlier in the decade estimated that
    New York had thirty associations devoted to housing issues. And those

groups helped pressure the city into implementing its housing laws, while agitating for newer legislation when they felt necessary. Carrol D. Wright, "Housing of the Working People," *Eighth Special Report of the Commissioner of Labor* (Washington, 1895), 88–89. For a full contemporary treatment of the tenement issue see Robert DeForrest and Lawrence Veiller, eds., *The Tenement House Problem* (2 vols., New York, 1903).

27. Matthew and Hannah Josephson, *Al Smith, Hero of the Cities* (Boston, 1969), 20. See also Peter J. Rose, ed., *The Ghetto and Beyond: Essays on Jewish Life in America* (New York, 1969); Sam Bass Warner and Colin Burke, "Cultural Change and the Ghetto," *Journal of Contemporary History,* IV (Oct. 1969), 173–87.

28. Harry Roskolenko, *The Time That Was Then* (New York, 1971), 34–35; Mario Puzo, "Choosing a Dream" in Thomas C. Wheeler, ed., *The Immigrant Experience* (New York, 1971), 36.

29. For a history of the attempt to build such a community see Arthur A. Goren, *New York Jews and the Quest for Community: The Kehillah Experiment, 1908–1922* (New York, 1970).

30. Bayrd Still, *Mirror for Gotham,* 113–15; Jay P. Dolan, "Immigrants in the City; New York's Irish and German Catholics," *Church History,* XXXXI (Sept. 1972), 308. For a fuller discussion of residential mobility in the Civil War period see Peter Knights, *The Plain People of Boston: 1830–1860.*

31. Dolan, "Immigrants in the City," 359. Two of every five Irish and two of every three Germans moved more than once.

32. *Trow's New York City Directory, 1881* (New York, 1881), iii.

33. *Ibid.,* 1880, iii–iv. Howard Chudacoff, *Mobile Americans* (New York, 1972), 25–26, 42, 57, 179, dismisses criticism of the directory and compares it with the census for thoroughness. "The spirit behind the compilation of the city directories resembled that associated with the 1890 census count." This is unlikely. Census canvassers could threaten legal consequences for evaders, scheduled their visits carefully, and often prepared the way by distributing foreign language leaflets to explain their work. See Carrol D. Wright assisted by William C. Hunt, *The History and Growth of the Census* (New York, reprint of 1900 ed., 1966), 66 and passim. Peter Knights discusses city directories and their usefulness in *The Plain People of Boston,* 127–39.

34. Chudacoff, *Mobile Americans,* 41; Richard J. Hopkins, "Status, Mobility, and the Dimensions of Change in a Southern City; Atlanta, 1870–1910" in Kenneth T. Jackson and Stanley K. Schultz, eds., *Cities in American History* (New York, 1972), 224; Stephan Thernstrom, *Poverty and Progress,* 31, 96, 85.

35. Kate H. Claghorn, "Foreign Immigrant and the Tenement House," 82.

36. For an example of this conventional view see Glazer and Moynihan, *Beyond the Melting Pot,* 187.

37. The procedure used to adjust the sample was to expand it by using Italians drawn from the 1880 Directory and adding those who could successfully be traced, to the original sample.
38. Data on Brooklyn and Manhattan are from Pratt, *Industrial Causes of Congestion*, 26; Italian and east European data from Billings, *Vital Statistics of New York City and Brooklyn*, 236–39.
39. David McCullough, *The Great Bridge* (New York, 1972), 480–84, 514–15, 519, 545; Billings, *Vital Statistics*, 165. Brooklyn with 82, 282 homes had 454 more than Manhattan. See also Alan Trachtenberg, *Brooklyn Bridge: Fact and Symbol* (New York, 1965).
40. Billings, *Vital Statistics*, 242–45. The four wards with the highest Russian and Polish concentrations were the Sixteenth and Fourteenth in Williamsburgh, the Twenty-Sixth in Brownsville, and the Eighth in South Central Brooklyn. Together they add up to 53 per cent. The real proportion of Jews is much higher because a number of Russian and Polish areas like the Seventeenth and Nineteenth Wards were almost completely Christian.
41. Harold C. Syrett, *The City of Brooklyn, 1865–1898* (New York, 1944), 19.
42. *Ibid.*, 236.
43. Alter Landesman, *Brownsville*, 37.
44. *Ibid.*, 38–44.
45. Quoted in Harold Syrett, *Brooklyn*, 237.
46. *Ibid.*, 11. See also Appendix B, Table 23.
47. Charles McCabe, *Lights and Shadows*, 686; Charles Loring Brace, *The Dangerous Classes of New York* (New York, 1880), 57–60; I. N. Phelps Stokes, *Iconography of Manhattan Island*, III, 805.
48. Stokes, *Iconography*, III, 812; Charles H. Cooley, "Statistics of Street Railway Transportation," in Henry C. Adams, ed., *Report on the Transportation Business in the United States: Transportation by Land, Eleventh Census*, XVIII (Washington, 1895), 681–84. See also Joel Arthur Tarr, "From City to Suburb: The Moral Influence of Transportation Technology," in Alexander Callow, ed., *American Urban History* (New York, 1973), 203–12.
49. Stokes, *Iconography*, III, 814, 1985, 2021; Con Edison Industrial and Economic Development Department, "Population Growth of New York City by Districts: 1910–1948," (New York, 1948).
50. Pratt, *Industrial Causes of Congestion*, 24, 84–86, 112; Jesse Pope, *Clothing Industry in New York*, 174; Leo Grebler, *Housing Market Behavior*, 111; George Filipetti, *The Wholesale Markets in New York and Its Environs* (New York, 1925), 15–60; Faith M. Williams, *The Food Manufacturing Industries in New York and Its Environs* (New York, 1924), 19, 23, 28, 44 and passim; Donald H. Davenport, et al., *The Retail Shopping and Financial Districts in New York and Its Environs* (New York, 1927), 26–27; Lucy Killough, *The Tobacco Products Indus-*

try in New York and Its Environs (New York, 1924), 18, 31, 37, 44, 47, 49.

51. Pratt, *Industrial Causes of Congestion*, 43; New York City Commission on Congestion of Population, *Report* (New York, 1910), 11.
52. Pratt, *Congestion*, 119–21, 127, 135, 246.
53. *Ibid.*; Grebler, *Housing Market Behavior*, 118–19, 135.
54. Herbert Gans, *The Urban Villagers* (New York, 1962), 197–225, 289–291; Walter Firey, *Land Use in Central Boston* (Cambridge, 1947), 170–225.
55. Edward Corsi, *In the Shadow of Liberty* (New York, 1935), 22–24; Phyllis Williams, *South Italian Folkways in Europe and America* (New Haven, 1938), 6; Humbert Nelli, *The Italians of Chicago, 1880–1930* (New York, 1970), 34; Indust. Comm., XV, 474, emphasis added. Asked if they could use a house-garden, a sample of 1,936 slum dwellers in Manhattan diverged along ethnic lines. Jews generally said no, Italians yes, Grebler, *Housing Market Behavior*, 141.
56. *Ibid.*, 142.
57. Louis Wirth, *The Ghetto*, 241–46; Gilbert Osofsky, *Harlem: The Making of a Ghetto*, 88.
58. Pratt, *Congestion*, 86; Grebler, *Housing Market Behavior*, 111, 114–16, 122, 126–27.
59. Indust. Comm., XV, 477.
60. Osofsky, *Harlem*, 89.
61. Paul Frederick Cressey, "Population Succession in Chicago, 1898–1930," *American Journal of Sociology*, XLIV (July 1938), 61.
62. Howard Chudacoff, *Mobile Americans*, 77–79; Humbert Nelli, *Italians in Chicago*, 44–46. See also Stanley Lieberson, *Ethnic Patterns in American Cities* (New York, 1963), 101–8.
63. If one defines an entire ward as a neighborhood and finds ward totals showing a variety of ethnic groups, he has not really shown that immigrants were mixed with no firm ethnic lines dividing them. Ward boundaries are too ample. In this regard see, Chudacoff, *Mobile Americans*, 67, and Nelli, *Italians in Chicago*, 30–33.
64. Lillian Betts, "The Italians in New York," quoted in George E. Pozzetta, "The Italians of New York City," 109; Stephan Thernstrom, *Poverty and Progress*, 85, 198–99; Stephan Thernstrom and Peter Knights, "Men in Motion, Some Data and Speculations about Urban Population Mobility in Nineteenth Century America," in Tamara K. Hareven, *Anonymous Americans* (Englewood Cliffs, 1971), 17–47; Clyde Griffin, "Workers Divided: Craft and Ethnic Differences in Poughkeepsie," in Stephan Thernstrom and Richard Sennet, eds., *Nineteenth Century Cities* (New Haven, 1969), 59–61; Peter Knights, *The Plain People of Boston*, 115–18.
65. Paul F. Cressey, "Population Succession," 68.
66. *Ibid.*, 67; Nelli, *Italians in Chicago*, 47; Grebler, *Housing Market Be-*

havior, 135–36, 249–53. See also Walter F. Laidlaw, *Statistical Sources for the Demographic Study of Greater New York: 1910* (2 vols., New York, 1912).
67. Chudacoff, *Mobile Americans*, 5–6.

CHAPTER VII—The New York Experience

1. Michel Guillaume St. Jean de Crèvecœur, *Letters from an American Farmer*, in Merle Curti et al., eds., *American Issues: The Social Record* (2 vols., 1971), I, 103–10.
2. Robert Foerster, *Italian Emigration of Our Times*, 374–77.
3. *Ibid.*
4. William Miller, "American Historians and the Business Elite" in William Miller, ed., *Men in Business: Essays on the Historical Role of the Entrepreneur* (New York, 1962), 309–28. See also Frances W. Gregory and Irene D. Neu, "The American Industrial Elite in the 1870's: Their Social Origins," in *ibid.*, 193–212. The less rigorously built sample of businessmen studied by C. Wright Mills and Richard Bendix with Frank Howton is discussed by Herbert G. Gutman, "The Reality of the Rags-to-Riches 'Myth': The Case of the Patterson, New Jersey Locomotive, Iron, and Machinery Manufacturers, 1830–1880," in Stephan Thernstrom and Richard Sennett, eds., *Nineteenth Century Cities*, 98–101.
5. Stephan Thernstrom, *Poverty and Progress*, 112–13, 162–65, 223.
6. Herbert Gutman, "The Reality of the Rags-to-Riches 'Myth',", 98–124; Clyde Griffin, "Workers Divided; The Effect of Craft and Ethnic Differences in Poughkeepsie, New York, 1850–1880" in Thernstrom and Sennett, eds., *Nineteenth Century Cities*, 93; Howard Chudacoff, *Mobile Americans*, 109; Humbert Nelli, *The Italians in Chicago*, 109; Richard Hopkins, "Status, Mobility and the Dimensions of Change in a Southern City: Atlanta, 1870–1890," in Kenneth Jackson and Stanley Schultz, eds., *Cities in American History* (New York, 1972), 223; Paul B. Worthman, "Working Class Mobility in Birmingham, Alabama, 1880–1914," in Tamara Hareven, ed., *Anonymous Americans: Explorations in Nineteenth Century Social History* (Englewood Cliffs, 1971), 193.
7. Stephan Thernstrom, "Reflections on the New Urban History," in Felix Gilbert and Stephen R. Graubard, eds., *Historical Studies Today* (New York, 1972), 329; Stephan Thernstrom, *The Other Bostonians: Poverty and Progress in the American Metropolis, 1880–1970* (Cambridge, 1973), 257–58.
8. Peter M. Blau and Otis D. Duncan, *The American Occupational Structure* (New York, 1967), 249.
9. An extremely useful summary of mobility findings is presented in Thernstrom, *Other Bostonians*, 234. The figures for upward mobility into the

white-collar class between 1880 and 1890 are: Atlanta, 22 per cent; Omaha, 21 per cent; Boston 12 per cent. Corresponding downward mobility figures are: 7 per cent; 2 per cent; 12 per cent. It is true that these figures must be understood within the perspective of the methodology that produced them. Thus they may be somewhat skewed because the better situated are more easily traced, but this problem is common to all these mobility studies and therefore the figures are valid in a comparative context.

10. *Ibid.*
11. Miriam K. Slater, "My Son the Doctor," 369.
12. "Letter of the Russian Emigrant Relief Fund to the Alliance Israelite Universelle, 1881," Appendix B to Zosa Szajkowski, "The Attitude of American Jews to East European Jewish Immigration (1881–1883)," *Publications of the American Jewish Historical Society*, XL (Sept. 1950), 265–66. Emphasis added.
13. Blau and Duncan, *American Occupational Structure*, 295–98, 361–99, quotes are on 367 and 428.
14. Sidney Goldstein and Calvin Goldscheider, *Jewish Americans: Three Generations in a Jewish Community* (Englewood Cliffs, 1968), 116, 121, 124. Emphasis added.
15. Salvatore LaGumina and Frank J. Cavaioli, eds., *The Ethnic Dimension in American Society* (Boston, 1974), 186–87.
16. Isaac M. Rubinow, "Economic and Industrial Condition in New York," in Charles Bernheimer, ed., *The Russian Jew in the United States*, 103–4; Ascoli quoted in Eugene P. Ericksen, Richard N. Juliani, and William Yancey, "Emergent Ethnicity: A Review and Reformulation," prepared by the authors at Temple University (1974), 33.
17. Herbert Gans, *Urban Villagers*, 123–212.
18. Moses Rischin, *Promised City*, 176; Joel Seidman, *The Needle Trades*, 43, 228.
19. Chudacoff, *Mobile Americans*, 157.
20. Thernstrom, *Poverty and Progress*, 1.
21. Daniel Bell, *The End of Ideology* (New York, 1960), 115–36; Humbert Nelli, *Italians in Chicago*, places heavy emphasis on the role of crime in mobility and analyzes it functionally, 125–55. Professor Nelli is now at work on a full-scale study of Italian crime entitled *The Business of Crime* to be published in the fall of 1976. Arthur Goren, *New York Jews and the Quest for Community: The Kehillah Experiment, 1908–1922* (New York, 1970), includes a chapter on crime in the Jewish quarter, 134–58, and Professor Goren is at work on a full study of that topic.
22. Abraham Cahan, *The Rise of David Levinsky* (New York, 1917), 525–30.
23. Mario Puzo, "Choosing a Dream," in T. C. Wheeler, ed., *The Immigrant Experience* (New York, 1971), 49.

Bibliographic Note

This bibliographic note is intended to identify some of the sources I found most useful in preparing this study. Secondary materials are cited in the footnotes and have not been repeated here. I would direct the reader seeking a conventional bibliographic listing of all sources to my doctoral dissertation which carries the same title as this book and was completed at Columbia University in 1975.

Two efficient guides to a variety of New York sources are: Rosalie Fellows Bailey, *Guide to Geneaological and Bibliographical Sources for New York City (Manhattan), 1783–1898* (New York, 1954), and Harold Eiberson with Sidney Ditzion, *Sources for the Study of the New York Area* (New York, 1960). In addition, a few of the less well-known bibliographies that are worthwhile include: Francesco Cordasco and Salvatore LaGumina, *Italians in the United States: A Bibliography* (New York, 1972); Moses Rischin, *An Inventory of American Jewish History* (Cambridge, Mass., 1954); Mary Van Kleeck, *Industrial Investigations of the Russell Sage Foundation* (New York, 1915); Henriette R. Walter, *Investigations of Industries in New York City, 1905–1915* (New York, 1916). Adelaide Rosalie Hasse, *Index of Economic Materials in Documents of New York State: 1789–1904* (Washington, 1917) is, despite its age, a comprehensive and valuable guide to economic sources; it is available for twelve other states besides New York.

Much of the basic statistical information for this study was drawn from an assortment of census sources. The Manuscript Federal Census Schedules of the Population for 1880 have been reproduced on microfilm and are readily available. The Genealogy and Local History Division of the New York Public Library, Main Research Branch has prepared an efficient "Guide to the Use of the Census of the United States: Tenth Census, 1880" (1963) to help the researcher locate specific neighborhoods, wards, election districts, and street addresses by microfilm reel. Scholars intending to use census sources will find Carrol D. Wright assisted by William C. Hunt, *The History and Growth of the Census* (New York, reprint of 1900 ed., 1966) helpful.

No federal census returns were available for New York beyond 1880 and I had to turn elsewhere for data. I consulted the "Police Census of Manhattan; 1890" at the New York Municipal Archives and Records Center. However, this census, narrowly concerned with assembling the names and addresses of respondents, is useless for occupational studies.

Fortunately, New York State conducted enumerations of the population and these listings have in many instances been preserved. These State Census schedules contain the name, address, occupation, nationality, age, sex, citizenship, and length of residence in the United States of each respondent family member. The 1892 returns for Manhattan no longer exist, but I was able to use the Brooklyn schedules which are housed in the office of the Kings County Clerk.

There is a little-known census of Manhattan's Jewish community that was conducted by the Baron de Hirsch Fund in 1890. This survey assembled information on 111,690 Jews and included occupational data. Some findings are reproduced in E. Tcherikower, *The Early Jewish Labor Movement in the United States,* translated by Aaron Antonovsky (New York, 1961), pp. 153-55.

For 1905, New York State conducted a state census, and I sampled the manuscript returns for Manhattan and Brooklyn. These fragile, bound volumes show the wear and tear of the intervening decades but are still quite useable. They can be found in the offices of the respective County Clerks. The New York County Clerk's office also contains a helpful system of files which translate Manhattan addresses into ward, assembly district, and election district locations, something the census-researcher will fully appreciate.

Other essential tools for constructing a census sample are ward, A.D., and E.D. maps. The boundaries changed often and maps must be secured for each census year. The New York Municipal Reference Center has a good collection of these maps on microfiche. The Main Research Branch of the New York Public Library, Map Room, also has a variety of these maps, and still other charts can be found in the County Clerk's offices.

The quantitative historian who wishes to exploit the computer's capabilities but lacks the requisite background in programming has a variety of "packaged" programs to choose from. Each research design differs and therefore some packages will prove more suitable than others (one important consideration: the computer center that is used must also have the package in its system). For this study I used the *Cross-Tabs* program which boasts a particularly powerful capability for multi-dimensional cross-tabulation. A close reading of the *User's Manual for Cross-Tabs* (Cambridge, Mass., revised, 1970), will provide the diligent neophyte with a working knowledge of the program and its application.

Published census materials proved very informative and helpful. The publications include long-range analyses, annual statistics, and a rich variety of monographs. These volumes bristle with ethnic, immigration, wage, manufacturing, population, health, death, and disease statistics, as well as others. I found the volume edited by Dr. John S. Billings, *Vital Statistics of New York City and Brooklyn Covering a Period of Six Years Ending May 31, 1890* (Washington, 1894), particularly valuable for its maps, short neighborhood descriptions, health statistics, and finely subdivided population data.

The first United States Commissioner of Labor, Carrol D. Wright, expanded and professionalized the collection of statistics on wages, labor, and employment. The *Seventh Special Report of The Commissioner of Labor: The Slums of Baltimore, Chicago, New York, and Philadelphia* (Washington, 1894) is perhaps one of the most useful of his compilations. The United States Industrial Commission *Reports* (19 vols., Washington, 1901–1902), contains several volumes on industrial and labor conditions, including VII and XIV, but the most helpful for my purposes was volume XV, which is devoted to immigration and has an entire section on New York City. The United States Bureau of Labor, *Report on the Conditions of Woman and Child Wage Earners in the United States* (19 vols., Washington, 1911), is another government study that offers much relevant material. I consulted Volumes II, VII, and IX most often.

The Progressive style which emphasized dense statistical studies as a means for solving complex social problems produced yet another multi-volume study in the forty-one-volume United States Immigration Commission *Report* (Washington, 1911–1912). Despite its transparent and persistent bias (briefly discussed in Chapter Two), it remains an indispensable source for the study of pre-World War I immigration. No study concerned with this period can afford to ignore this impressive compilation of statistical and narrative data.

Other sources include: New York State Commissioners of Immigration, *Annual Reports,* United States Treasury Department, Bureau of Statistics, *Tables Showing the Arrival of Alien Passengers and Immigrants to the United States from 1820 to 1888* (Washington, 1889); United States Commissioner General of Immigration, *Annual Reports;* United States Congress, House of Representatives, *Letter from the Secretary of Treasury Transmitting a Report of the Commissioners of Immigration upon the Causes Which Incite Immigration to the United States: Volume I—Reports of the Commissioners* (Washington, 1892).

The urban ecology of New York City is best seen in land use maps. Published sporadically and under various titles they provide structural profiles of the city's real estate. A good collection of these maps is available in the New York Public Library Main Research Branch, Map Room. One bound volume of such maps to which I referred often was Roger H. Pidgeon, *Atlas of the City of New York Lying South of Fourteenth Street* (New York, 1881).

Index

Adams, Charlotte, 53
Adams, Henry, 39n.
Adelphi College, 98
Alexander II, 17
Alliance Israelite Universelle, 168
"amoral familism," 172
area of second settlement, 156, 157-59
artificial flower industry, 73, 73n., 74, 79
Ascoli, Max, 172
Association for Improvement of the Conditions of the Poor, 13, 20, 131
Atlanta, Georgia, xii, 142, 164, 165
A. T. Stewart's department store, 10-11

Bailey, W. B., 42
Banfield, Edward, 172
Barnes, Charles, 56-57
Barondess, Jacob, 69
Bartholdi, Frédéric A., 3
Bell, Dr. A. N., 21
Bell, Daniel, 176
"Birds of Passage." See transiency; Bailey, W. B.
Birmingham, Alabama, xii, 164
Blau, Peter, 116-17, 165, 170
boarders. See lodgers
Boardman, James, 140
Boston, xiv, 5n., 67, 120-21, 164-65, 165-66, 172
Brace, Charles L., 15, 148
Brandt, Lillian, 80
Brecht, Berthold, 44
Breckinridge, Sophonisba P., 151
Bronx, 119, 153, 154, 155, 175
Bronx Aqueduct, 58
Brooklyn, 21, 49, 66, 143, 144-47, 149, 152, 153-58, 166, 175, 179-80. See also Brownsville; Coney Island; New York City; Wallabout

Brooklyn Bridge, 21, 141, 143-44
Brooklyn Polytechnic, 98
Brownsville, 146-47, 149, 152, 153, 157-58, 175
Burgess, Ernest W., 136n., 159

Cahan, Abraham, 69, 70, 88, 89, 129
capillarité sociale theory, 170
Carito, Diomede, 29
Carpi, Leone, 27-28
Castle Garden, 23, 41, 127
census, xiv, xv, 44, 48, 49, 50, 67, 72, 78, 82, 106, 132, 146, 157, 159, 175, 176, 179-80
Century of Progress Exposition, 3
Chicago, 17, 152, 156, 157, 164
chiffonniers. See rag picking
Children's Aid Society, 80
Chudacoff, Howard P., 157, 164, 175
cigarmaking, 46, 87
City College of New York, 98
city directories. See directory
Claghorn, Kate, 14, 132
clothing industry, 9-10, 19, 56-59, 61-63, 64, 65, 69, 72, 75, 76, 86, 91-92, 110, 111, 130, 146-47, 149, 150, 168, 171
clothing trades, 37, 48, 56, 59, 61-65, 69-70, 91, 168, 171
college, 98. See also under specific college
Columbia University, 98
Coney Island, 118
contadini, 36-37, 39, 39n.
Conwell, Russell A., 12, 12n.
Corsi, Edward T., 151
Cotello, Salvatore, 138n.
Covello, Leonard, 94, 96
Cressey, Paul F., 156-59
Crèvecœur, Michel Guillaume St. Jean de, 161-62

Davitt, Michael, 18
De Conde, Alexander, xiii

217

semiskilled class, 51, 52, 56-57, 60,
63, 65, 66, 68-69, 79, 81, 85,
89, 90, 92, 101, 102, 107-9,
110, 111, 113-18, 121-26, 174,
175
shtetl, 46, 64, 76, 88, 94, 139, 147,
172, 175
skilled class, 51, 52, 55, 57, 60, 62-
63, 68-69, 75, 78, 79, 81, 85,
89, 90, 91, 92, 93, 101, 102,
106, 107-8, 110, 111, 113-18,
121-26, 145, 147
Sklare, Marshall, xiv
slum housing, 13-17, 20-21, 62, 98,
127-29, 131-34, 137-38, 141,
145, 147, 148, 152. *See also*
dumb-bell tenements; homeworkers
Smith, Al, 138
Smyth, Rev. Newman, 115
social economic grouping, 50-51
southern European immigration. *See*
Italians; New Immigrants
Standard International Occupational
Prestige Scale, xv
Staten Island, 118. *See also* Rich-
mond
Statue of Liberty, 4, 176
steamship rates, 26-27
Steiner, Edward, 120, 130
Stewart, A. T., 10-12
surface transit, 32. *See also* rapid
transit
"sweater," 62-63, 64, 70, 76, 131,
136, 171

tailor, 46, 52, 61-63, 65, 79, 86, 111,
165
tenements. *See* dumb-bell tenements;
slum housing
Tenement Commission, 132
Thernstrom, Stephan, xii, xiv, 42-43,
66, 67, 125, 158, 161, 163, 164-65
Time on the Cross, xvi
transiency, 26-32, 42, 70, 101, 142
"birds of passage," 26-27, 31, 42
difference between Italians and
Russian Jews, 27-32, 166
difference between Old and New
Immigrants, 26-27

and mobility, 27, 29, 31, 42
transitional zone, 156, 157. *See also*
residential mobility
Treiman, Donald, xv
Triangle Fire, 152
Tuoti, Guiseppe, 118

"Unguarded Gates, The," 25n.
United Hebrew Charities, 31-32
United Hebrew Trades, 69, 173
unskilled labor, 27, 33-34, 36, 39,
45, 46, 48, 50, 51, 53, 58, 59,
60, 63, 65, 67, 68, 70, 72, 75,
78, 79, 82, 83, 85, 87, 89, 90,
92, 93, 101, 102, 107-9, 110,
111, 113, 114, 115, 116-17, 121,
122, 123, 124, 125, 126, 145,
167, 168, 174; *See also* con-
tadini

Van Kleeck Mary, 72, 91
Veblen, Thorstein, 88
Veiller, Lawrence, 138

wages, 58, 62, 73, 74, 87, 110, 171
average annual wage in New York
City, 66
Wallabout, 149, 152
Warner, Lloyd, 88
Washington, Booker T., 35
western European immigration. *See*
Old Immigrants
Whitman, Walt, 5n.
Wiener, Norbert, xvi
Willet, Mabel H., 73
Williams, Phyllis, 151
Williamsburg, 45, 146, 152, 175
Wilson, Woodrow, 25
Wirth, Louis, 152
women, 30-32, 37, 56, 63, 71-77, 83-
85, 90-93, 99, 128-29. *See also*
working wives
Woodridge, New Jersey, 118
working wives, 48, 56, 63, 71-75, 77,
109
Worthman, Paul, 164
Wright, Carrol D., 58

Yelverton, Therese, 5

Zborowski, Mark, 94